AMERICA'S FOLKLORIST

America's Folklorist:
B. A. Botkin and American Culture

EDITED BY

Lawrence Rodgers and Jerrold Hirsch

University of Oklahoma Press : Norman

This book is published with the generous assistance of the Center for Digital Research, University of Nebraska, Lincoln.

Library of Congress Cataloging-in-Publication Data
America's folklorist : B. A. Botkin and American culture / edited by Lawrence Rodgers and Jerrold Hirsch.
   p. cm.
   Includes bibliographical references and index.
   ISBN 978-0-8061-4111-4 (hardcover : alk. paper)
   1. Botkin, Benjamin Albert, 1901–1975. 2. Folklorists—United States—Biography. 3. Folklore—United States. 4. United States—Social life and customs. I. Rodgers, Lawrence R. (Lawrence Richard), 1960–   II. Hirsch, Jerrold, 1948–
   GR55.B65A44   2010
   398.092—dc22
   [B]   2009048983

1   2   3   4   5   6   7   8   9   10

Old man, what are you planting?
Good tales—root crops—
And myself who lived them,
In the dark of the moon.
Anything you want to grow in the ground,
Plant in the dark of the moon.

Old man, I am planting a fence,
A crazy worm fence,
With songs for rails,
With men and regions for songs—
Myself the ground rail—
In the light of the moon
So it will stay on top always
Until it rots—
To bridge the now and the then and the still-to-come,
To climb from hell to heaven.
Anything you want to stay on top of the ground,
Plant in the light of the moon.

Grow down, old man;
Grow in and under, old tales;
Grow up, my songs;
Grow together and in and out, myself, men, and regions—
In the dark of the moon,
In the light of the moon.

Botkin 1931h

Contents

Acknowledgments

Our largest debt is to Ben Botkin himself. While our focus has been on his in-tellectual legacy, it is Botkin's personality that has made this volume a pleasure to put together. We continue to be struck by the deep well of loyalty, affection, and goodwill that he inspired among those who were fortunate enough to be a part of his wide orbit. He was a man worth knowing who knew a lot.

Special gratitude goes to Katherine Walker, who chairs the University of Nebraska–Lincoln Libraries' Special Collections and Preservation Depart-ment, which is home to the Benjamin A. Botkin Collection of Applied Ameri-can Folklore. In addition to being the moving force behind creating the Botkin collection, she organized and oversaw the symposium to celebrate the anniversary of Benjamin Botkin's 100th birthday at the University of Nebraska in January 2001. Several of the essays in this volume originated as papers at that symposium. In addition, this volume was published with a generous contribution from the University of Nebraska–Lincoln Libraries in support of the Benjamin A. Botkin Collection of Applied American Folklore. Without the steady support of Katherine and the University of Nebraska, this volume would not exist.

The bibliographic entries for Botkin's primary writing originally appeared in *Folklore & Society: Essays in Honor of Benj. A. Botkin*, edited by Bruce Jackson. At first we planned to bring that work up to date. To our pleasure, we came to find that the original bibliography had been done so thoroughly and so well that it continued to stand on its own four decades later. We have updated it to reflect current bibliographic conventions, made minor correc-tions and alterations, and added the few pieces that Botkin published at the end of his life. It is incorporated in the bibliography, with our gratitude to Professor Jackson for the meticulous hard work it reflects.

The volume was improved substantially by the astute comments of four outside readers for the press. Thanks to Heather Rae Bremicker, a graduate student in Oregon State University's English Department, for preparing the index. This book passed through the hands of a number of able editors. For their oversight and support, we thank Karen Wieder, Matt Bokovoy, Kirk

Bjornsgaard, Julie Schilling, and Steven Baker, as well as our meticulous copy-editor, Kathy Lewis. Special thanks to Kirk, whose untimely passing we note with sadness. We would also like to thank Karen Duncan and Hanna Wilcox at Kansas State's College of Arts and Sciences for clerical help.

Slight editorial changes were made to the previously published works (including Botkin's) to reflect press style and modern usage and for consistency. Essays are reprinted with permission from the following sources:

Ronna Lee Widner, "Lore for the Folk: Benjamin A. Botkin and the Development of Folklore Scholarship in America." Reprinted from *New York Folklore* 12.3–4 (1986): 1–22.

Bruce Jackson, "Benjamin A. Botkin (1901–1975)." Reprinted from *Journal of American Folklore* 89 (January–March 1976): 1–6.

Ellen Stekert, "Obituary: Benjamin Albert Botkin, 1901–1975." Reprinted from *Journal of Western Folklore* 34.4 (October 1975): 335–38.

"Growing Up in Folklore: A Conversation with Ben Botkin's Children, Dorothy Rosenthal and Daniel Botkin." Reprinted from *Voices: The Journal of New York Folklore* 27 (Fall–Winter 2001): 11–15.

Introduction

JERROLD HIRSCH AND LAWRENCE RODGERS

> [F]or every form of folk fantasy that dies, a new one is being created, as
> culture in decay is balanced by folklore in the making.
>
> *Botkin 1937c*

B. A. Botkin lived a life of intellectual adventure, engaging in bold undertakings that he regarded as opportunities to help his countrymen and coun-
trywomen look at American culture in a new way. Like all grand adventures,
this life was fraught, for with opportunities also came uncertainty and risk.
Botkin eagerly crossed ethnic, cultural, geographic, and socioeconomic borders and explored the terrain of what we today often see as distinctly separate
academic worlds. His goal was to reach the widest possible audience, whether
they were writers, poets, regionalists, historians, social scientists, or even folklorists. We say folklorists last because most writers, scholars, and general
readers, then and now, do not think of folklore as relevant to their concerns or
as material that can provide answers to questions important to them. Botkin
acknowledged that most of his audience thought of folklore as "dead or phony
stuff," when he knew that it was a form of art and culture that was still being
created (Botkin 1939e: 14). It could, he maintained, speak to everyone: poets
and other creative writers, regionalists who wanted to understand and preserve their local traditions, historians who wanted to include an account of
daily life in their study of the past, and social scientists who aimed to understand diversity. Botkin's willingness to listen, speak, and engage with such
audiences makes this volume of essays possible and necessary.

Botkin's work as a poet, literary critic, regionalist, student of anthropology,
social historian, and folklorist might at first appear random, but in reality it
was eclectic. He was trying to get beyond what he saw as approaches that were
too formal and limited to explain a dynamic American culture. To do that,
Botkin was prepared to draw on whatever cultural and intellectual resources

he felt illuminated his case. He tied his interests together in a democratic, egalitarian, and pluralistic vision of American culture founded on a widely shared understanding of the facts, the value, and the folklore of the American experience. Botkin believed fervidly that if the American people understood their interconnected history, their shared lore, and the relationships between their seemingly diverse experiences and backgrounds, they could embrace their diversity and fulfill their democratic and egalitarian ideals. Such understanding, he also thought, would revitalize their expressive culture in ways that could help them understand each other and articulate and achieve their democratic visions. In the grandest terms, Botkin engaged in a lifelong project of redefining national identity.

Who was Botkin that he thought he could accomplish all of this? Although the child of poor Lithuanian Jewish immigrants, Botkin (born in Boston, Massachusetts, in 1901) made a career in American cultural studies that took him from the urban Northeast to Oklahoma and the Southwest and back again to the Northeast. He received degrees from Harvard (B.A., 1920), Columbia (M.A., 1921), and the University of Nebraska (Ph.D., 1931) and was an English professor at the University of Oklahoma (OU) from 1921 to 1939. He held important positions in governmental cultural programs, serving as national folklore editor of the New Deal's Federal Writers' Project (FWP, 1938–39), chief editor of the Writers' Unit of the Library of Congress Project (1939–41), and head of the Archive of American Folk Song (1942–44). He resigned from the archive in 1944, settled in Croton-on-Hudson, New York, and spent the last thirty years of his life as a self-employed professional writer on American culture and folklore.

Throughout his career, Botkin worked to broaden the subject matter of American folklore and the role of the American folklorist. He always insisted on approaches to folklore that did not separate the lore from the folk who created it. He saw the study and use of American folklore as contributing to creative writing, an understanding of history, and cultural renewal. Botkin sought to reconcile a legacy of romantic nationalism with an emerging emphasis in the social sciences of the 1920s on cultural pluralism. He worked to overcome the division between literary and anthropological approaches to folklore and to break down the separation between scholarship and what he initially called utilization and later called applied folklore. He attempted to formulate an approach to the study of American folklore that took into account the nation's different regions, races, and classes and showed the interrelationship of folk, popular, and high culture. Botkin continuously sought new ways to establish a new view of the role of the folklorist in American culture, whether through his work on the interregional *Folk-Say* anthologies (1929–32), as an editor and archivist, or as the author of numerous folklore treasuries, starting with *A Treasury of American Folklore* (1944).

Beginning in his Oklahoma years, Botkin challenged what throughout his career was commonly referred to as the "science of folklore." He rejected traditional folklore scholars' privileged hierarchies regarding what constituted acceptable objects of study: the lore over the folk, the past over the present, the rural over the urban, the agrarian over the industrial, survivals over revivals, older genres over newer emergent forms, oral transmission over technological media, homogeneous groups over heterogeneous ones. Yet it was in studying many of those subjects that were not deemed academically legitimate that Botkin saw folklore's richest avenues for comprehending modern American life. Thus he had every reason to subvert, or even ignore, folklorists' claims regarding the authentic and the spurious, the traditional and the nontraditional, the pure and the "contaminated." As a professor at the University of Oklahoma, as a government official, and as a self-employed professional writer from 1944 until his death in 1975, Botkin used the university, the federal government, and commercial publishing to produce his experiments in cultural representation and to further his goal of reframing public discourse about these matters.

To understand Botkin involves comprehending the degree to which he moved between being an insider and an outsider. Each phase of his career involved not only crossing borders but also addressing criticisms from those who viewed him as violating boundaries that they thought needed to be maintained and respected. Being the son of poor Jewish immigrants might not seem a promising beginning for someone who wanted to be a poet and interpreter of the American experience, but Botkin turned it into one. He found a path into major American institutions while remaining a cosmopolitan outsider who was never totally assimilated by any of them. Scholarships enabled him to enter Harvard University at the age of sixteen as a student who lived at home and commuted to his classes. He majored in English and studied and wrote poetry. His undergraduate papers on William Wordsworth and Carl Sandburg reveal an aspiring poet focusing on writers he thought had renewed the language of poetry by turning to rural scenes or to urban-industrial life (Botkin 1967a: 18). He also wrote essays for his composition classes about the diverse immigrant folklore that he had encountered growing up in Boston.[1] At the same time, his relative poverty, his commuting to school, and not least of all his ethnicity kept him on the margins of Harvard undergraduate life. Shortly after Botkin graduated, Harvard adopted strict quotas to limit the number of Jewish undergraduates (see Synnott 1979).

Botkin's next move took him from Boston and Harvard to New York City and Columbia University, from the city that had been America's first cultural capital to its newly emerging successor. His brother Harry was already in New York, working as a commercial artist and spending days with their soon-to-be-famous cousins, George and Ira Gershwin. Throughout his life Botkin would explore in scholarly terms the relationship of high, popular, and folk art that Harry and the Gershwins explored in practice. In 1921 Botkin completed a master's degree in English at Columbia University, where Franz Boas taught anthropology. From Boasian anthropology, Botkin learned how the particular historical experience of different groups resulted in cultures that were both products of and responses to specific conditions. This constituted a challenge to the romantic nationalist and evolutionary anthropological assumptions that he had encountered in his developing interest in folklore studies.[2] The romantic nationalist aspect of folklore studies stressed that the folk of a nation represented an isolated and homogeneous rural group whose lore provided the basis for national identity and unity and the stimulus for a great national artistic flowering. Evolutionary anthropology saw lore as predominantly the survivals of earlier stages in development, useful only in reconstructing the history of human progress.

Botkin knew from both lived experience and study that American culture was heterogeneous, composed of a multiplicity of cultural groups who not only kept old lore alive for reasons that were important to them but also were creating new lore in response to new circumstances. He was ready to synthesize his romantic faith in lore as the basis of national cultural expression and cultural pluralism. From his point of view, the very heterogeneity of American culture constituted an advantage in developing American art. While studying literature and anthropology was important to Botkin, he could leave behind literature departments' emphasis on European folklore texts and anthropology departments' focus on fieldwork among, for example, American Indians. He may well have left Columbia after completing his master's thesis because its English department in those years was unsympathetic to someone whose work was moving in an interdisciplinary direction and whose vision embraced cultural diversity.

When Botkin began teaching at the University of Oklahoma in 1921, what he wanted most was to be a poet who contributed to a new American literature that would help in "restoring the oral popular tradition to poetry" (Botkin

1935b: 324–25). It was not long before he became president of the Oklahoma Folklore Society and the Oklahoma Poetry Society. When he became president of the Oklahoma Authors' League he could not resist writing his in-laws: "and that's not so bad for a Jew, is it?"—and, we might add, an easterner and a Harvard Man.[3] He would find, however, that anti-Semitism was hardly absent from the university or even his own department.

Botkin participated in the poetry and ballad revival on the University of Oklahoma campus. He later wrote that from these experiences "grew my interest in folk-song, particularly the play-party song"—a form of adult recreation that combined song and movement while avoiding religious objections to dancing (Botkin 1935b: 323–34). He welcomed the use of play-party songs and the descriptions of these social gatherings in the work of contemporary novelists, a development that he saw as having ample and distinguished precedents. In his 1937 dissertation on the Oklahoma play-party, Botkin argued that this lore was created not by a classless community that existed only in the distant past but rather by one that was constantly being re-created on the edge of the advancing frontier by an increasingly stratified and heterogeneous community (Botkin 1937b).

Botkin's numerous contributions to the cultural life of the University of Oklahoma and the state have not been recognized to the degree that they deserve. Throughout the 1920s in the pages of the Sunday *Daily Oklahoman* Botkin engaged in what he called a "two-fold pioneering" (Botkin 1935b: 322) in his book reviews. He introduced and fostered interest in contemporary modernist writers such as W. B. Yeats, D. H. Lawrence, and T. S. Eliot, while also reviewing work that helped Oklahomans value their own heritage.[4] The first book that the newly created University of Oklahoma Press published in 1929 was *Folk-Say: A Regional Miscellany*, edited by Botkin, which was followed by three more volumes. The publication of the fourth volume was halted, however, when influential state residents attacked its treatment of sexuality and economic unrest (Botkin 1935b: 329). As Botkin moved further to the left during the Great Depression, he came under increasing attack. University officials and students, trustees, state newspapers, and even legislators made him a target. By the time he left OU in 1939, there was little goodwill left on the part of either Botkin or the university.[5] In his last few years there, he was cast in the by now familiar role of an academic who leaned too far left in a conservative state. Such a legacy, however, obscures his very substantial contribution to the university and his stature as one of the Oklahoma's most important cultural advocates.

Botkin publicly joined the regionalist discussion in 1929 when he edited the first volume of *Folk-Say*, which began with one of his most notable essays,

"The Folk in Literature: An Introduction to the New Regionalism" (Botkin 1929b). The essay centered on questions about American art and culture and the writer's relationship to his or her culture. In it he made clear his position that folklore was a form of literature and that folk, high, and popular culture always interacted. The regionalist literary movements of the 1920s and 1930s were part of the debate between the genteel critics and romantic nationalists. If it was time to declare America's coming of age in relation to Europe, it was also time to declare provincial America's coming of age in relation to the urban centers of the Northeast. Regionalism was a variation on the romantic nationalist theme. In its literary dimension, Botkin declared, regionalism was "an inclusive term for a variety of movements to relate the artist to his region" (Botkin 1935b: 321).

Regionalists like Botkin rejected the argument that American culture offered limited sustenance to its artists. Instead they argued that regional landscapes, history, and folk culture offered writers an adequate culture. These regionalists, like earlier American romantic nationalists, were issuing a declaration of cultural independence. Thus Botkin was part of a tradition that had its roots in the work of Ralph Waldo Emerson and Walt Whitman and in the twentieth century in the writings of Van Wyck Brooks, Randolph Bourne, and Lewis Mumford. Mumford especially influenced what Botkin came to call his "culturalist" approach to regionalism, which saw a role for cities in organizing a regional culture and economy. Botkin wore the cosmopolitan regionalist mantle of these men. His ideas about regionalism bore none of the conservative cultural chauvinism that characterized the views of some regionalists.

In the early years of the Depression, Botkin argued that cultural diversity was not a danger but a source of vitality: "There is not one folk in [in America] but many folk groups—as many as there are regional cultures or racial or occupational groups within a region" (Botkin 1929b: 19). He insisted that it was time "to recognize that we have in America a variety of folk cultures, representing racial, regional, and even industrial cultures; that this very variety . . . constitutes the strength and richness in American lore, and that in the very process of transplanting, these imported cultures and traditions have undergone changes that make them a new tradition" (Botkin 1930c: 16).

In 1937 Botkin argued in deeper theoretical and more leftist formulations for rejecting the view of folklore as merely survivals. His first move was to attack evolutionary anthropology. Seizing on the functionalism in the work of ethnographer Bronislaw Malinowski and the pluralism of Boas, Botkin insisted that the "modern folklorist has come to see that folk phenomena . . . are the product of a complicated process of cultural isolation, conflict, change, and adaptation rather than of simple survival—the results of acculturation as well as diffusion" (Botkin 1937c: 466). He shifted the argument from an evolutionary view of culture to a view of the function of lore in the history of a group's past and contemporary life: "our many folk cultures are not behind us at all but right under us. Below the surface of the dominant pattern are the popular life and fantasy of our cultural minorities and other nondominant groups—nondominant but not recessive, not static but dynamic and transitional, on their way up" (Botkin 1938b: 126). If writers acted like ethnographers, Botkin argued, they not only would be performing important cultural work but also would be modernists who would aid in "restoring the basic integration of work patterns and ethical patterns" and thereby also show that the source of modernist dreams could be fulfilled: "Then the breach between expression and experience, universality and personality, the artificer and the maker, the subjective and the objective will be healed" (Botkin 1938b: 128–29). Ultimately the ideal is romantic, liberal, and reformist:

> And these are the values that folklore can restore to the individual and that the individual should seek to recover from folklore for literature—a sense of the continuity of human nature; a sense of art as a response instead of a commodity; a sense of social structure, based on social intelligence and good will; and a sense of pattern in its primitive use as a model and a guide rather than a limit. (Botkin 1938b: 135)

In the spring of 1938, when Botkin was offered the position of national folklore editor of the New Deal's Federal Writers' Project (FWP), he eagerly accepted it. The University of Oklahoma granted him a leave of absence (Hirsch 2003a: 232–33). Botkin probably did not note that congressional hearings had already begun that were hostile to all Works Progress Administration (WPA; later Works Projects Administration) arts projects and would lead to curtailing the activities of the FWP little over a year later (see Hirsch 2003a: 197–212). His eye was on the possibilities, on the opportunities to continue the work he had begun in Oklahoma. The demise of *Folk-Say* and *Space* (an experimental literary magazine he had edited) convinced him that he had not successfully stimulated the new literature and work of folklore that he wanted to see take root and flower. The *Folk-Say* experiment, which combined folk literature and literature about the folk, had not found a wide audience and had not solved the problem of the writer's relation to society or reinvigorated the culture of the larger society by reintroducing it to the diversity and richness of its folk traditions (Botkin 1935b: 321–30). Now the FWP was offering him an opportunity to have the assistance of the federal government in implementing what might be seen as a revised version of the folklore and literature program that he had first tried out in Oklahoma.

One of the attractions of the position was that the project was run by officials who, like him, were committed to redefining American identity in pluralistic and egalitarian terms (a point developed fully in Hirsch 2003a). National FWP officials knew that they could not follow the direction of national folklorists in Europe, who had maintained that the peasants (the largest group in the rural areas of their nations) were the bearers of the folk traditions that would provide a basis for a national identity and art. Yet, as romantic nationalists, FWP officials rejected the idea that the United States had no folklore. Botkin proved particularly helpful here. He argued that there were distinctive and diverse forms of lore that grew out of the experience of American folks. By also asserting that lore was still being created, Botkin was one of the first American folklorists who did not see modernity as the mortal enemy of folklore. While geographic isolation was no longer possible, he pointed out, it was not necessary for the creation of new lore, because class and ethnicity were among the new factors that led to partial isolation of groups. Unlike many other folklorists, Botkin was not looking for pure, uncontaminated lore. He maintained that interaction between cultural levels and different groups produced a new hybrid of lore. With its implications of cultural interaction, this concept was a controversial one that many of his fellow Americans were unwilling to accept in the face of conversations inside fascist states about cultural and racial purity. As national FWP officials sought to take a deeper look into contemporary culture, ethnicity, and occupational life, Botkin would be able to show them the relevance of folklore to their studies.

Botkin used the FWP to collect, preserve, and disseminate American folklore and hoped that his work would lead to the creation of a permanent federal folklore program. In his new position he established a committee to coordinate all the folklore programs and activities going on within the myriad of New Deal agencies. The committee was charged with preparing a new folklore manual for FWP workers and implementing new projects. The manual was written not with fellow scholars in mind but to help ordinary fieldworkers. Though the manual's emphasis does not appear very startling today, in 1938 it was groundbreaking.[6] In part it embodied traditional views of the field, but it also insisted that folklore was not confined to the ignorant and the isolated and had to be understood in terms of its meaning in group life.

> Folklore is a body of traditional belief, custom, and expression handed
> down largely by word of mouth and circulating chiefly outside of com-

mercial and academic means of communication and instruction. Every group bound together by common interests and purposes, whether educated or uneducated, rural or urban, possesses a body of traditions which may be called its folklore. Into these traditions enter many elements, individual, popular, and even "literary," but all are absorbed and assimilated through repetition and variation into a pattern which has value and continuity for the group as a whole.[7]

In his work with the FWP Botkin moved toward an idea of folk-say and life histories as a contribution to folk history. This was a social history told from a folk perspective: as he put it (after editing the FWP interviews with former slaves), he envisioned a new American "history from the bottom up," based on the assumption "that history must study the inarticulate many as well as the articulate few" (Botkin 1945g: xiii).

In the fall of 1938 Botkin was able to establish special Living Lore Units in New York City, Chicago, and New England (see Botkin 1946d and Botkin 1958k). Creative writers, some of whom would become famous (like Nelson Algren and Ralph Ellison), worked on these special units, which Botkin frequently visited. In the very naming of these units Botkin made a scholarly and ironic point. William Wells Newell, one of the founders of the American Folklore Society, had used the term "living lore" to make a distinction between what he saw as the living culture of American Indians and folklore survivals, the dead or dying remnants of earlier stages in the evolution of culture, found in "civilized" society (Newell 1888: 5–6). Botkin encouraged those who wrote on the Living Lore Units to focus on the collection of urban and industrial lore and to explore the relationship between lore and creative writing that had long concerned him. Writers would learn more than merely how to place folk items in their own work; they would learn how to represent, transform, and draw out the implications of folkloric events.

Congressional conservatives, charging New Deal arts projects with promoting communism, eliminated the Federal Theatre Project and curtailed other projects. What had seemed like a long-term intellectual avenue for Botkin to pursue proved only a temporary base from which to operate. In 1939 he was appointed to head the Writers' Program Unit at the Library of Congress. For two years he worked to catalogue Federal Writers' Project materials and also to give the study of folk culture a kind of sanctioned stature in the federal government (Hirsch 2003a: 229–37). In this latter effort Botkin failed, though he recognized the failure as a learning experience. When he discussed returning to the University of Oklahoma, the administration let him know that he would have to answer questions from the trustees, who viewed with alarm his participation in leftist cultural politics.[8] After extended periods of shuttling between Washington and Norman, Botkin left the University of Oklahoma, and the academic world, permanently.

In 1941 Botkin was appointed a fellow at the Library of Congress, with the support of a Carnegie grant. His knowledge of folklore had impressed Archibald MacLeish, the well-known poet who was serving as head of the library. The next year Botkin was made the assistant director of the Archive of American Folk Song. In 1944 he became director and followed a policy that treated "folk-song activity . . . as arc, with collection at one end and publication at the other" (Botkin 1944a: 24). He tried to shape archive policy along the lines that he had outlined in his 1939 presentation "WPA and Folklore Research: 'Bread and Song' " (Botkin 1939e) before the Modern Language Association (MLA). Specifically Botkin contended that folklore collecting should be "research not for research's sake but for use and enjoyment by the many," that such research should be seen "as a public function and folklore as public, not private property," and that folklorists had the moral obligation to give back to the people the lore "that rightfully belongs to them, in a form which they can understand and use" (Botkin 1939e: 10–14).

Botkin probably could have stayed at the Archive of American Folk Song permanently. But he was still committed to introducing Americans to their folklore in the broader ways that he had been articulating since the publication of his first volume of *Folk-Say* in 1929. In 1940 he began working on a project that would be the most important of his career if judged solely by its national impact. Published in 1944, *A Treasury of American Folklore* become a bestseller and gained him a small measure of genuine fame. The volume's enormous commercial success gave him the financial security to leave Washington in 1944 and devote himself full time to his own projects. Recognizing a substantial reading audience for his work, he continued to produce a diverse series of regional and topical folklore anthologies, including *A Treasury of New England Folklore* (1947), *A Treasury of Western Folklore* (1951), and *Sidewalks of America* (1954).

With the popular and critical success of his treasuries, it might seem that Botkin was about to assume a position as a wise eminence in the study of American culture in general and American folklore in particular. But perhaps there is always something about writing aimed at popular audiences that strikes some academics as vulgar. Indeed, Botkin had sensed this back in 1938 when he spoke to the Modern Language Association and not only laid out his ideas but anticipated how they might be attacked: "if giving back to the people what we have taken from them and what rightfully belongs to them, in a form which they can understand and use, is vulgarization then we need more of it" (Botkin 1939e: 10). Given the defensive and marginal position of folklore studies in the academic world, some were bound to perceive Botkin's views and practices as a threat to the scholarly status of folklore as a field. It did not help that folklore in the 1950s was only beginning to undergo the academic professionalization that often meant driving amateurs out of learned societies, which had occurred in fields such as history half a century earlier. Increasingly, areas of study that did not have their own university departments were at risk of being marginalized or even eliminated. These high stakes were clear to Richard Dorson, who was determined to establish folklore as a fully funded university discipline that granted doctoral degrees. In such an atmosphere, Dorson would view Botkin's border crossings as transgressions.

Dorson led the charge to bring down Botkin's reputation, to marginalize his influence, and to ensure that scholars from other fields would not regard him as a reputable folklorist. The irony that the two men shared a common viewpoint about the centrality of American folklore in comprehending American history was seemingly lost on Dorson. He called Botkin a "fakelorist" and his work "fakelore" (Dorson 1950a). However clever the terms sounded as neologisms, in the long run they would not delimit Botkin's ultimate legacy. Even at the height of Dorson's influence, Botkin had a respectful audience among some folklorists, especially the generation that emerged with the postwar folksong revival. Nonetheless, the belittling labels caused Botkin considerable pain during the last twenty-five years of his life.

Botkin observed the folksong revival and concluded that his views regarding the direction that folklore study should take were not yet defeated, despite the vituperative campaign being waged against him by Dorson's folklore department at Indiana University. What pleased Botkin most was that the revival stimulated new questions about the meaning and use of tradition: "What is the relation of the individual to the group? of urban to rural groups? of tradition to change?" (Botkin 1963f: 62). These were questions that Botkin had been asking since the 1920s and 1930s. By 1959, he concluded, the positive influence of the folksong revival was spilling over into the American Folklore Society and was playing a major role in encouraging new approaches among younger folklore scholars (Botkin 1959e). He held onto the hope that a new generation of scholars, many of whom were deeply involved in the revival, might heal the divisions among older folklorists. Botkin saw these divisions as standing in the way of both scholarly innovation and the utilization of folklore. This new generation of folklorists would improve academic folklore's relations with the public and move beyond what he saw as false dichotomies. As a supportive critic of the revival, Botkin reiterated the main themes of his lifelong work in folklore. He viewed the folksong revival as a sign that the work he had been doing in folklore might be continued by others, that his legacy (although he did not use this term) would be expanded by others.

Botkin's position that the revival raised profound issues about the study and use of folklore had roots in the vision and theories that he had been articulating since the publication of his first volume of *Folk-Say*. In keeping with his commitment to a Popular Front alliance of liberals and leftists, Botkin had told his MLA audience in 1938 that the challenge facing a democratic scholarship and art was to study and use folklore to understand and strengthen democracy: "Upon us devolves the tremendous responsibility of studying folklore as a living culture and of understanding its meaning and function not only in its immediate setting but in progressive and democratic society as a whole" (Botkin 1939e: 14). Almost twenty-five years later Botkin insisted that for the new folksong revival to survive it had to "ally itself with the egalitarian 'urban majority' on the side of the dynamic creative forces of cultural pluralism and equality against the forces of conformity and reaction" (Botkin 1966a: 15).

For a long time, little effort was made to assess Botkin's legacy. One reason may be that the controversies surrounding his work cast him as a kind of hands-off object of scrutiny in academic folklore settings. The very folklore students who would have been most likely to study and perpetuate Botkin's theories were also invested in establishing themselves in a profession that had resisted much of his thinking. Another reason has to do with what we now call Botkin's multidisciplinarity. A scholar would have to move deftly within many fields to place Botkin and his work in the broad historical context it deserves.

But it was perhaps inevitable that someone who participated in so many cultural and intellectual discourses in the twentieth century could not be ignored indefinitely. Two conferences held on the hundredth anniversary of Botkin's birth in 2001, one at the University of Nebraska–Lincoln in February and one at the Library of Congress's American Folklife Center in November, indicated that—if there was not a subfield of Botkin studies—at least emerging numbers of scholars from different fields were finding him relevant to their research interests. Botkin would have been pleased if he had known that both events included musical performances and personal reminiscences as well as scholarly papers. Such a structure reflected the value that he attached not only to studying folklore but also to presenting the lore itself in a way that integrated it back into life. Botkin was willing to listen and learn from anyone, so it would also have pleased him to know that amid the scholars who attended were a number of nonscholars who came only because they wanted to learn more about American folklore and culture, wanted to understand, appreciate, and enjoy.

Pack rat that he was, Botkin would have been happy to learn that his personal library of over 8,000 books and 700 recordings (including some of his field recordings) and nearly 500 linear feet of papers would all be shared with anyone who visited the newly established University of Nebraska Love Library's Benjamin A. Botkin Collection of Applied American Folklore. The collection's contents point to Botkin as a book hound, a collector of all kinds of published Americana, and someone who saved bits and pieces of old papers. Like most collectors, he probably felt that he was preserving material for later generations. And he was right if he imagined that in time others would want to read what he had saved. This collection includes correspondence with figures as diverse and culturally significant and prominent as Ira and George Gershwin, H. L. Mencken, Lewis Mumford, Woody Guthrie, Sterling Brown, Henry Nash Smith, Katherine Ann Porter, Alan Lomax, Charles Seeger, Ruth Crawford Seeger, Pete Seeger, Mari Sandoz, Richard Dorson, Norman Rockwell, Archibald MacLeish, Langston Hughes, and Carl Sandburg. And this list barely skims the surface. The collection will be useful to anyone interested in twentieth-century American cultural and intellectual life. It would have made sense to Botkin that his working cultural business archives are now at the University of Nebraska. He had come to Lincoln from Norman, Oklahoma, in the 1930s to study with the noted folklorist and local legend Louise Pound, whom he always admired. Complementing the University of Nebraska's Botkin Collection is the American Folklife Center at the Library of Congress, which is perhaps the most complete fulfillment of some of the intellectual adventures and risks that Botkin had been willing to undertake. The American Folklife Center was proud to honor Botkin in 2001 and will continue to draw on his language, vision, and work.

The great advantage of this volume of essays is that a group of scholars can explore facets of Botkin's career and examine his vision and work from very different perspectives. This collection is intentionally organized around Botkin's wide-ranging interests and therefore is not focused on a specific theme or on a particular aspect of his work or career. Nor does it approach Botkin's work from the viewpoint of one particular discipline. Instead literary scholars, folklorists, musicologists, and historians contribute to a book that focuses on Botkin's eclectic but interrelated concerns, work, and vision. Scholarly papers that were prepared especially for the Nebraska conference are found alongside classic treatments of Botkin by scholars, friends, and relatives. Arguably the most exciting part of the volume comes in allowing Botkin to speak directly to readers in his own voice through his poetry and essays. These works have never been brought together before in a single collection. In so prolific a career there is always the wish to include more, to add, not edit: we left out more far more than we could put in. If our intent has been to include a variety of Botkin's best-known writings alongside some lesser-known gems, our hope is to give readers an opportunity to appreciate his wide-ranging mind as he made illuminating connections among diverse topics in clear and often memorable prose.

This volume is divided into three parts: biography and folklore contexts; Botkin and his contemporaries; and Botkin in his own words. The first section examines themes that tie together Botkin's life and work. Throughout his life he worked with a variety of contemporaries who were part of different intellectual discourses that he was able to see as interrelated. The second section highlights that fact. Botkin always insisted it was important to listen creatively to informants. The last section allows readers to hear Botkin's own voice.

In part I Lawrence Rodgers offers the first extended analysis of Botkin's poetry. This chapter is also an account of his academic career as a poet and English professor. Rodgers finds in these's early creative writings a theory of art and culture that Botkin would incorporate into his theoretical thinking about folklore, especially the part that addressed the role of the creative writer.

Ronna Lee Widner Sharpe provides one of the first scholarly accounts of Botkin's career. She places his work in the context of a history of conflict between purists and popularizers in the study of folklore. She also finds a connection between Botkin's concerns with utilization and applied folklore and the growth of public folklore, which had just begun to develop when she wrote the essay. For her and for other public sector folklorists who work for the kind of governmental and not-for-profit agencies that directly interface with the general public, Botkin is an inspiring figure.

Jerrold Hirsch examines *The Treasury of American Folklore* (1944), Botkin's most popular work and the most popular folklore book ever published in the United States. He looks at the book as an outgrowth of Botkin's career-long reflection on the place of folklore in American culture. Hirsch also discusses the history of praise and criticism of the book and what its reception reveals about larger historical trends.

Bruce Jackson and Ellen Stekert were among the many folklorists who came of age in the sixties and seventies who found Botkin to be an inspiring figure. They sought out his advice, became friends, and in the broadest and truest sense of the term became Botkin's students, although he was not then teaching at any university. When he died in 1975, just as Jackson's and Stekert's own impressive careers were going forward, they wrote the moving obituaries included here. Both of them argue for the respect that Botkin deserves because of his broad poetic vision. Jackson also points out the heuristic value of Botkin's career for other folklorists and for anyone interested in American culture. Stekert includes some revealing personal observations about Botkin's shyness, his sense of humor, and his maverick nature. The biographical section concludes with a conversation with Botkin's adult children, Dorothy Botkin Rosenthal and Daniel Botkin, recalling what it meant to grow up in a household where folklore, books about folklore, and students and performers of folklore were a palpable presence. This chapter can be read both for the personal glimpse it gives of Botkin and his family and for its revelation of the richness and joys of participating in a family world that was in no small part shaped by the interconnectedness of life and lore.

Part II provides a rich sense of the fruitful relationships that Botkin had with leading musicologists, composers, poets, and intellectuals of his day. Music historian Judith Tick's essay uses a neologism "twistification" as a metaphor for the working friendship between Botkin and the composer Ruth Crawford Seeger. The essay positions this friendship in the context of the folk revival movement in its formative decades to show how Botkin and Crawford Seeger both challenged the categories of "purist" and "popularizer" within folklore and folksong scholarship. Nancy Cassell McEntire examines Botkin's first book (based on his doctoral dissertation), *The American Play-Party Song* (1937). Musicologist Taylor Greer's discussion of the long friendship between Botkin and Charles Seeger describes how both men moved away from the great nineteenth-century science of classification and evolution, constructed and looked at from the allegedly all-knowing perspective of a singular observer. In contrast, Botkin and Seeger embraced a more relativistic, multiperspective, uncertain, and intuitive set of views on science and art.

Including two essays on Botkin and Sterling Brown side by side allows for a more thorough consideration of their relationship. As Brown's critical stature has deservedly increased over the past decade, he joins Botkin as a fellow intellectual and artist whose shared contributions to mid-century conversations about American diversity have only recently begun to be fully appreciated. Brown and Botkin were lifelong friends at a time when close personal friendships between whites and blacks were less common. In the midst of recognizing Brown as a major American poetic voice, Steven B. Shively and John Edgar Tidwell together flesh out Botkin's connection with Brown and his influence on the poet. Employing fresh archival material, Shively provides a formal analysis of Brown's poem "Ma Rainey," first published in *Folk-Say II* in 1930 as the second of three sections of his masterful poem "Dark of the Moon." Shively also examines the extensive correspondence between Botkin and Brown about "Ma Rainey." Botkin suggested changes in the poem and even rewrote parts of it. His role is especially important in light of the contention of Houston Baker, Jr., that "Ma Rainey" is a defining achievement in modernist African American poetry.

The relationship between Brown and Botkin affirms the breadth of Botkin's national network. It also bolsters Brown's contention that however much Harlem was the "show window, the cashier's till" of the New Negro Renaissance, it was a nationwide phenomenon that extended well beyond Lenox Avenue (Brown 1955: 57). Tidwell's chapter focuses on the crucial role that Botkin, as sometime editor, played in Brown's career and more generally establishes his significant role in promoting African American scholarship and art. Tidwell makes a strong case for the ways in which Botkin's view of literature and theories of folklore were useful to Brown in his poetry about African American life and lore.

Botkin's own writing is as eclectic as the subjects he studied. Part III is a selection of his essays and poetry. He is a serious folklorist, an astute essayist and observer of casual human behavior, an intellectual of the mid-century American Left, an editor, a well-published poet, and a literary artist. Botkin moves from the serious and analytical to the playful and informal, from writing that is deeply personal to writing that is pointedly detached. He was prolific enough to offer more than a single volume of works that deserve rereading and studying. But choices had to be made, so this section showcases an introduction to his writing intended to open doors, not close them. Together the essays reflect the development of Botkin's consistently democratic, egalitarian, and pluralistic vision of American culture and the role that folklore should play in that culture. Amid the astounding variety of Botkin's writing, it is easy to overlook the unifying thread that binds his career. Whatever his tone and subject, the unifying feature of the writing is the clarity and accessibility of his voice. Botkin insisted that old ways of thinking about folklore stood in the way of studying and utilizing American lore.

Botkin's poetry took diverse forms, reflecting both his affinity for a romanticism born out of British sources and a place-oriented poetics of American regionalism. For nearly two decades Botkin published poems in some of the country's most distinguished poetry venues. Some of these poems are reprinted together here for the first time. The complete list of Botkin's works in the bibliography provides a sense of the great range of his intellectual curiosity and an opportunity for readers to explore his and their common interests. It is still too early for a full understanding of Botkin's influence, but we can see it emerging. And the work being done in response to the ongoing study of Botkin is creating a legacy in the making. We think Ben Botkin, the student of folklore in the making, would have been pleased.

Notes

1. B. A. Botkin, "The Autobiography of a Boy" (unpublished manuscript, 1918, in Hirsch's possession).

2. For a still classic account of evolutionary anthropology and the impact of Franz Boas's views, see Stocking 1968, especially 64–90, 195–223.

3. Botkin to parents-in-law, April 24, 1927, Botkin Papers (hereafter BP), copy in Hirsch's possession.

4. For a list of Botkin's reviews in the *Daily Oklahoman*, see the bibliography.

5. Gertrude Botkin to Ben Botkin, September 7, 1939, Botkin Papers, University of Nebraska, Lincoln.

6. Folklorist Kenneth Goldstein in a conversation in 1982 referred to Botkin's definition of folklore and his manual in general as the best definition of and introduction to the field.

7. Botkin, "Manual for Folklore Studies," August 15, 1938, Box 69, Federal Writers' Project files, Works Progress Administration, Records Group 69, Federal Writers' Project, National Archives, Washington, D.C.

8. B. A. Botkin (Ben) to Gertrude Botkin, August 21, 1939; Gertrude to Ben, September 7, 1939; Ben to Gertrude, November 3, 1939; Ben to Gertrude, n.d. [fall 1939]; B. A. to Gertrude, February 19, 1941, Botkin Papers, University of Nebraska, Lincoln.

PART ONE

Biographical Backgrounds and Folklore Contexts

"In the beginning lore and literature were one"

B. A. Botkin's Literary Legacy

LAWRENCE RODGERS

Benjamin Botkin's work in folklore will no doubt remain his most lasting legacy. However, long before he became a folklorist, at least a professional one, he was a poet. His undergraduate studies at Harvard—begun when he was only sixteen—exhibited an abiding interest in literature, especially in William Wordsworth's romantic circle and in Carl Sandburg. He wrote his Columbia master's thesis on Thomas Edward Brown, a Victorian lyricist and the national poet of the Isle of Man. Botkin's earliest publications were poems. His first job, as an English professor at the University of Oklahoma, cast him, in his own words, in the role of "press-agent" for the "promotion" of regional poetry (Botkin 1927j). While in Oklahoma, he reviewed any number of poets in the Sunday pages of the *Daily Oklahoman,* including W. B. Yeats, T. S. Eliot, D. H. Lawrence, and Countee Cullen (see the introduction). Indeed, he would come to play a central role in bringing national attention to Oklahoma literature, not only as a promoter but as a theorist of how creative writing could develop out of an immersion into regional culture.

Although it is tempting to bifurcate Botkin's career trajectory into two phases—the youthful poet maturing into the distinguished folklorist—in reality his legacy as a man of letters reflects a seamless melding of the sometimes contentious arenas of folklore and literature. His vision was grand. Nothing less than the basis for a new renaissance in American culture and writing could be found at the intersections of folklore, literature, and regionalism.

Botkin's creative vision both distinguished him as a folklorist and set him apart from some of the conventional, if narrow, academic views that have constituted the literary and anthropological wings of the field. Botkin viewed folklore as more than either the "unlettered" detritus of real literature or an unmediated, aesthetically inferior mirror of local culture. It occupied an artistic middle ground whose significance was to be measured in its essential connections to the region in which it was produced. Botkin had little interest in defining the science of folklore via either evolutionary anthropology or geographical historical methods. Folklore was not, as he conceived it, so much a scientific record of culture as a means to interpret and comprehend cultural phenomena, especially since he maintained that "in the beginning lore and literature were one" (Botkin 1929b: 9). To encapsulate Botkin himself is to personalize that statement: he brought a poet's gaze to the field of folklore.

Botkin's artistic ethos would make him a lifelong renegade in academic folklore circles, which in his era tended to pay attention to local cultural artifacts and attributes not in terms of whether they possessed aesthetic merit but as the building blocks of systems of cultural classification. This made professional folklorists, by their own estimation, scientific, scholarly, and worthy of harborage in university departments, while Botkin was cast in the role of popularizer, a "fakelorist" in Richard Dorson's coinage (Dorson 1950a). But even as Botkin's detractors were guilty, as one of his obituaries phrased it, of "ideological tunnel vision inculcated by grim professionalism" (Jackson 1976: 4), Botkin did not seek to mollify his detractors. He chose instead to follow his own path, a synthetic approach that allowed his sources to document their lives on their own terms and that has found a firm enough disciplinary toehold to render him, with the benefit of a generation of hindsight, a visionary practitioner, especially in the study of urban lore. An adherent of "impure" applied folklore that mixed "both life and literature," Botkin was, by his own characterization, "half-literary and half-anthropological in my interests."[1]

I am interested in the less studied part of this equation, Botkin's literary half, not so much because he deserves critical resuscitation as an undiscovered poetic genius but because his early participation in literary culture, as student, poet, and editor, offers a revealing starting point for gaining insight into the folklore work of his mature years. His artistic sensibility had a significant impact on the unfolding of his theories of folklore. It ingrained in him the tools that made him an astute editor able to nurture dozens of fellow poets, folklorists, and other scholars. And it accounted for his emergence as an important contributor to the movement of literary regionalism during the 1920s. To broaden the portrait of Botkin the folklorist, this chapter briefly sets out three examples that showcase his literary side: his graduate work on Thomas Brown, several examples of his own poetry, and his first major editing project, *Folk-Say*, which represents a model melding of regional folklore and literature. If this sampling reinforces a sense of Botkin as a figure attracted to out-of-the-way places, bypassed communities, and things outside the mainstream, his literary work also underscores the merits of his fundamentally pluralistic conception of society. He emerges, to my mind, not only as a unique bridge between literature and anthropology but also as a one-of-a-kind vantage point for comprehending the relationship of art, whether high or low, rural or urban, with the surroundings from which it emanates.

Twenty-year-old Botkin completed his Columbia master's thesis on Thomas Edward Brown in 1921, the same year he saw his first three published poems appear in the *New York Evening Post*. By present terms, Brown is a second-tier nineteenth-century regional writer who, as the National Poet of the Isle of Man, offers historical insight into an isolated corner of the British Isles. Rarely anthologized and invisible to all but the most widely read Victorianists, Brown nonetheless remains (as a poet, letter writer, columnist, and general observer of Manx life) a crucial repository of the island's past. Brown's relative obscurity would have rendered him an appealing choice for Botkin. The Isle of Man, a self-governed dot of land, rises out of the Irish Sea at the halfway point of a line drawn from Belfast to Liverpool. Although it has its own church, money, stamps, tax system, and parliament, it is thoroughly enough British to make its independence "a patriotic and legal fiction." Brown, by his own account, sought to write "in the language really used by men" in an effort to "unlock the treasures of the Island heart" (Tobias 1988: 16–18). About four of every five poems he wrote are in the English dialect spoken by the modern Manx. Mostly lyrics, they address island topics and are attuned to the region's Celtic past. Like the Scots in the poetry of Robert Burns, the person to whom Brown invites easy comparison, he portrays the Manx as simple, untaught people challenged by the stresses of modern life. His characteristic blend of provincial and religious subject matter is in evidence in one of his more widely read poems, "Mater Dolorosa," a doleful maternal lament on the loss of a son, Billy, "The sweetest lamb of all our fold." The mother takes consolation in the "good sowl" who "naver knew sin" because he has gone to the angels in a "yandhar place." In the last stanza, Billy's six-year-old sister "knelt upon her brother's grave" and "so unto the turf her ear she laid," only to find that "Death's silence is profound!" In final consolation, the grieving mother concludes that "If this is as it ought to be, / My God, I leave it unto Thee" (Tobias 1988: 19).

Although Brown was born on the Isle of Man, his Scottish parents were not. Educated at Oxford and later a Fellow there, he was considered a relative newcomer and an outsider to an isolated locale where pedigree was measured less in years than in centuries. As such, his motives and credentials as a native writer were constantly under scrutiny even as long-time residents welcomed the recognition he brought to them. Botkin's master's thesis tends to focus, like most critical projects of the day, almost entirely on formal aspects of individual poems. While praising poems in high-blown language for their romantic virtuosity, the thesis pays little attention to situating Brown in his own cultural milieu. Nonetheless, we can observe in hindsight an almost uncanny affinity between Brown's inside/outside status on the Isle of Man and the situation Botkin would find himself in when he left Boston to come west to Oklahoma and Nebraska. Both were well-educated men with strong credentials from distinguished universities; both exhibited a joint passion for poetry and scholarship; and both found their most lasting intellectual inspiration in regional enclaves far afield from the dominant cultural centers that other people of their intellectual pedigrees tended to favor. One can find in Brown's 1887 dedication to *The Doctor and Other Poems* a nearly perfectly worded summary of Botkin's own career motives. Here Brown promised to fix Manx life on the page: "That so the coming age, Lost in the empire's mass, / . . . here / May see, as in a glass, / What they held dear" (quoted in Tobias 1988: 16). Had Brown been born in a more recent age, he might be looked upon less as a poet and essayist than as a practical folklorist who, like Botkin, brought an artistic perspective to preserving the indigenous habits, cultural patterns, and local meanings of his surroundings.

On finishing his thesis, Botkin spent a year with his family in New York, deeply entrenched in reading poetry. He left for Norman in fall 1921, when he accepted a job as an instructor of English at the University of Oklahoma, a relatively young university in a new state that must have seemed as remote, to Botkin, as the Isle of Man. As the son of Yiddish-speaking Lithuanian Jews (with the family name Rabotnick), Botkin would have seemed more destined for the East Coast intellectual world inhabited by his cousins George and Ira Gershwin than for an outpost of frontier temperament located in the midst of the windy plains. His failure to warm to the Norman scene immediately is hardly surprising. Oklahoma's ethnic and racial insularity guaranteed that, as the second Jew to teach at the university, he was not likely to be readily embraced. But he had a teaching job, which gave him, in his words, "students to mold." And his new position appealed to his sense of being an outside observer of an exotic scene, even as he lamented the dearth of cultural and intellectual opportunities to which he was accustomed. "Culture in Norman is illusory," he wrote soon after arriving. Yet soon enough Oklahoma began to awaken something in him and gradually would become one of the more enduring sources of scholarly and poetic inspiration. Following a two-year hiatus back east from 1923 to 1925, Botkin returned to Norman. "[I]n spite of the physical and spiritual flatness of the place," the region had become a fertile source of artistic inspiration (quoted in Dorman 1993: 45). The basis of what would turn out to be his most productive literary period lay in the landscape of his adopted region. He had, as he later put it, a near religious conversion to the power of western topography: "The possibilities of Oklahoma as literary material struck me with the force of the Oklahoma wind and stuck to me like a sandbur" (Botkin 1930c: vi).

The timing of Botkin's arrival was auspicious, coinciding as it did with a burgeoning poetry movement that would, in a few short years, bring national attention to a group of state writers. Botkin joined two other figures, an Oklahoma poet named John McClure and the prominent Baltimore editor H. L. Mencken, as the midwives most responsible for this run of statewide literary fortune. Mencken's curious role has been fully described elsewhere (Rodgers 2000–2001), but a brief summary helps account for the part that Botkin played in this small-scale renaissance. In 1917 Mencken published a now-infamous denunciation of southern culture, "The Sahara of the Bozart," wherein he wrote that the South was as "sterile, artistically, intellectually, culturally, as the Sahara Desert" (Mencken 1920: 136). In a passing reference, he contrasted what he denounced as the South's "neighborhood rhymesters" with McClure, a relatively unknown Oklahoma versifier. Earlier he had ac-claimed McClure for writing "the best recent American poetry" and put his work in the same class as Carl Sandburg's much acclaimed *Chicago Poems*. More remarkably, based on McClure's single book *Airs and Ballads,* Mencken proclaimed him to be the finest "lyric poet the United States has produced in fifty years" (Bode 1977: 102). Botkin found the best of McClure's poems to be filled with "fragile music," steeped in "peculiar Celtic glamor" (Botkin 1927j: 29), but generally did not have the same high praise for McClure's verse, which seemed to him limited in style and subject.

Nonetheless, Botkin encountered an enthusiastic group of McClure de-votees in the Oklahoma English Department, even though McClure himself had moved away. Botkin quickly emerged as the leader of this talented as-sembly of writers. They were featured (together with a host of other young writers) in a 1921 university poetry anthology, which, though uneven in qual-ity, was successful enough to spur a more substantial second volume in 1924. (A third volume followed in 1929.) The second anthology caught the eye of

Mencken, who liked what he saw well enough to make what turned out to be a kind of birth announcement of Oklahoma writing:

> Oklahoma, though it came in before Arizona and New Mexico, is actually the youngest state in the union. Until 1889 it was a sort of No Man's Land. Yet I can testify as an editor that it produces ten times as many likely manuscripts a year as Maine, which was admitted in 1820, or Delaware, which was one of the original thirteen colonies, and it has already thrown off such men as John McClure, the poet, and Burton Rascoe, the critic.
>
> The reason I don't know, but the fact is brilliantly plain that many young Oklahomans are taking to the pen, and that not a few of them have talent. There is almost, indeed, an Oklahoma literature, or, at all events, an Oklahoma manner. (Mencken 1925: 9)

Like most things Mencken wrote, the statement (especially the final sentence) was publicized, which led Botkin to publish a follow-up article examining "The Oklahoma Manner in Poetry" (Botkin 1925a). While the article showcased his impressive critical faculties, it was clearly promotional in intent. In a lively descriptive framework, two distinct groups emerged from what Botkin would call "a rough-and-ready botanical classification" of the region's poetry. One, in a "vein of clever whimsy," was "the harlequin school of sophisticated lyrists fostered by John McClure, which is after all an exotic transplanted to Oklahoma soil." The other was a region-based "homespun local-color school" that focused on "pioneer work with frontier material." In an effort to counter the eastern seaboard's literary dominance, he proclaimed the "hope and promise of an 'enlightened regional consciousness'" in the country's interior (Botkin 1925a: 27). After reading the piece, Mencken asked Botkin for a group of samples, which were featured in the *American Mercury*. Despite appearing with nine other poets in the May 1926 issue, Botkin was not wholly pleased. Although he had a hand in selecting the poems, he had some second thoughts about whether they shed the best possible light on the group of writers he later christened "Oklahoma Poets, *inc.*" He claimed that the "Oklahoma manner could not exist apart from an Oklahoma subject-matter; and that the only justification of the existence of these poets, individually and collectively, as Oklahoma poets, lay in their development and even systematic exploitation of local material." By Botkin's measure, the *American Mercury* poems failed to demonstrate sufficient "sectional consciousness," which was his way of saying that they contained too much McClure and not enough Oklahoma (Botkin 1927j: 29–30).

In fact, a similar appraisal helps sort out Botkin's own poetry, which is at its best when it expresses an awareness of local surroundings and is less successful when it expresses conventional lyrical pieties through traditional verse forms. Although he may not qualify as a major poet, he wrote his share of excellent poems. Most of his poems appeared in the 1920s and early 1930s, and he quit submitting poetry for publication altogether after leaving Oklahoma for Washington, D.C., in 1937. (His last published poem, "Carnival," appeared in 1938.) Botkin's work tends, on occasion, to reflect the uneven stylistic traces of youth. Consider, for example, two poems that similarly chart the vicissitudes of love. Although both display less depth of insight than cleverness and jocose punch lines, "Villanelle a Deux" evinces Botkin's genuine wit and sets out his sophisticated understanding of form. The other poem, "Values," is a simplistic rendering of the paradoxes of attraction:

> At first, because I thought you deep,
> You rightly held my wisdom cheap.
>
> And since I found you too, too dear.
> You kept me in a constant fear.
>
> But now it's you who are afraid,
> Since I see through the game you played.
>
> And now I hold your charms so cheap,
> You think me very, very deep.
> (Botkin 1923c: 14)

The poem's limitation is twofold. It asserts in its final line a depth that is nowhere in evidence in its content. And it assumes a singsong meter whose consistency relies on lapsing into needless repetition of intensifiers ("too, too," "very, very").

A far more successful approach to a similar subject is "Villanelle a Deux." The poem follows that notoriously intricate nineteen-line form, originally French. It employs an exact pattern of only two rhymes that repeat throughout, line one repeating as six, twelve, and eighteen; line three as nine, fifteen, and nineteen. The rhyme scheme is *aba aba aba aba aba abaa*. The most famous example, Dylan Thomas's "Do Not Go Gentle into That Good Night," is anomalous because of its lofty seriousness. More generally, villanelles are light-hearted, since their obsessive repetition points to typically hyperbolic preoccupations, as is the case with Botkin's rendition of a he said/she said moment in a relationship:

He: And that's the end of that.
        I am not wanted here.
     It must be tit for tat.

She: I know he'll leave me flat.
         They always disappear,
      And that's the end of that.

He: I take my stick and hat.
        "It's getting late, I fear."
     It must be tit for tat.

She: How terribly long he sat!
         Who will it be next year?
      And that's the end of that!

He: I give my gloves a pat.
        We're both bored stiff, it's clear.
     It must be tit for tat.

     I straighten my cravat.—
        "Good night!" (Good-bye my dear!)
     And that's the end of that!
     It must be tit for tat
     (Botkin 1923c: 14)

The poem bears, in every way, the mark of a young writer not only experi-
menting with form but willing to be original enough in his writing to move
beyond the excesses, what he called the "heartfire and singing," of the lyric
mood. As he would write elsewhere "the lyric mood is capable of infinite
modulations of temper and tone, from the sardonic to the saccharine, its
prevailing note being subjectivity—preoccupation with self or inability to
escape from self" (Botkin 1927d: 34). Botkin's suspicion of McClure-style
lyrics came from reading widely enough to know that poetry, even from
provincials like Thomas Brown, needed more than "the strange sweet sadness
of Celtic magic" to avoid degenerating into "flippant mannerism." Indeed,
poetry needed a sense of grounding in the real. One tires, he would note, of
trivial subjects like "clowns and elves" and overwrought language that sounds
like a "bassoon crying in darkness" (Botkin 1927d: 34). When Botkin wrote
that "the pure lyricist does not worry much about people; he finds more
company in himself than in a crowd," he was not offering a compliment.
While the young romantic in him, the lover of Wordsworth, may, for a time,

have embraced the preoccupation with the self, the nascent folklore collector knew enough about art to find poetry more appealing when its preoccupation moved outward into the world.

Botkin's interest in making such a move is illustrated in his 1928 poem "Going to the Store." Botkin employs the sonnet—the formal embodiment of self-conscious, inward-gazing poetry—to write about the simple appeal of local life. He exhibits a knack for extracting meaning from the kinds of every-day details, the "small delights," that could easily be overlooked. In the poem's beginning lines, Botkin's character sounds decidedly like a folklorist, especially one interested in urban folklore:

> Out of the walk he snatches small delights,
> Constructing plots and patterns in the streets
> And seeing strangeness in accustomed sights,
> At whose new sense his heart more quickly beats.

Finding meaning in life less in "distant war" than in "small-town thrills," Botkin turns the modest act of going to a store into an adventure that opens up a life to the "latest plunder."

This sonnet, and his poetry in general, suggests that Botkin's attentions were moving more toward subjects associated with folklore than toward romantic lyrics. His work on behalf of others—his "creative editing" and "creative conservation of human resources"—reflects an even more profound embrace of what he later identified as "my loyalty to the native tradition" (Botkin 1930c: vii). Oklahoma writers benefited greatly from his support. Having determined that "Oklahoma suffered no lack of sweet singers," Botkin set out to make them both better writers and better known. Before long, with the zeal of one newly converted to the landscape, with the sensibility and the general frontier temper of the country's Middle West, Botkin would stake a legitimate claim as the era's most astute observer and avid advocate of Oklahoma writers. State writers employing the "Oklahoma Manner" had gained a reputation for an impressive body of quality verse, displaying a distinct regional flavor.

Under Botkin's enthusiastic guidance, poetry continued to thrive. In 1927 he became president of the nascent (if short-lived) group Oklahoma Writers, which, continuing in the regional vein, was explicitly interested in fostering "Oklahoma backgrounds and materials" (Botkin 1927j: 29). The capstone of his involvement in Oklahoma poetry came in 1931 when he edited and published an anthology of regional verse, *The Southwest Scene* (1931i): eighteen of the twenty-nine featured poets were Oklahomans. Botkin's participation went a long way toward reaching his goal of making "Oklahoma culture-conscious and Oklahoma-conscious (a two fold pioneering)" (Botkin 1930c: v–vi). It also gave him a forum in which to air his midwestern, folk-based theories of culture vis-à-vis the heated contemporaneous scholarly debates on regionalism. Impressive in its own right, *The Southwest Scene* joined a range of other major regional texts, including Benton MacKaye's exploration of indigenous New England, *The New Exploration* (1928), and Walter Prescott Webb's historical assay of western regionalism, *The Great Plains* (1931). All of these combined to help map an alternative American landscape indebted, in Constance Rourke's words, to "the slow accretions of folk elements" necessary to define "the spirit of a region, its customs, folklore, and native speech" (Rourke 1933: 149).

The issue of regionalism, which "has been raging since the Republic's beginning" (Odum and Moore 1938: 228), deserves elaboration for two reasons. First, the debates reached an especially fevered pitch among intellectuals of the 1920s and 1930s. Second, and more to the point, this issue suggests the way in which Botkin considered Oklahoma as a literary locale to represent an exemplar of the cultural possibilities that a regional ethos would inspire.[2] The names affiliated with regionalism (including Walter Prescott Webb, Mary Austin, Donald Davidson, Angie Debo, J. Frank Dobie, Lewis Mumford, Howard Odum, and Mari Sandoz) were as diverse as the locations and subjects they represented. At stake were issues greater than scholarly ownership of a concept. They revolved around a looming cultural crisis over the changing nature of American identity. Representing a critical juncture in how that identity was to be constructed, the 1920 census had proclaimed for the first time that more Americans lived in the city than in the country. In response to the deficiencies of a culture at large that seemed increasingly urban, corporate, consumerist, and homogeneous, a core of like-minded intellectuals (including Botkin) rallied to proclaim the need to reassert pluralistic alternatives, a quintessential Americanness, born out of the political and cultural possibilities of local cultures, traditions, and landscapes. The geographic rootstock of this counter-response to the atomization of mass consumer society was the region, a *place*-oriented designation whose boundaries included a state like Oklahoma (hence Botkin's desire to showcase "local material").

The regional movement produced an array of alternative means for reconstructing society, all of them attuned to some form of diversity that celebrated the movement's ethic of pluralism. The realignment of values underpinning the regionalist project was hardly neutral, resting as it did on the not-always-popular political assumption that American diversity should be viewed as a cultural asset. Insofar as the very idea of being "regional" amounted to residing on the periphery of a dominant sphere, the call for ascribing value and status to things regional (whether writers, places, or indigenous practices) deemphasized the normative cultural and geographic center from which those things had been excluded. Examining something in regional terms, thus, was at once an empowering and transgressive act. Botkin would offer his own definition of regionalism: "The traditional forces of custom, belief, locality, and speech which within a region constitutes the peculiar disposition and expressiveness of a people, considered as a composite of racial and geographic influence and a component of national culture" (Botkin 1930c: 15). Oklahoma, by such measures, was less a frontier outpost on the fringe of *real* American culture than a legitimate repository of a particular regional branch of national culture. One of Botkin's most controversial positions held that regional folklore was not about people culturally, geographically, and/or socially isolated from the mainstream; rather, folklore was a relevant facet of almost all groups, regardless of whether they resided in the middle of Appalachia or in midtown Manhattan. Through the process of identifying these diverse folkloric traits, folklorists, in Botkin's terms, helped all citizens to recognize and come to appreciate the kind of cultural differences that constituted the bedrock of the country's pluralistic culture.

Oklahoma's dominant terms of identity—agriculture, Indian affairs, ranching, oil, western migration and settlement, rural and small-town concerns—were very much in sync with the larger range of issues around which the regional movement tended to converge. The regionalists expressed the need to protect regional inheritances (through emphasizing older America and its folk-rural cultures) from the encroaching throes of modernity. They set the country's interior, including the less-populated Midwest and Southwest, on an equal cultural footing with the coasts. They collapsed the cultural hierarchy between country and city, while simultaneously recognizing that folklore was not only a rural but an urban enterprise. Botkin hardly minced words in formulating such a sentiment: "America to-day is divided between the metropolitan civilization of our large industrial centers, where life is uprooted and disharmonious, and the indigenous culture of rural and small-town America, where people have roots in the soil or at least ties with their fellow beings" (Botkin 1931i: v). The regionalists showcased the expressive possibilities of African American and Native American cultures (embodied, for example, not only in the Harlem Renaissance and Santa Fe pottery but also in Jimmy Rushing's Oklahoma City Deep Deuce jazz sounds and Lynn Riggs's Oklahoma folk drama), while refusing to sugarcoat the exploitive realities of southern agrarianism and western expansion. Perhaps most significantly, they placed their faith in the power of art to help bring about this radical cultural transformation.[3]

Botkin's intellectual values, which put a premium on examining culture in egalitarian, relativistic, and pluralist terms (see Hirsch 1987: 5–9), meshed well with the tenets of this regional ethos. Commenting on the appeal of Oklahoma, he articulated the allure of the place to his friend Mary Austin in expressly regional terms: "I see in it an equilibrium of man and nature, for nature triumphs over man's attempts to mechanize the life of the region with the ubiquitous standardization of automobile, radio, talkies, electrical conveniences. . . . This is where I have learned and am applying what I flatter myself with calling a regional philosophy; and I am not only attached to this place but grateful to it" (quoted in Dorman 1993: 44–46).

The most extended application of that philosophy was *Folk-Say,* Botkin's compendium of four regional miscellanies, whose approach to folklore and linkage to literary and regionalism would turn into a career preoccupation. A neologism coined by Botkin, "Folk-Say" is an extension of an Anglo-Saxon term for preface ("Fore-Say") that includes "literature about the folk as well as of the folk" (Botkin 1930c: viii). When the first volume of *Folk-Say* was published in June 1929, it represented an attempt not only to bring together a range of material from Oklahoma and surrounding states but also to offer a case study in how such material could dissolve the division between folklore and literature. In an introduction focusing on "New Regionalism," Botkin phrased the project's goal in grand terms. "By setting the scholar and the artist at work upon oral tradition," he announced, "it is creating a genuine American myth and fable" (Botkin 1929b: 9–10).

Indeed, on one level *Folk-Say* seems mostly folkloric, containing, in Botkin's own colorful description, a "native medley of Indian legends, tall tales, old-timers' reminiscences, old songs, folk cures, dialect, slang, and local-color sketches and poems, adorned with a buffalo-head colophon and cowboy, Indian, and oil-field motifs" (Botkin 1929b: 10). On another level, the best of the sketches and poems moved well beyond folklore's initial impulse merely to record the verbal remnants of unlettered cultures. In no small part this is because of their willingness to address lyrically the everyday challenges and somber images of life among common folk, whose spiritual anxieties, though inarticulately expressed, are no less potent than those of more "enlightened" regions. The volume exemplifies why literary critics—who retain disciplinary sympathies with the tenor of the oft-quoted observation by William Carlos Williams: "The classic is the local fully realized, words marked by a place" (Williams 1970: 358)—find so much value in Botkin's brand of folklore. If there is an overarching thematic thread to the various genres and subjects that Botkin cobbled together to create the *Folk-Say* volumes, it is bound up in two things: a recognition of the diversity of the population that inhabits the country's middle region and an apprehension of the array of challenges that must be confronted on a day-to-day level. In their collective expression of those challenges, the various contributors to *Folk-Say* helped create, in Botkin's view, a collective means of making sense of and adding coherence to the otherwise disorienting nature of frontier experience.

Botkin added his own lasting contribution to this sense-making exercise via "Home Town," which appeared in *Prairie Schooner* in 1930. The poem is an appropriate end point for considering Botkin's literary side for several reasons. As his most enduring literary piece, it marks his willingness to embrace sophisticated intellectual questions about the modern self, in this case through simple, unadorned verse. It also stands as a brilliant, upbeat answer to the prevailing mood of spiritual alienation prevalent among Botkin's poetic contemporaries. Addressing terrain similarly covered by T. S. Eliot in "The Love Song of J. Alfred Prufrock," "Home Town" can be cited both to demonstrate Botkin's rebellion against the stylistic fragmentation and hyperethereality found in Eliot's modernist circle and also, more generally, to register Botkin's disgust with modernist writing's "blighted expressionistic philosophy of disintegration and disenchantment" (Botkin 1927t: 5).

The poem reframes the fragmented scraps and pieces of modernity, as Eliot expresses them, in the kind of communal small-town terms that let the "narrow walls and lonely rooms . . . shut out defeats." Eliot's narrator, whose words are also predominantly in couplets, tries to regain some sense of coherence by articulating the experience of disorientation. But he feels only indecision and paralysis as he has walked "at dusk through narrow streets / And watched the smoke that rises from the pipes / Of lonely men" (Eliot 1962: 5). In contrast, Botkin's persona moves comfortably through the town, absorbing the daily scene:

> . . . folk
> In casual encounters at their doors;
> Genie-like tradesmen, women doing chores,
> Old men on sticks who hugged the sunny side,
> Children on swings and carts and skates who cried
> A tuneless song; dogs running out to sniff
> Or bark at him; the titillating whiff
> Of cooking meals and burning trash.

Such disparate images conjure up, for Botkin, not estrangement but the basis of meaning and the appeal of local life, which delivers each day "With shining subtlety new evidence / Of people's likeness and their difference."

In the poem's most important line, which counters the "stray fragments, hints, mute words" (Eliot 1962: 6) so characteristic of Eliot's verse, Botkin spells out his confidence in shoring up the fragments as well as his belief in the power of absorbing and comprehending local knowledge: "He pieced together bits that he collected." When he left Norman in 1937 to take on the most important job of his career, as chief editor of the Writers' Unit for the Library of Congress, he might well have imagined that he was answering a call to continue his life-long project of making sense of the world by means of this simple line, by "piecing together bits."

Notes

1. Quoted in Hirsch 1996: 310.

2. For my understanding of regionalism during the 1930s, I am especially indebted to Robert L. Dorman, whose account is definitive, and John L. Thomas, who pointed me to Constance Rourke's article. In addressing this topic, I have incorporated some of the same language from an earlier essay I authored on George Milburn, an Oklahoma regional writer whom Botkin mentored. See "Oklahoma on His Mind: The Folklore Legacy of George Milburn," *Folklore Historian* 21 (2004): 5–7.

3. On the importance of art as the basis for transformation, Botkin writes that "the conception of a regionally differentiated and interregionally related culture has something to offer to literature, namely, a subject matter (the physical and cultural landscape, local customs, character, speech, etc.), a technique (folk and native modes of expression, style, rhythm, imagery, symbolism), a point of view (the social ideal of a planned society and the cultural values derived from tradition as 'the liberator, not the confiner')" (chapter 12).

Lore for the Folk

Benjamin A. Botkin and the Development of Folklore Scholarship in America

RONNA LEE WIDNER (SHARPE)

Images of voluminous treasuries of American regional, national, and topical folklore spring readily to mind at the mention of the name Benjamin A. Botkin. Public acceptance of these panoramic collections was immediate and enduring. Professional opinion of the philosophy they embodied varied and vacillated. The interaction of these elements provoked an intense debate electrifying the atmosphere in which the discipline of American folklore scholarship evolved during the twentieth century.

Succinctly stated, this confrontation pitted "purist" against "popularizer." Seeking institutional credibility, purists demanded scholarly perfection and encouraged scientific methodology. In essence, they sought to extract the lore from the folk and to examine it under laboratory-like conditions. Rigorous research methods and the data they generated would serve to confirm the validity of their discipline and ensure its continued existence.

As a popularizer, Botkin based his work on principles that may indeed have appeared subversive to such ivory tower ideals. More practical applications of folklore, perhaps not condoned by and certainly not confined to academic edicts, underlay Botkin's approach. Aggregation of folk and lore was imperative, for in the doctrine of the popularizer the two were inseparable.

Originally published in 1986, this essay was one of the first following Botkin's death to address his contributions to the field of American folklore. The approach is less theoretical than summative and biographical. It originally appeared as Ronna Lee Widner, "Lore for the Folk: Benjamin A. Botkin and the Development of Folklore Scholarship in America," *New York Folklore* 12.3–4 (1986): 1–22.

More important to Botkin than exacting analysis was sharing the harvested lore with the folk who provided it in a form they could understand and appreciate. More important than disciplinary integrity was the creation of an awareness among the folk of their inherent importance, of their worth as individuals, and of their social value as a community. In light of his tenacious belief in the cultural wealth of America's folk it is fitting that the major products of Botkin's work are called "treasuries." In light of the discrepancy between the philosophies of the man devoted to producing those treasuries and the individuals struggling to institutionalize folklore studies, the conflict that engaged them seems inevitable.

The details of Benjamin Botkin's career help to explain how he came to assume his role as popularizer. And the details of his debate with the purists illustrate the roles of individuals, their work, and their philosophies as they approached the fundamental task of defining the essence of a discipline. Following is an overview of the career of one scholar as it influenced and was influenced by the evolution of American folklore scholarship.

————

Benjamin A. Botkin's career spanned a period of fifty years. Two major aspects of that lengthy career are especially helpful in interpreting his impact upon the discipline. Through his work with the Works Progress Administration's Federal Writers' Project in the 1930s he gained notoriety as a folklorist. Through the publication of his many treasuries between the 1940s and the 1960s he gained public acclaim and professional skepticism for his work. But understanding the professional and personal equipment he brought to these tasks requires some familiarity with the conditions surrounding his earlier life and work that help to explain the impetus for his career.

By the 1930s disciplinary trends and personal experiences had already been at work for many years shaping Botkin's views about the study of folklore. Testing the boundaries and surpassing the limitations of conventional approaches resulted in the selection and combination of some techniques, the abandonment of others, and the emergence of an approach that was uniquely Botkin. Clear representations of his attitudes can be observed in his responses to his contemporaries' views of regionalism, anthropological methodology, and the study of "survivals."

When at last scholars deemed American folk and lore subjects worthy of study, two distinct regionalist approaches emerged. In one, local folklorists with personal affinity for a given region identified representative literary forms and samples seeking to inspire regional pride and self-identification.

A second approach presupposed that genuine folk traditions survived only among social groups that had remained isolated and unexposed to mass culture (Bauman, Abrahams, and Kalcik 1976: 366). Through their titles alone the treasuries reveal that Botkin's studies were limited neither to areas to which he enjoyed close personal proximity nor to those groups outside the mainstream of mass culture.

Similarly, he resisted the limitations of Boasian-style identification and classification imposed by the anthropological approach to folklore. While many of his peers were devoting their efforts to scientizing folklore study, Botkin begged them to augment their research with creative interpretation. Assuming the folk to be everywhere and everyone, he also yearned to extend research horizons beyond the quest for survivals of European traditions that had constituted the bulk of early folklore study in America. In encouraging these changes Botkin sought nothing less than a fundamental redefinition of research methodology.

Unwilling to stop there, he devoted much of his career to identifying previously discounted sources of lore. Not only seeking folklore from a wider variety of sources than those sanctioned by his colleagues (those encountered in written material for example). Botkin also labored to redefine the concept of "the folk." Relocation through early teaching career moves had introduced him to the western environment of rural Oklahoma and to the urban milieu of New York City's ethnic neighborhoods. Although the two cultures were significantly different in content, he determined early on that both the frontier culture of the West and the cosmopolitan culture of the urban East had unique and equally valuable contributions to make in exploring the lore of the land.

By the 1930s these forerunners had set the stage for Botkin's life's pursuit. Useful elements had been identified and extracted from established approaches and personal experiences and his unorthodox manner brought a fresh outlook to folklore scholarship. He encountered a welcome chance to exercise his novel ideas during a period in America's history when opportunity was far from the norm.

While the Great Depression offered only adversity to much of American society it presented folklore scholarship with an unprecedented chance to take to the field. A part of the Works Progress Administration (WPA) effort to curtail crippling unemployment between 1935 and 1943, the Federal Writers' Project (FWP) was aimed at preserving the nation's literary talent. Compilation of descriptive material for state and regional guidebooks was the main task assigned to FWP writers. As it became clear that animating descriptions of streets and structures with images of living individuals and their stories could enhance the product, folklorists joined the ranks.

Like other WPA projects the FWP sought to furnish social benefits beyond the mere provision of employment opportunities for writers and folklorists. Born in the midst of economic depression, in a nation whose people were grasping for both financial and spiritual revival, the folklore project's primary goal was to help all Americans rediscover their sense of pride and self worth. Gathering fact and folk tale from rich and poor, the project "brought its audience face to face with the factual, rich diversity called America and her people" (Penkower 1977: 243–44). Those who initiated and administered the program

> saw that the country lacked a feeling of unity; they saw that there were conflicts between various kinds of racial, regional and class groups in this country. They hoped that the cultivation of folk music, and the spread of the feeling of cultural unity . . . would give Americans the feeling that they all belong to the same kind of culture. (Williams 1975: 218)

With these concepts foremost in their minds, enthusiastic fieldworkers set out to do what they could to heal the wounds of a nation in distress.

Philosophically, the FWP and Benjamin Botkin were well suited to one another's needs. Such an overwhelming task required a special type of leadership and found in Botkin its "guiding spirit" (Mangione 1972: 275–76). As "one of the most thoroughly and extensively educated folklorists in the country . . . schooled in the areas of literary criticism, fieldwork, teaching, archiving, and editing" (Stekert 1975: 335–36), Botkin lent the position of project director an aura of respectability it needed (Mangione 1972: 275–76).[1]

In turn, the project offered Botkin an ideal opportunity to practice and refine his approach to folklore. The program's treatment of folklore as public domain rather than as the private property of scholars dovetailed perfectly with his own sympathies. Through sensitive research, collection, and distribution of material, Botkin and the FWP aspired to give "back to the people what we have taken from them and what rightfully belongs to them, in a form in which they can understand and use [it]" (Botkin, 1938f: 10).

As Botkin set about reorganizing the folklore project he was also able to satisfy other goals he held for the field of study. Not only could he encourage returning the lore to the folk, he was also able to exercise his predilection toward creative interpretation. Surpassing mere collection and indexing of material, the program further attempted to assimilate "folklore to the local and national life by understanding . . . the relation between the lore and the life out of which it springs; and by translating the lore back into terms of daily living and leisure-time activity" (Botkin 1938f: 10).

Additionally, he guided the project toward the study of yet untapped resources. His earlier acknowledgment of the existence and importance of urban and industrial lore at last gained institutional support. Perhaps more than any of his other contributions this one served to nudge folklore scholarship in new directions. Collectors were no longer restrained by "pristine society" prejudices that preached that genuine folklore persisted only in isolated communities. Instead, they ventured forth pursuing lore on the streets of New York City, in the industrial plants of Chicago, and among various occupational, ethnic, and regional groups of New England (McDonald 1969: 714–15).

"We Called It 'Living Lore,'" Botkin recalled some twenty years later, and "[t]he key to living lore was the relating of the foreground, lore, to its background in life." Collecting living lore and relating it to life demanded much more than passive listening and recording, and project guidelines introduced workers to the new techniques required.

> You gather folklore between shifts or during the lunch hour, from members of Compressed Air Local No. 147, in the hoghouse or locker rooms of the construction company engaged in building the Queens Mid-town tunnel. Or in the hiring hall of the National Maritime Union, with the windows overlooking the piers, and the ships' funnels. Or on the picket line. (Botkin 1958j: 189, 191, 193)

Collectors were encouraged to look everywhere for material. And exemplifying their supervisor's sympathies they were instructed to evaluate material in new ways, considering its interest to the general public to be of equal importance as its suitability for the guidebooks and its usefulness to folklore scholars. Project guidelines emphasized human values as well as literary importance (McDonald 1969: 711). Whether its end product was "old wine in new bottles" or "folklore in the making" (Botkin 1946d: 256) the research conducted under this project was entrusted with respecting and reflecting the intimate relationship between art and life, between work and culture (Botkin 1938f: 7). Many years later, Botkin reflected on the Living Lore experiment that permitted him to apply his ideal approach to folklore. In his analysis it was "perhaps the most important achievement of the Folklore Studies of the Federal Writers' Project" (Botkin 1958j: 198). Even so, his realistic evaluation admitted that the project faced the same problems that plagued other WPA programs. As a consequence, he noted, the results were less than perfect.

Financial instability, irregular project distribution, and the use of inexperienced fieldworkers (McDonald 1969: 707) produced material that "was necessarily uneven, and a good deal of it was unreliable." Despite its shortcomings, however, "as a record of folklore as a living culture and living literature, and for the understanding of the meaning and function of folklore in a democratic society, it is invaluable" (Botkin 1958j: 198).

Project insecurity aside, Botkin was able to effect administrative improvements that complemented the project's academic and humanitarian contributions. From the beginning of his assignment, he purposefully cultivated and nurtured an atmosphere of close cooperation among communities, collectors, and colleagues. Professional advice was sought from colleagues outside the project (McDonald 1969: 711–18). And cooperation was encouraged between the folklore unit and the social-ethnic unit of the FWP.

Perhaps most noteworthy of these enterprises was his role in forming the Joint Committee on Folk Arts within the WPA. The committee that ultimately elected Botkin as its president (Mangione 1972: 275–76) "provided a formalized structure for the exchange of information and ideas relating to folklore, folk music and folk arts" (Dwyer-Shick 1976: 484). Botkin's association with this committee not only facilitated communication within the WPA but also inspired a growing respect for the project in the opinion of the American Folklore Society.

A legacy of skepticism lingered from the project's early days when the AFS proclaimed they would acknowledge FWP materials "only if their evaluation, supervision, and continuation were placed under expert guidance." Suggestively they had added "we proffer our help in this endeavor." In a later statement, recognition by the AFS that the Joint Committee had been organized by "a trained folklorist, Dr. B. A. Botkin," was accompanied by an expression of their willingness to work with that committee. A new avenue of communication was thus opened between the AFS and the FWP. While maintaining its demand that project materials be subjected to the close scrutiny of folklore scholars, the AFS admitted that " 'it would seem not impossible that the voluminous collections made by the project from every state might form a nucleus for a more comprehensive national archive' " (Dwyer-Shick 1976: 483–84).

Obstacles and opportunities faced those entrusted with determining the value, location, purpose, and ultimate use of that "national archive." Later assessments of the project have expressed disappointment that the folklore program never reached its full potential and that indifference to the unpublished material generated by the FWP "constituted a shocking waste of a precious national resource" (Mangione 1972: 371). The regrettable fact that "the creative arts were supported by the American government only in time of dire need" (Penkower 1977: 248) perhaps explains in part the underutilization of these rich resources. While admirable efforts have made use of some of the raw material gathered in the 1930s,[2] the majority remains to be examined, assessed, and utilized.

Nevertheless, the contributions of the project were pervasive and integral to the development of American folklore scholarship. Its lessons were many, and they bear reviewing from time to time.

> For one thing, it has taught folklorists that they can work together; that folklore collection and editing can be a cooperative undertaking, not only on a group basis but also on a nationwide scale. It has also taught folklorists that there is an art as well as a science of folklore—that the art consists of selecting and presenting aesthetically as well as socially valid expressions by folksayers—the individual creative geniuses and trans-mitters of the folk group or community. And it has taught folklorists that folklore is, as I have written elsewhere, "an activity or experience . . . an interchange between cultural groups or levels, between the folk and the student of folklore," bringing together the disciplines of literature, history, and anthropology, for the understanding of the science and art of society. Folklore is not only of, for, and by people; it is *with* people. (Botkin 1958j: 199)

The folklore project, as described above by Botkin, clearly bore the imprint of its "guiding spirit" and of his philosophy regarding methodology and the intended use of folklore. In view of the controversy just over the horizon, it is ironic that the folklore project established such a model of cooperation and dedication that would be well-nigh irretrievable under later circumstances.

Just as the folklore project bore the mark of Botkin's inspiration, so too did the next major phase of its guiding spirit's career exhibit vestiges of the proj-ect's influence. Exposed to the wealth of material amassed during the Depres-sion years, Botkin yearned personally to take the treasures of folklore to the public. His continued mission to return the lore to the folk took form in the several popularly successful treasuries that in essence represented folklore of, for, by, and with the people.

While rewarding in many ways, this part of Botkin's career was also fraught with controversy. The FWP era's spirit of benevolence among folklorists be-gan a steady decline as polarization between purist and popularizer ideals intensified. Disagreements between the two camps over folklore fundamentals

—a sanctioned definition, agreement on suitable sources and proper uses of folklore—culminated in the 1950s "Battle of the Books/War of the Folklorists" (Williams 1975: 225).

Botkin's approach, of course, epitomized the doctrine of the popularizer. Purist philosophy found its opposing voice in the words and works of his harshest critic, Richard Dorson. Nothing less than the future security of folklore study in America consumed Dorson's diligent efforts. By ensuring its rigor and purity, his goal was to professionalize the discipline, thereby justifying permanent financial and academic support for its continuation. Botkin's treasuries formed the eye of a turbulent storm that relentlessly pitted these contrasting views against one another for decades.

A full embodiment of folklore according to Botkin materialized in his pioneering collection *A Treasury of American Folklore*. Introductory remarks concretized his definition of folklore and clarified its influence over his choice of source materials. Botkin's comments, and the book itself, attested to a folklore methodology inspired by his early academic and personal experiences and nurtured by his FWP work.

At the heart of that methodology was a commitment to include material that others chose to exclude, and to pursue material from sources, both human and literary, that others chose to discount. His belief that "[a] book of American folklore . . . should be as big as this country of ours" (Botkin 1944j: xxi) was manifested in this initial volume of nearly one thousand pages. Even so its composer worried over omissions. But endorsement of sundry types of lore engendered a wide array of material and the unabashed placement of "Tall Tales of the Mines" and "Sidewalk Rhymes of New York" just chapters away from more traditional "Songs of the Farmers" and stories of "Backwoods Boasters."

Frank admission that many of these songs, rhymes, and tales had been culled from newspapers, books, or magazines and not obtained directly from oral sources paved the way for future criticism of his techniques. But written sources were integral to his approach and in fact were an essential element in his working definition of folklore.

> The term "American Folklore" is employed here in the sense that one speaks of American literature, language, humor, etc., as an expression of the land, the people, and their experience. The same images and symbols have permeated all parts of this expression, so that folklore, literature, language, and humor are inseparable. (Botkin 1944j: xxiv)

Commercial success and critical acclaim were nearly instantaneous for *A Treasury of American Folklore,* the first true representation of this definition of folklore. Reviewer Wayland D. Hand showered author and book with praise, identifying a major contribution to be "the attention which the author has given to the relationship between literature and folklore." Likewise, Hand lauded its multiplicity of tales, of sources, and of folk groups, which effectively challenged the misconception that the scope of American folklore could be summed up in "a few old time songs and some stories about Paul Bunyan." In the final analysis the author's credibility and motives for publishing the book were pronounced impeccable.

> Botkin has not allowed his passion for a popular acceptance of his book, and of folklore, to preclude so-called "scholarly" considerations, with which, by virtue of training in the science of folklore as well as in literature, he is thoroughly competent to deal. (Hand 1944: 56)

Upon its debut, then, the first collection was embraced as a public treasure and certified a scholarly success, a commendable accomplishment for its popularizer author. Commercial success and public fondness for this type of work endured.[3] Critical acclaim, however, proved more fickle as commendation presently yielded to condemnation. Each wielding his own precious philosophy, adversaries Botkin and Dorson faced off in the 1950s and the War of the Folklorists had begun.

Battle lines were drawn around fundamental questions. What constituted folklore? Where was it to be found? How should it be collected? And how should it be used? Popularizer and purist answers to these queries shared little common ground, and no aspect of Botkin's methodology escaped Dorson's reproof.

Characteristically, Botkin answered these ponderous questions in book form. Published in 1949, *A Treasury of Southern Folklore* depicted folklore as a living process. Botkin did not limit his focus to the traditional agrarian lifestyle and the isolated existence of the mountaineer, as his colleagues might have done. Rather, he examined their responses to the encroaching industrialism that threatened their integrity. As the culture of the cotton mill, its barons, and its workers encountered the age-old traditions of the South, labor conflicts "created a new folklore-in-the-making" (Botkin 1949f: xxii). Instead of recording survivals of passing cultural traditions, *A Treasury of Southern Folklore* chronicled the processes of change and adaptation that occurred as dissimilar cultures collided and struggled to coexist.

Under these conditions, Botkin argued, the appearance of folk expressions in print did not signal their demise. Instead, it signified the adaptability, durability, and continued utility of folk elements in the presence of stressful circumstances. Where industrial and agrarian traditions tested their usefulness to one another, Botkin found a cultural milieu suitable for analyzing the resilience of folk expressions and practices as they suffered the strains of modernization.

Diametrically opposed to these principles and the methodology that Botkin summoned to explore the South's "folklore in the making," Richard Dorson leapt eagerly at the opportunity to publicize his criticism. The tone and meaning of Dorson's evaluation of the author and of his work are suggested by the initial volley of his scathing review.

> For his latest collection, Mr. Botkin has done fieldwork—ten days in North and South Carolina. But his basic techniques remain the same, stripping all kinds of volumes of their frothy stories—often ones recently published and of a popular nature . . . and reshuffling them in his files under snappy headings. (Dorson 1950b: 480–81)

The assault proceeded to discredit the book's content as well as its intent. Dubbing it "a rehash of rehashes" Dorson charged that its "excessively flat and dull and badly written" stories had "nothing to do with folklore." In place of academic rigor Botkin catered "to his audience much as do newspapers, digests and omnibuses, with short, breezy selections, good for a laugh or a human-interest angle, that also appeal to superficial regional patriotism with familiar names and places" (Dorson 1950b: 481).

Material, sources, and presentation equally bore the brunt of the review's criticism. Dorson held out a faint glimmer of hope at such inclusions as a description of ritual tobacco auctioning, a piece more closely reflecting his own principles of folklore scholarship. Nevertheless, authentic folkways were inadequately represented to fully redeem the work. In the final analysis, the reviewer found Botkin to be concerned with little more than the successful promotion of a book, and certainly not with its scholastic rigor. "And what drugstore bookbuyer," he asked, "will cavil at disparity of sources or the many removes from oral tradition?" (Dorson 1950b: 481).

While the explicit target of this barrage was Botkin's most recent treasury, the discord itself suffused the professional attitudes of both men. One refused to separate American folklore, language, literature, and humor from one another and used them in whatever form they were encountered. The other proclaimed the only genuine wellspring of folklore to be oral sources. Botkin the popularizer viewed those who created, transmitted, and perpetuated the lore as equal partners in his work. Dorson the purist confined the lore and its use strictly to academic purposes. Indeed, their answers to the basic questions of folklore—what, where, how, and why—could hardly have differed more.

In broadcasting his chagrin over Botkin's techniques, Dorson's caustic review marked a turning point in the professional evaluation of Botkin's work. While less vindictive than Dorson's, subsequent reviews were far less complimentary than Hand's 1944 analysis of the first treasury. The appearance in 1953 of a review of the latest treasury revealed the spread of Dorson's attitude to other folklore scholars.

Gustave O. Arlt chided *A Treasury of Western Folklore*, published in 1951, for its inclusion of "something for everyone, except possibly for the student of folklore." Such a miscellany, which gave equal reign to the Donner Expedition and to stories about the Lone Ranger and Tonto, might represent an entertaining and valuable "anthology of Western literature," but rendered "a distinct disservice to the cause of folklore by creating a totally false impression of the nature of folk material." Arlt echoed Dorson's analysis of *A Treasury of Southern Folklore* with the concession that "an occasional nugget" rescued the work from total worthlessness. But in the overall assessment, *A Treasury of Western Folklore* fared little better than its southern counterpart (Arlt 1953: 177).

Perhaps more than any of the other treasuries it was this of western folklore that epitomized Botkin's professional posture and accentuated the philosophical rift. Aspiring to present a panoramic view of western American culture, the author rejected any distinction between the literature of and about the people. In compiling resources he consulted oral sources, formal literature, and published folklore as well as subliterature of dime novels, guidebooks, and diaries. Like its fellow collections, *A Treasury of Western Folklore* identified folk elements within popular culture and declared folklore to be "an imaginative expression that is a part of, not apart from, the main stream of culture in a given time and place" (Botkin 1951g: xxiii).

In addition to expressing the current state of its author's approach to folklore, *A Treasury of Western Folklore* also reflected the influence of his past experiences. Reminiscent of the FWP Living Lore concept of relating lore to its background in life, this book represented his continuing commitment to "relating the lore to ways of living, ways of making a living, and ways of looking at life." And his personal familiarity with the West provided the intimacy and incentive for producing a book that "aims to give a folk's eye view of the region—the land, the people, and their history" (Botkin 1951g: xxiii). But the method represented by Botkin and his treasuries for capturing and interpreting that folk's eye view was anathema to his peers who demanded a more scholarly methodology for their discipline.

Dorson's and Arlt's reviews demonstrate that Botkin's critics perceived his folk's eye views as serious misrepresentations of the definition and intent of folklore during the 1950s. In a concise summary of the difference of opinion Dorson later explained that his objective had been to draw "a distinction between properly documented oral folklore collected directly in the field from the tellers of the tales and the singers of folksongs, and the rewritten, saccharine versions of fakelore" (Dorson 1976: 5), a term he claimed to have publicized "directly as a consequence of these treasuries and their influence" (Dorson 1971a: 5). Dorson's method demanded selectivity and exclusion in its pursuit of folklore directly from its perpetuators. Conversely, the treasuries advocated catholicity and inclusion, even to the extent of eliciting the folk's eye view from the printed word.

These tenets that guided Botkin's research and writing remained relatively consistent throughout his career. Less inveterate was the state of the discipline. Its fundamental philosophy and even its purist proponents were by no means exempt from the forces of disciplinary evolution. As the values that inspired Botkin and infused his books became more palatable to his critics, popularizer and purist viewpoints eventually began to converge.

Over time even Richard Dorson's strict biases succumbed. Traditional purist philosophy dictated the complete disengagement of authentic folklore from the surrounding milieu of mass culture. Formal institutions and folk elements (tales, art, songs, customs, speech, and wisdom) were treated as mutually exclusive phenomena (Dorson 1976: 11). But by the mid-1970s Dorson's teaching methods had incorporated Botkin's persistent belief that mass culture and traditional folk characteristics coexist and reveal important information about each other.

> For the past several years I have assigned graduate students an exercise of culling folklore from the mass media. They clip items from printed sources and note examples from television, radio, and films. Their directions are, first, to identify folkloristic themes; second, to comment on the relation of these themes to oral folk sources; and, third, to interpret the use or purpose to which the mediated folklore is being put. Most students compile intriguing scrapbooks that reveal the wealth of folk stuff encountered in their daily exposure to the media over a period of a couple of months. (Dorson 1976: 63–64)

Dorson's description of the projects assigned to his students bespeaks decades of disciplinary development. In the mind of the purist professor the relationship between folklore and mass culture had evolved from a state of mutual exclusivity to one of complementary coexistence. His admission of the media as a source of folklore reiterated Botkin's precept that the appearance of folk elements in mass culture represented not their demise but their resilience in the face of challenge. Obviously a quarter-century of disciplinary evolution had mediated some major theoretical differences between the principals of the "War of the Folklorists."

The polarization between popularizer and purist principles had spawned a lengthy debate during a critical period in the metamorphosis of American folklore scholarship. Dorson was driven by his resolve to define and justify once and for all folklore as an independent and respectable discipline. At times his staunch defense against invasion by commercializers resembled a personal vendetta against Botkin, whose popularizations of folk material appeared at a time that may best be described as inopportune.

Some thirty years after the appearance of the first treasury Dorson reflected back over these foregoing events. By then a product of his own professional evolution influenced in part by Botkin and their conflicting ideals, he enumerated his adversary's personal and professional contributions to the discipline.

> In any history of the American folklore scene Ben Botkin deserves a respected place. His first series of *Folk-Say* volumes, published annually in Oklahoma from 1929–1932, directed general attention to indigenous oral traditions as a source for regional literature. When as a callow graduate student in 1939 I first met Ben in Washington, D.C., he showed me every kindness, and he has always generously assisted younger folklorists. (Dorson 1971a: 13–14)

In assessing the treasuries' commercial success, Dorson suggested that they "made an impact on the public imagination that is in itself a phenomenon for the folklorist to contemplate." Analyzing their academic merits, he admitted that "they do point to sources that the folklorist can consider and screen." And finally divulging the basic cause of the debate they perpetuated, he claimed that his "quarrel is less with Botkin than with the folklorists who praise his patchworks as models of research." Indeed, "[h]ad they not received such extravagant praise, no controversy would have arisen" (Dorson 1971a: 14, 27).

Given the legacy of the controversy that did arise, however, it is not surprising that Dorson declared: "No subject of study in the United States is more misunderstood than folklore" (Dorson 1976: 1). It seems that folklorists could hardly agree among themselves about its essential nature. Continual bickering over definition and incessant struggle for supremacy of methodology prolonged the controversy. The righteousness of each argument eluded the other.

Complicating matters further, folk and folklorist were equally confusing to one another. In the 1940s Botkin suggested that the folk "know the nature and meaning but not the name—and certainly not the scholarship—of folklore." But scholars' efforts to define folklore to their liking certainly conveyed the advantage to the folklorist.

> Because the word denotes both the material and its study, and has come to stand more for the study of the thing than for the thing itself, folklore, in fact, seems to have become the possession of the few who study it rather than the many who make or use it. (Botkin 1944j: xxi)

Benjamin Botkin dedicated his entire career to helping the folk understand their lore and regain possession of it. During the Great Depression, Botkin's FWP efforts had labored to use the lore to reinstill a sense of worth among a financially and emotionally depressed population. Later, the treasuries aspired to apprise various regional and occupational folk groups of their uniquenesses and similarities, to teach them the value of their culture, and to present its verbal manifestations to them for their education and enjoyment. Perhaps it was Dorson's inability to sympathize with these commitments that most effectively hindered his ability to accept Botkin's work.

And to accept and appreciate what Botkin's work was about, it was imperative that one understand his philosophy. Throughout his career he cherished three convictions first introduced in *A Treasury of American Folklore* in 1944. First, Botkin imparted his belief that "the industrial folktales and songs in this book are evidence enough that machinery does not destroy folklore" (Botkin 1944j: xxii). Hence the search for lore led Botkin to previously unacknowledged sources far removed from the pristine, isolated communities that had furnished his predecessors with European survivals.

Second, Botkin described his collections of this type of urban, labor, and occupational lore as "a species of living literature which has no fixed form . . . and which is constantly shifting back and forth between written and unwritten tradition." But he did admit that "folklore is most alive or at home out of print, and in its purest form is associated with the 'grapevine' and the bookless world" (Botkin 1944j: xxii). Dorson originally insisted that folklore lived *only* out of print, and for his proposition that it could be found in written form Botkin suffered dearly.

Lastly, he voiced his eternal ambition to bestow upon the folk who created and nurtured it his special variety of living literature. Ideally, his publicly accessible treasuries provided everyone the opportunity for "an enjoyment and understanding of living American folklore for what it is and what it is worth" (Botkin 1944j: xxii). "What it is" and "What it is worth," of course, varied from folklorist to folklorist and from folk group to folk group. But to Botkin it was the folk's eye view of the land, and what it was worth depended to a great extent upon his ability to share it with the folk.

———

In the aftermath of this particular controversy over what folklore is and what it is worth much remains to be sorted out. Thorough unraveling of the many phases and complex aspects of Botkin's lengthy career is in its early stages. Folklore journal obituaries following his death in 1975, the Festschrift dedicated to him in the 1960s, and current ventures of folklorists in the 1980s indicate that interpretation and analysis have begun. These materials provide strong evidence of enduring and escalating interest in Botkin's work and philosophy, the meaning of his career to the discipline, and its impact upon the direction of folklore scholarship in America.

Ben Botkin was a scholar with many talents, a man with many dreams. Perhaps first and always he was a poet. And it was with the heart, the mind, and the sensitivity of the poet that he approached his life's work. Representing much more than collections of folklore, his treasuries are a poetic tribute to the land he loved.

It was the poet in Botkin that other folklore scholars often failed to comprehend. "It's not just that those poets insist on dancing to their different drum, but that they have the arrogance of refusing to tell us how to interpret it. They just keep saying, *Listen, listen, listen*" (Jackson 1976: 1). As fellow folklorists were trying to improve their techniques for recording, codifying, indexing, and filing their growing resource base, he asked them to transcend those tasks, to give a listen to the human aspect of their work. "If the folklorist would only content himself with being a listener, he might be able to hear the folk voices speak more clearly and more truly" (Botkin 1958j: 199).

Botkin himself looked for and listened to the folk voices of the common man, the laborer, the underdog. He chose to work with and to study foreign immigrants, rural common folk, the urban worker, the pioneer. A sort of self-appointed middle-man between folk, lore, and scholar, he worked on the one hand to break down "popular resistance to folklore as dead and phony stuff and on the other hand academic resistance to its broader interpretation and utilization" (Williams 1975: 221). He loved the stuff of the lore and wanted desperately to be able to share it with its rightful owners. Just as desperately he wanted to convince his colleagues that it should be shared.

The conflict between this poet/folklorist and his purist colleagues owes much to their fundamental differences in vision. Purists "were looking for texts that could be properly annotated and indexed; Ben was trying to document the soul of a land" (Jackson 1976: 1). In his search for the soul of the land he loved, Botkin wanted to look at everything resulting in the aggregation that characterized his unorthodox vision of folklore. Subtle were his "distinctions between popular and folk traditions, regionalism, applied folklore, folklore, and mass media" (Stekert 1975: 337) And out of this milieu emerged what another folklorist described as "Ben's field," consisting of the "complex of high and low and mass and pop and folk culture we sometimes call the American Experience" (Jackson 1976: 4).

Controversies that arose around "Ben's field" and his work were ignited by this holistic approach and its popular success. For the purists struggling to define folklore as an academic pursuit worthy of funding and respect it was convenient to have at hand an example of what in their opinion was *not* folklore. Botkin's treasuries surfaced at the perfect time to serve as useful weapons in this philosophic duel.

During the course of the duel, Botkin argued that *too* much social science methodology would ruin the essence of folklore (Stekert 1975: 336). Meanwhile, his contemporaries engaged in a hearty effort to bolster their image through increasingly scientific research methods. Botkin's type of folklore was part and parcel of the folk. Purist methodology entrenched folklore within the hallowed halls, confined it to the ivory tower.

The obituaries cited above clearly show that by the time of Botkin's death his type of folklore was deemed praiseworthy. Bruce Jackson eulogized Botkin's work, claiming that it "taught millions about the legitimate place of folklore in the American cultural continuum" (Jackson 1976: 4). Ellen Stekert had agreed, noting that his "work helped gain public recognition and respect for the field of folklore" (Stekert 1975: 335).

In addition to professional accomplishments his personal contributions have also been duly noted. "Above all, Ben Botkin was a humanist" (Stekert 1975: 336). He gave unselfishly of himself in the 1920s to aid immigrants struggling under unfamiliar conditions. And later he assisted students struggling to meet the academic and financial demands of graduate school. Even

Richard Dorson admitted that he had been a recipient of Botkin's kindness and generosity.

The words of praise that suffused Botkin's obituaries were not the first voiced in his favor, nor would they be the last. In 1966 fellow folklorists had collaborated on *Folklore & Society: Essays in Honor of Benj. A. Botkin,* edited by Bruce Jackson, to commemorate his sixty-fifth birthday. Jackson's introduction to the Festschrift reveals that this published testament to Botkin's life and work embodied a long tradition of admiration and acceptance of his personal and philosophical contributions to the field.

> In presenting Ben with this small collection of essays, we acknowledge the work he has done for and in the field of folklore and, more personally, our pleasure in having him as colleague, teacher, and friend. (Jackson 1966: xii)

Folklore & Society paid homage to a long and bountiful career, one still productive in the mid-1960s. In progress at that time was an ambitious project Botkin "regards as the fulfillment of his long career as teacher, poet, critic, folklorist and social historian" (Jackson 1966: viii). *American Myths and Symbols,* he felt, would

> integrate and culminate my thinking on applied folklore in an analysis of folk and popular assumptions and their symbolic expression in heroes, idols, butts, scapegoats, archetypes, stereotypes, totemic creatures and objects, fictitious personalities, cliches, catchwords, shibboleths, slogans, phrases, historical traditions, legends, myths, fables, anecdotes, jests, codes and rituals. (Jackson 1966: ix)

Before all his ambitions for this project could be realized, Botkin's life and his active contributions to the field ceased in 1975. Unfortunately, the book he considered to be the fulfillment of his bountiful career, the crystallization of his philosophy on applied folklore, was left unfinished. But fortunately, contemporary trends in American folklore scholarship demonstrate that Botkin's legacy has been embraced by kindred spirits.

Botkin-style urban and applied folklore activities are intensifying, especially in New York. On a personal level this would surely have pleased the man who chose to make his permanent home in that state. But it is even more fitting that many of his hopes and aspirations for the field are being realized in the state and city where his professional involvement was most profound.

In many ways Botkin shaped the nature of folklore research in New York. Working with the New York City Writers' Project in the 1930s he guided research efforts toward the collection of living urban lore in New York City. And by the time the New York Folklore Society (NYFS) was officially established in 1944, his experience with the region's folklore was extensive. As one of the society's early guiding spirits, Botkin helped to plan its annual meetings and contributed frequently to its activities during the formative years (Stevens 1985: 5–6, 17).

Both the society and its journal enjoyed Botkin's faithful support and in their fundamentals resounded the philosophy of the popularizer. *New York Folklore Quarterly* pledged not only to publish the work of professional folklorists but also to produce what founding editor Louis Jones described as a "readable magazine for the true amateurs, those who love folklore but are not professionally dependent upon it" (Stevens 1985: 1). Furthermore, in an effort to foster understanding and communication between folklorist and folk, the society aspired to coordinate and legitimize the work of amateur collectors. Clearly, the NYFS supported Botkin's belief that folklore belonged not in the sterile kingdom of the ivory tower but rather in the vital realm of the folk community.

Among New York's most vital folk communities, of course, are those located in urban centers. Botkin's collection of the lore of its major city appeared in 1956. Beyond merely documenting their lore *New York City Folklore* aimed "[t]o get under the collective skin of New Yorkers, to feel their traditional pulse and heartbeat, and to catch the folk 'voice of the city'" (Botkin 1956b: xv).

But Botkin hoped that folklore could do more than record and replay the folk voice of America. His ultimate goal was to put the field to work for the good of humanity, to apply "folklore for understanding and creating understanding." Of all his concepts that of applied folklore "gives me the most satisfaction because of its multi-disciplinary broadening and deepening of my perspective and insight" (quoted in Jackson 1976: 3).

And it was not only the broadening and deepening of his own perspective and insight that he had in mind. Applied folklore should accomplish no less than the encouragement of interdisciplinary, cross-cultural, and even international understanding. New York City's cultural "unity in diversity" and its "two-way flow of national and world influence" (Botkin 1956b: xvii) rendered it an ideal testing ground for folklore's ability to foster understanding. Establishment of an Applied Folklore Center there was a special dream of Botkin's.

His plans included specific recommendations for creating an Applied Folklore Center. Its philosophical foundation would be designed to facilitate the "exchange [of] cultural gifts" and the "rediscovery of group heritages." Its activities would serve as deterrents against cultural conformity and the eventual "loss of cultural diversity" (Botkin 1961i: 152).

Its practical foundation would be established through the assumption of three specific roles. As a centralized repository the center would collect and organize scattered and duplicated materials. As a clearinghouse and service bureau it would ensure the "collection, documentation, preservation, and dissemination of folklore material." As an information center it would share the spirit and products of folklore research with the folk (Botkin 1961i: 152).

Addressing the question of its organizational foundation Botkin suggested that "one way for the center to get started is through a New York City chapter or committee of the New York Folklore Society" (Botkin 1961i: 154). In 1979, some forty years after Botkin had first enunciated the idea, the New York City Chapter of the New York Folklore Society was established. Recently rededicated under its new name, City Lore: The New York Center for Urban Folk Culture is indeed a crystallization of Botkin's ideals for urban and applied folklore.[4]

Perpetuating the spirit he inspired through the 1930s New York City Writers' Project, City Lore focuses on the living urban folklore of New York. The organization also maintains the legacy of the New York Folklore Society's interest in urban lore fostered by Elaine Lambert Lewis's 1940s *NYFQ* column "City Billet: Folklore News and Notes from New York City" (Stevens 1985: 6). And by assuming the roles Botkin delineated in 1961 it is becoming the applied folklore center he envisioned.

City Lore is establishing an archive to assemble audio, visual, and written information on the traditional culture of New York. It serves as a resource center for exploring New York's traditional culture, offering the services of folklore consultants to help identify folk arts and folk cultures in New York City and state. And it serves as a clearinghouse for information about relevant major folklore and folklife collections. Through these activities City Lore pledges its dedication "to the preservation, documentation and presentation of New York's living cultural heritage; it seeks to make the City's culture and the culture of cities more accessible to all" (City Lore Information Pamphlet). Botkin's legacy could hardly be more comfortably housed.

Folklorists have taken their time accepting Botkin's concepts of urban and applied folklore to the extent that an organization named City Lore is now possible. In the introduction to his 1954 *Sidewalks of America* Botkin recognized among his colleagues "those used to thinking of folklore as something belonging to the past and to the country," to whom " 'city folklore' may come as a surprise if not a shock" (Botkin 1954n: viii). Even thirty-one years later

City Lore's director Steven Zeitlin was compelled to admit that "[u]rban folklore is a new field" (NYFS 1985: 1).

Early on, folklorists were advised that folklore could be found "all around them on the sidewalks of America" (Botkin 1954n: vii). While Americans commonly perceive the sidewalks of New York City as the domain of mass culture and the preserve of elite culture, City Lore folklorists insist that the culture there is far more diverse. Like Botkin they assert that "another side of the city is the beauty and significance of the culture of ordinary people who live here. And that is something that City Lore can serve to highlight and foster" (NYFS 1985: 2).

The official inauguration of City Lore in May 1986 was appropriately accompanied by a program entitled "The Sidewalks of New York Revisited: A Tribute to Benjamin Botkin." In 1953 Botkin had written that "applied folklore involves an interchange . . . between the folk and the student of folklore" (Botkin 1953a: 201). In testimony to continuing support for that attitude representatives of the folk community were invited to participate in the meeting not only as performers but also as peers.

Botkin's successors in the field assembled at the 1986 meeting to learn of recent research in the field from one another and from the folk. In doing so they celebrated the man who contributed so much to New York's folklore scholarship. Carrying on the spirit expressed in the 1960s Festschrift and the 1970s obituaries, they represented the most recent, but surely not the last, chorus of voices raised in support of Botkin and his work.

Within the discipline today, the definition and sources of folklore continue to evolve, exhibiting traces of the humanistic/poetic/popularistic/folkloristic philosophy that was Ben Botkin's guiding spirit. The new, bottom-up social history attempts to let the folk speak for themselves, elaborating on Botkin's folk-say themes. And recording and distributing material of, for, by, and with the people echoes the 1930s Living Lore efforts to illuminate those lives that would otherwise remain unnoted in America's historical record.

Botkin's pioneering question "Is there a folk in the city?" (Bauman, Abrahams, and Kalcik 1976: 373) cleared the path to new sources of research materials for studying historically voiceless groups and individuals. A discipline that once limited its focus to the pursuit of Child Ballad versions among isolated communities is taking to the city streets and country fields to study the messages of folk architecture. Clearly having traveled far from former doubt that an urban industrial environment could sustain its own lore, folklorists are even beginning to explore the lore of the air traffic controller and the auto mechanic (Bauman, Abrahams, and Kalcik 1976: 374).

Folklore, its definition, and its practitioners have changed overwhelmingly during the twentieth century. Benjamin Botkin's influence upon folklore scholarship and upon these changes cannot be overlooked and should be duly acknowledged as one of the major influences in the evolution of the discipline. To be sure, folklore study in America would be quite different today if not for a great national Depression, a scholarly sparring match that spanned several years, and the literature that grew out of one man's love for the lore and for the folk.

Notes

1. Differing interpretations have obscured the specifics of Botkin's assumption of the role of project director. Mangione implies that Botkin was actively sought to unseat predecessor John Lomax. But this assumption was later challenged by Susan Dwyer-Shick (1976: 482–83). Dwyer-Shick points out that Mangione's "chatty style" interfered with factual presentation, resulting in a somewhat creative ordering of events. Lomax's term as "national advisor on folklore and folkways" had, according to Dwyer-Shick, concluded two months before director Henry Alsberg confessed his concerns regarding the folklore program to the American Folklore Society. At that time he formally expressed his perception of the need for greater respectability in the program.

2. Penkower (1977: 154) notes Botkin's use of ex-slave narrative material and folktales from the project in his two books *Lay My Burden Down: A Folk History of Slavery* (1945) and *A Treasury of American Folklore* (1944). Ann Banks's *First Person America* (1980) represents a commendable recent use of FWP collections.

3. Half a million copies of *A Treasury of American Folklore* were sold during the first three years of publication. Some twenty editions had appeared by 1971, and more than forty years after its initial appearance the book remains in print.

4. Two publications provided most of the written information about City Lore that was used here. The *New York Folklore Newsletter* contained interview information obtained from City Lore folklorists. And an informational pamphlet prepared by City Lore explained its purpose and activities. Further information about City Lore may be obtained from the NYFS or City Lore (72 E. First Street, New York, N.Y.).

The "Ben Botkin Bulldozer"

Toward a Reassessment of
A Treasury of American Folklore

Jerrold Hirsch

A Treasury of American Folklore (1944) has been the uninvited, and probably unwanted, guest in what might be called the Botkin reassessment festivities of the last twenty years. Public folklorists have all but declared him a patron saint whose name can be called up to give prestige and legitimacy to their work; but they have not been interested in talking about Botkin's folklore treasuries. Increasingly, historians are examining specific aspects of Botkin's career—his role in the interwar regionalist movement (see Dorman 1993), contribution to the Harlem Renaissance (see Hutchinson 1995), participation in the literary battles of the 1930s (see Wixson 1994), work on the New Deal's Federal Writers' Project (see Hirsch 2003a), and activity in the cultural work of the Popular Front of the late 1930s (see Denning 1996). It could be argued that these historians simply have an interest in Botkin that does not include his 1944 treasury. But when historian Robert Dorman asserts without providing evidence that Botkin's "popular" *Treasury of American Folklore* (*TAF*) is a prime example of how the quality of the work of the interwar regionalists declined in their later years (Dorman 1993: 308), one has to wonder if scholars have not accepted without question a negative assessment of this work.

And yet any meaningful reassessment of Botkin's work cannot ignore his most popular and influential book, which Botkin saw as the capstone to the first phase of his career and which marked a new direction in his role as a folklore editor, what he called his "special bracket."[1] Perhaps some of us who are engaged in reexamining Botkin's work as a folklorist, litterateur, and social historian are ashamed of Botkin "the treasury manufacturer," as Richard Dorson contemptuously referred to him (Dorson 1959: 202). In this way, we give an awesome power to Dorson in this area. It needs to be recalled that *TAF*

56

was initially praised by leading folklore scholars. Dorson's campaign to label Botkin a fakelorist was itself a reassessment that he used to try to define what he considered the scholarly study of folklore and the proper role of folklorists. Thus subsequent reassessments of Botkin's work were also reassessments of Dorson and initially implicit or explicit challenges to Dorson's only now waning authority in constructing the modern discipline of American folklore studies.

Pride and shame should not be the hallmarks of our new assessment of Botkin. On the one hand, such attitudes suggest a fan club. On the other hand, Botkin and our understanding of history would both benefit from a more disinterested approach. The purpose of this chapter is to bring *TAF*—the most popular book ever published on American folklore—into the ongoing discussion of Botkin's work and legacy and the history of American folklore studies. This requires that we put aside for the moment the criticism of Botkin's scholarship, or lack of scholarship, that Richard Dorson began in a series of influential and withering reviews of Botkin's various treasuries. It is not that Dorson's criticisms should be ignored, for they raise important methodological issues for folklorists and are important in the history of the field. Rather, the problem is that they have overshadowed all other questions about the place of *TAF* in the history of folklore studies in particular and American cultural studies in general.[2]

This chapter is only an opening foray, for what may seem to be merely the examination of one book is nevertheless a huge topic that other scholars will also need to address. It seeks to reopen aspects of this topic that have remained closed, to create a space for work that remains to be done. The Dorson-dominated debate about Botkin's treasuries was too narrowly focused to help us understand important aspects of Botkin's aims and the world of folklore studies in which he pursued his goals. If we continue to avoid reassessing *TAF* because of the subliminal, or not so subliminal, influence of Dorson's critique of that volume and subsequent treasuries, we will understand neither Botkin's purposes in a book that marked a turning point in American culture nor Dorson's critique. Such a scenario would be disappointing in several ironic ways. For one thing, Dorson had wanted to promote a debate—a clash of ideas—rather than to sweep matters under the rug. Whatever conclusion we may ultimately arrive at regarding Dorson's motives, his attack on Botkin has much to tell us about *TAF* in relationship to the development of American folklore studies.

Ultimately, it is necessary to place Botkin and Dorson in a larger historical perspective than either of them may have been able to envision. That larger perspective will involve understanding *TAF* in relationship to the world of folklore studies, from which it emerged and which it rejected in significant ways. As scholars pursue this work, they will in time be in a position to examine the ideas inherent in the treasury's form and content and to understand its success in relation to the celebratory American nationalism of the late 1930s and early 1940s, which could be either a cultural component of a call to reform or an endorsement of the status quo.

We need to imagine the history of *TAF* before Dorson began his relentless campaign against Botkin's treasuries. It is important to understand how the success of the book helped Botkin reshape the folklore agenda to which he dedicated the rest of his life, an agenda that had its roots in his work in the years between the two world wars. In reading about Botkin, Dorson, and the history of American folklore studies one might get the impression that Dorson was the first and only scholar to review Botkin's work, which is not true. Actually, the initial scholarly reviews placed the book in the context of what they saw as Botkin's already significant contributions to American folklore studies. That context was lost and now has to be retrieved. Revisiting Botkin's goals and recovering the initial reception that *TAF* received can provide fresh insights into Botkin's work and a historical moment when the idea of scholarship and professionalism not linked to university-based departments was still imaginable.

————

For Botkin, *TAF* was a logical extension of the work he had done in the *Folk-Say* anthologies when he was a professor at the University of Oklahoma (1921 to 1939) and his later work on the Federal Writers' Project (1938 to 1939). This is clear in his thinking about the nature of American folklore, the role of the folklorist, and the means that the folklorist could use to reach a wide audience. From the beginning, Botkin's program involved recognizing and overcoming what he saw as an arbitrary division between folklore and literature that obscured the relationship between the two. In the first two pages of "The Folk in Literature: An Introduction to the New Regionalism" (the 1929 introduction to the first volume of *Folk-Say*), Botkin laid out the themes and issues of his life's work. He suggested that "in the beginning lore and literature were one." It was only with such modern developments as "the invention of writing and printing, the stratification of society, and the growth of modern individualism . . . [that] the two have become separated" (Botkin 1929b: 9–10). Therefore, in his view, the real distinction was between "folk literature" and "culture literature." It was, Botkin insisted, a difference in form, not in kind or content. There were two intermediate classes that played back and forth between folk and culture literature. Botkin identified these as popular culture and "that part of culture literature which, brooding over folk materials and motifs, rehandles and recreates them." The first needed to be studied. The latter was to play a key role in reuniting the two streams of literature into one, as they had been in the beginning and could be, in a new way, once again. This was a cultural nationalist vision that looked forward to a better world, rather than nostalgically backward to a world that had been lost (Botkin 1929b).

Botkin further explored the relationship between folk literature, culture literature, and popular culture in his essay "The Folk and the Individual" (Botkin 1938b) and in the introduction to *TAF*. Here, too, the goal was not so much analysis for its own sake but analysis designed to promote a vision of cultural reintegration. In the introduction, Botkin declared that "if this book is intended to bring the reader back to anything, it is not to the 'good old days,' but to an enjoyment and understanding of living American folklore for what it is and what it is worth" (Botkin 1944j: xxii).

Botkin's cultural nationalism clearly linked his discussion of American folklore to a larger debate in the interwar years about whether America had the cultural traditions from which a national culture could be created. Botkin took the affirmative point of view in this debate. His thinking about folklore helped him answer affirmatively a question that Van Wyck Brooks had famously answered in the negative.[3] He worked to reconcile romantic nationalist views, which usually stressed purity and homogeneity, with an affirmation of diversity—"racial, regional, and even industrial cultures" as the source of American folklore, a "new creation" (Botkin 1930c: 16), a "Living Lore" (Botkin 1946d, 1958j),[4] a "folklore-in-the-making" (Botkin 1937c: 469). To make American folklore part of an affirmative answer Botkin had to reject much of the traditional folklore scholarship he was familiar with—he had, in the end, to create *TAF*.

From the beginning, Botkin engaged in living and defining what he saw as the role of the American folklorist. Throughout his career he revisited questions about the role of the folklorist as he thought about the changing America around him. As early as 1930, he stated the theme on which he would build variations in answering this question, when he insisted that collection and classification were not ends but means. He always disagreed with those folklorists in America who argued that questions of interpretation and utilization had to be deferred for the foreseeable future. The question that should concern writers, critics, and folklorists, he contended, is "not what is the folk and what is folklore but what can they do for our culture and literature" (Botkin

1930c: 16–18). And yet this central concern did not keep him from pondering the terms "folk" and "lore" in the Oklahoma, New Deal, and treasury-editing phases of his career. In *TAF* he found both academic and lay terms for discussing folklore: "patterned by common experience; varied by individual repetition, inventive or forgetful; and cherished because somehow characteristic or expressive" or, put another way, "complementary to the 'Stop me if you've heard this' aspect of folklore is the trait implied in the comeback: 'That's not the way I heard it'" (Botkin 1944j: xxi).

Botkin understood the resistance he would face from ordinary folk (here defined as the lay reader) and academics in promoting a folklore program of utilization and interpretation. Explaining the challenge that WPA folklore programs had taken on, he declared before a scholarly audience at the annual meeting of the Modern Language Association that these New Deal programs were bent on "breaking down on the one hand popular resistance to folklore as dead or phony stuff and on the other hand academic resistance to its broader interpretation and utilization." Anticipating scholarly critics, he maintained that "it is idle to talk of the dangers of vulgarization and amateurishness. If giving back to the people what we have taken from them and what rightfully belongs to them, in a form in which they can understand and use, is vulgarization, then we need more of it" (Botkin 1939e: 10, 14).

TAF was a response to the same challenges that Botkin had been addressing regarding folklore both in Oklahoma and on the WPA. Clearly, he sought to help Americans enjoy a folklore that he feared they rejected: "Because folklore is so elemental and folk songs and stories are such good neighbors and pleasant companions, it is hard to understand why American folklore is not more widely known and appreciated." Part of the problem was folklore scholars: "folklore . . . seems to have become the possession of the few who study it rather than the many who make or use it." While folklore scholars, in what Botkin called "a kind of class-consciousness," gave classic folk literature a status they denied to a still emerging American lore, he also recognized that "in our rapid development from a rural and agricultural to an urban and industrial folk, we have become estranged from the folklore of the past, which we cannot help feeling a little self-conscious or antiquarian about, without yet being able to recognize or appreciate the folklore of the present" (Botkin 1944j: xxi–xxii).

Given Botkin's thinking about the role of the American folklorist, the question of how folklorists could reach a wide audience was never far from his mind. In his Oklahoma days he had focused on what folklore could do for creative writers and America's diverse regional cultures. In the FWP in the thirties, he later wrote, he began to move from thinking of "folk-say as literature to folk-say as history," without abandoning his earlier concerns (Botkin 1958j: 198). The opportunity to work on the FWP was for Botkin a new chance to realize his vision. When the government withdrew support for the FWP, Botkin at first found a position in the Library of Congress that could help him pursue his vision. In the end, however, neither the academy nor the government would support his work and vision in the way it turned out that commercial publishers could.

In 1938 Botkin brought to the FWP a greater sense of urgency about the economic and political problems facing the society in which he lived than he had at the beginning of the *Folk-Say* venture in 1929. Based on his experience editing *Folk-Say,* Botkin had become convinced that as an individual editor and writer he could neither successfully stimulate the folklore studies that he thought needed to be done nor encourage a new literature. He had already tried and, in his own harsh self-assessment, failed (Botkin 1935b). Then Henry Alsberg, national FWP director, offered Botkin a position as the project's folklore editor in 1938. This gave Botkin the opportunity to have the assistance of the federal government in implementing what might be seen as a revised version of the folklore and literature program he had first tried out in Oklahoma. Most significantly, it was also an opportunity to help create national folklore institutions in the United States. Botkin was the pivotal figure in the FWP's effort to move beyond work on the state guidebooks and to reconcile cultural nationalism with pluralism and modernism. Botkin had initially linked turning to the academy and later to the government for support with a critique of commercial publishing. The alternatives to the marketplace, however, proved to have their own severe limitations, as both the University of Oklahoma and the New Deal proved to be less than supportive.

In some ways *TAF,* Botkin's first major commercial success, is a less experimental and less politically radical venture than his *Folk-Say* and FWP folklore projects. *TAF* was not primarily an experiment in creative writing using folk images, motifs, and symbols; nor was it primarily an example of what Botkin had called proletarian regionalism during his participation in the FWP and in radical cultural activities, including the Popular Front (the loose alliance of left-leaning radicals whose antifascist sentiments were reflected in their collective efforts to transform the means of cultural production toward progressive ends and thus help influence the social democratic reforms of the New Deal). Nevertheless, it not only showed the impact of these earlier efforts but also had its own large ambitions. Building on his earlier work in folklore, Botkin's book included examples of "that small body of masterpieces of 'folk art' mined out of the collective experience and imagination by writers, known and unknown, who have succeeded in identifying themselves with their folk tradition," of "industrial folk tales and songs," and "of folklore in the making." As in his Popular Front cultural activities, in *TAF* Botkin celebrated the creativity of ordinary Americans and rejected the view of those who wanted to look at "folklore in terms of the 'racial heritage' " or who "insist[ed] that a particular folk group or body of folk tradition is 'superior' or 'pure.' " For Popular Front intellectuals like Botkin, opposition to fascism was part of their cultural politics (Botkin 1944j: xxii–xxv).

By the spring of 1940 Botkin was working with Crown publishers on *TAF*. At the same time, he continued to work for the Writers' Program Library of Congress Unit, a part of what remained for a while of the whittled down Federal Writers' Project. The Librarian of Congress, poet Archibald MacLeish, took a special interest in Botkin's work, appointing him a folklore fellow in 1941 and head of the Archive of American Folk Song in 1942. It was through MacLeish that Botkin and Crown came together. As Botkin wrote James Aswell (a friend from his FWP experience) in May 1940:

> The only good news I have is a contract to edit an anthology of American folklore for the Crown publishers of New York City, which came about, oddly enough, through the Library. The publishers came down in May to ask MacLeish to edit or write the introduction for the book, and he referred them to Alan Lomax and me, and Alan, being busy enough with his own books and programs, withdrew in my favor.[5]

It would be wildly inaccurate, however, to conclude that *TAF* was only the result of an opportunity that had fortuitously dropped into Botkin's lap. In the beginning, his editors at Crown may have seen matters in that way. They initially thought of Botkin as "the editorial manager" of their anthology of American folklore.[6] Botkin insisted that this designation did not fit his conception of his role as an editor creating an interpretation of American folklore:

> As I told you, I have always wanted to do a book of this type, and before getting into it I want to be sure that we agree on the type of book that, independently, we seem to have been thinking about.
>
> This is to be a critical selection of American folklore as an expression of America's cultural diversity. It is not just another book "In Search of America" or a book about the American tradition. Nor is it a pedantic compilation of folklore treated purely as science or as literature. The stress is on American life, realistically portrayed through folk activities and imaginatively interpreted in folk fantasy.[7]

On their part, Crown editors were convinced that they needed, in addition to Botkin, " 'a box-office name' to enable the book to get the popular acceptance which is necessary."[8] In the end, Carl Sandburg wrote the foreword to Botkin's book.

MacLeish's support of Botkin flowed logically from his own cultural commitments as reflected in *America Was Promises,* a book-length poem-photomontage about the disparity between promise and reality in Depression America, and his role as an active figure in the Popular Front. As historian Michael Denning points out, culture industry workers involved in the Popular Front influenced mass culture in the direction of empathy for the creativity of ordinary Americans (especially industrial workers) and advocacy of democratic cultural pluralism in opposition to both fascism and traditional Protestant versions of Americanism (Denning 1996: 2–66 passim). From this point of view, it was not an accident that Jewish American editors at Crown publishers, a relative newcomer in the staid world of the book trade, worked with Botkin, himself the child of immigrant Jews, on *TAF.*

During the years when Botkin was working on the book, he remained deeply involved in the conflicts over the method, role, and purpose of folklore study—the cultural politics of folklore scholarship. As his earlier work had contributed to his thinking about how to edit an anthology of American folklore, his work editing *TAF* contributed to his thinking about the work that folklorists should be doing. As part of its effort to reassess and promote work in the study of American culture, the American Council of Learned Societies sponsored the 1942 "Conference on the Character and State of Studies in Folklore," in which Botkin participated. Botkin, Sterling Brown, Herbert Halpert, Alan Lomax, and Charles Seeger all took issue with a view that divorced the lore from the folk and regarded "the folk as ignorant and simple-minded receptacles for traditions and ideas which they do not themselves understand." They called instead for "recording and interpreting [folklore as] a living human tradition," which had "a function within the context of its social environment." From this point of view, the study of the tales and stories could not be separated from the study of those who created them and kept them alive, as Ralph Boggs advised. The lore, as Botkin had been saying for over decade, could not be separated from the folk. Those folklorists who refused to do so insisted that their approach was as scholarly as that of their opponents ("Conference" 1946: 507).

Boggs recommended postponing questions about the utilization of folklore. He and his supporters opposed efforts "to apply folklore to its ultimate ends and to get the last values out of it before there has been any very substantial basis of conclusions from the science upon which to proceed with that artistic application." A focus on both the folk and the lore, such as Botkin, Lomax, and Brown advocated, led to an interdisciplinary approach and a concern with the lives of those who preserved and created folklore ("Conference" 1946: 503).

At this conference, Botkin made clear the importance in his view of the connection between collection, publication, popularization, and scholarship. The creative editing of folklore anthologies, he argued, had a major role to play in linking the collecting and publishing aspects of folklore study and in contributing to both popularization and scholarship. Botkin complained that "in no other science save folklore is the worker so likely to stop where he began—with collection, or rather with the publication of collections" that do not draw "inferences and conclusions" (Botkin 1946f: 520–22). Botkin saw *TAF* as an interpretation of the American experience based on inferences and conclusions about the nation's folklore.

Drawing on previous experience, Botkin pointed to the need for developing means other than books and scholarly journals for publishing folklore materials. Here he noted the relevance of the WPA's mimeographed studies, such as the Nebraska Folklore Pamphlets of the Nebraska Writers' Project. No doubt with work on *TAF* in mind, he commented on both publisher and reader resistance to folklore as something of little interest. More attention to the integration and arrangement of materials would help: "texts per se only interest other folklorists." Folklorists, Botkin suggested, should move away from the simple division between the introduction and texts. It was necessary to try to integrate texts, documentation, and commentary in a way that helped the reader learn about both the lore and its cultural background. Folklorists needed to avoid "an unfortunate compromise between public appeal, popular appeal, and scholarly value" that was "the result of most commercial publication of folklore." By following a functionalist approach folklorists could edit collections in a way that went beyond "folklorists talking to themselves, or folklore *in vacuo*," and instead spoke to the general reader. Botkin's discussion of the publication of folklore at this conference drew on his Oklahoma and FWP experiences, set out what may be viewed in hindsight as a rationale for his future treasuries, and indicated the close connections between his effort to have folklore publications reach a large audience and the approach of the functionalists (Botkin 1946f: 222).

Both Botkin and the first popular and scholarly reviewers of *TAF* saw the book in relation to previous folklore collections. Botkin's book was the first substantial collection of American folklore that did not confine itself to a single region or a single genre. Indeed, Botkin did not rely on traditional genre categories in arranging his material or provide detailed comparative notes and numerous variant texts or refer to standard motif indexes. This was not merely an effort to make the book appeal to a popular audience. Rather, it was part of Botkin's argument that American folklore had to be approached in a different way because it developed contemporaneously with literacy, print, and machinery and involved a diversity of folk groups, unlike more homogeneous societies. Focusing in *TAF* on folklore "as the stuff that travels and the stuff that sticks," Botkin recognized not only the role of print, machinery, and diversity in the creation of American folklore but also the emergent folklore "stuff that travels without sticking or sticks without traveling" (Botkin 1944j: xxiv–xxv). Botkin wanted categories that he thought emerged from the study and interpretation of American folklore. "Backwoods Boasters," "Local Cracks and Slams," and "Tall Talk" were in his view more useful categories than allegedly universally valid genre classifications. Critics recognized that the book, rather than shunning "inferences and conclusions," was rich in interpretation, that Botkin had not been content to simply publish texts *in vacuo*. Instead, he had integrated texts, documentation, and commentary.

Crown publishers advertised *TAF* as a celebration of America, of "the glorious, virile, and earthy American language," of "the imagination and vigor of an irrepressible people," and of "the nation at work and at play, loving, boasting, singing, laughing."[9] The language of the popular reviews also reflected the romantic nationalist and Popular Front ethos that persisted through the war years. For Stewart Holbrook, writing in the *New York Herald Tribune*, Botkin's anthology demonstrated that "the United States has produced in the past three centuries a folklore which could have originated nowhere else."[10] The headline of one review claimed: "These Stories and Songs Give America Its Own Mythology."[11] And the reviewer in the *New Masses*, an organ of the Communist Party of the United States, asked: "breathes there an American who can't find something closely identified with his way of living—his memories, too—in this gargantuan storehouse of tall tales, legends, traditions, ballads and songs of the United States?"[12]

Scholars, with few exceptions, hailed the appearance of *TAF* while at the same time raising important questions about Botkin's approach. They recognized his status and experience in folklore studies. In *Southern Folklore Quarterly*, Arthur Palmer Hudson pointed to Botkin's *The American Play-Party* as "demonstrat[ing] his competency to handle folklore in a scientific way" and to his work editing *Folk-Say* as evidence "that he knew how to handle [folklore] creatively and popularly."[13] Reflecting on Botkin's editorial introductions and comments, Wayland Hand declared in the *Journal of American Folklore* that Botkin "has not allowed his passion for a popular acceptance of his book, and of folklore, to preclude so-called 'scholarly' considerations, with which by virtue of training in the science of folklore as well as the literature, he is thoroughly competent to deal" (Hand 1945: 56). In the *Musical Quarterly*, George Pullen Jackson insisted that when a folklorist with Botkin's qualifications edited a 900-plus-page anthology it merited the attention of other scholars, for the result "is bound to be significant" (Jackson 1944: 496).

These scholars assumed that the views of Botkin, then the newly elected president of the American Folklore Society, deserved respectful attention, even as they examined, probed, and questioned his approach to folklore. They did not fear the popularization of folklore as a threat to the work of folklore scholars. Like Botkin, Wayland Hand felt that folklore was too important to be left exclusively to the academicians: "Folklore is gradually coming before the public eye in this country, and what once fell by default to the attention of but a few antiquarian scholars and specialists is now becoming the conscious property and the proud heritage of the whole American people." From Hand's point of view, Botkin's anthology was a major achievement that would nurture the growing public interest in folklore: "In this development, long overdue, Botkin's book is destined to play a significant part, constituting, as it does, the first serious attempt to provide a general anthology of American folklore" (Hand 1944: 57). Arthur Palmer Hudson was equally enthusiastic: *TAF* "comes nearer to representing the traditional roots of American culture than any other one volume book has done. . . . The people are reading *A Treasury of American Folklore* and will continue to do so. Folklorists who fail to read it will do so to their own loss" (Hudson review, n.d.).

The folklorists who reviewed *TAF* did not question the validity of the role Botkin had assumed in bringing American folklore before the public. They gave no indication that they saw the work that folklorists addressed to fellow scholars and work that they did for a larger audience as divided into separate spheres of academic and public folklore. They did, however, want to see a continuation of the discussion of what should be covered by the term "folklore." Botkin's approach raised questions about the relationship between oral tradition and written literature, between lore and popular culture. They wondered when oral utterance became folklore. How essential was the geographic spread of this material over time in making it traditional and in sifting out the aesthetically significant from the banal?

The "science of folklore" was a term that once had a meaning and prestige that folklorists who used it easily recognized without having to define it. This comes across clearly in the scholarly reviews of *TAF*. A clear sense of what was meant by the term "science of folklore" is contained in the transcript of the "Conference on the Character and State of Studies in Folklore," where Ralph Boggs, Alexander Krappe, and Stith Thompson argued that folklore was a "historical science" mainly concerned with trying to classify and analyze stories, songs, and beliefs in order "to determine what the laws are which have governed their origin, their growth, and their structure" ("Conference" 1946: 499, 501). It was, as the reviewers understood, an approach to the study of folklore that neither fitted nor encouraged the study of American folklore.

And yet even as scholarly reviewers were willing to challenge the science of folklore in expressing their admiration for *TAF*, they were also aware of its prestige and power. Thus Hudson pointed out that while Botkin's "conception of folklore as 'a species of living literature which has no fixed form . . . and which is constantly shifting back and forth between written and unwritten tradition' is consistent with the views of Continental scholars," he thought Botkin's "estimate of the range of variation in folklore as it shifts between the top and bottom layers of culture . . . is likely to get him into trouble with the scientific folklorists." The same was true regarding Botkin's "hospitality toward the current entertainments" (stage, radio, press, films, jazz, comic strips), which according to Botkin "have a folk basis or give rise to new folk creations such as Mickey Mouse and Donald Duck" (Hudson review, n.d.).

Folklorist Levette Davidson highlighted the stimulating questions that Botkin raised, which he thought made the book not only a source of entertainment but theoretically stimulating: "Where does 'folk' literature leave off and 'popular' or 'standard' literature begin? What differentiates 'popular' literature from 'sophisticated' or 'standard' literature. . . . Have Stephen Foster's songs passed over into folklore? Are Popeye and Donald Duck legitimate folk figures, to be associated with Sinbad and Brer Rabbit?"[14]

Scholarly reviewers found the question of when and how oral utterance became folklore as significant as questions about the relationships among folklore, written literature, and popular culture. This question raised issues from both a science of folklore and a literary aesthetic perspective. Hudson noted that Botkin included only two of the Child ballads, English songs known in America in "thousands of variants" and "some of them in words and music the most beautiful in the world," in favor of occupational and "Negro" songs, "all excellent in their kind" (Hudson review, n.d.).

George Pullen Jackson, a student of white spirituals, oscillated between praise for *TAF* and unease over the editorial choices that Botkin's approach led him to make, such as giving little space to older ballads while including more of "the ditties of cowboys, sailors, lumberjacks, miners, hoboes, and Negro convict-campers"—even finding "space for some of the lowest forms of song like those of Huddie Leady Belly [*sic*]" (Jackson 1944: 496). Jackson's aesthetic judgments blended with his understanding of the science of folklore: "Folklore is to Mr. Botkin Volkskunde, whether that means the ways and wisdom of the folk or our knowledge of those ways and that wisdom" (497). From this it followed, Jackson pointed out, that "folklore is . . . a broad thing to the editor. And since broad things have a way of lacking depth (historical depth, for this material), the editor is frankly willing to let the old folklore go and to underscore the new." Although he thought Botkin's preference for the new over the old, for distinctly American materials, "was healthy and long overdue" and was willing to "hail the editor's move in this direction," Jackson declared: "I can not follow him all the way" (498). In his view, the process by which folklore varied over time and space was not only at the heart of the science of folklore but also key to the artistic achievement of the folk: "Botkin and we will of course remember that folklore-on-the-make is an endless, ruthless, and almost automatic elimination of ninety-nine-hundredths of that which travels and may appear to stick. I think the folk will eliminate, for example, those 'Little Audreyisms' which are clever and urbane" (498).

While folklorists initially praised *TAF*, they had also noted the issues that Botkin's approach raised and the debates they thought would follow from that approach. They did not claim, however, as Dorson later would, that Botkin was doing the study of folklore a disservice. Rather, they insisted that his treasury aided the cause and study of folklore for both lay readers and scholars.

Botkin had good reason to savor the publication of *TAF* as a triumph that had followed a long, hard struggle, a triumph not merely in a commercial sense but in developing his vision of how to "assimilate folklore to the local and national life" (Botkin 1939e: 11). *TAF* was the capstone to all Botkin had learned in his Oklahoma *Folk-Say* period and in his years in Washington at the FWP and in the Library of Congress.

The Ben Botkin "bulldozer," as Jackson referred to *TAF*, was more than a personal triumph for Botkin, as the initial reviewers recognized. None, however, put it quite so dramatically as Jackson. Botkin, in his view, had leveled the traditional academic barriers that professors had erected when they "patented 'folklore.'" According to Jackson, it was about time for someone to push aside the existing "academic limitations" by which the professional folklorists had defined their field. Nevertheless, he was somewhat rueful about the consequences for folklorists of becoming "free," along the lines outlined in *TAF*. While

Jackson did not find an altogether comfortable home for his scholarly concerns in the existing folklore synthesis, he also appeared to have feared that he would not find one in the synthesis Botkin was working to create. In our terms, Jackson simultaneously welcomed yet feared a paradigm shift (Jackson 1944).

What Jackson and the other reviewers recognized more or less explicitly was that Botkin had created a new synthesis for the study of American folklore. As a synthesis, *TAF* drew on functionalist anthropology, the study of American popular literature, the search in the interwar years for indigenous American traditions, and earlier challenges not only to what constituted the folklorist's object of study but also to the role of the folklorist in American culture. Perhaps most startlingly, it silently dismissed as at best irrelevant to American folklore the syntheses being built by evolutionary folklorists and by the historical-geographic school, with their mammoth and ongoing motif indexes. Like all synthesizers, Botkin incorporated what he learned even from folklorists he disagreed with on larger issues, for he was interested in their information and insights, if not in the overarching structures that they thought provided a structure for the field.

As a work of synthesis, *TAF* not only built on the earlier work and experience of Botkin and folklorists who shared his outlook but also suggested an agenda for future work in the field. One part of that agenda was that folklorists needed to strive to make the lore of a diverse America a respected part of the nation's culture by sharing the materials of their study with the general public. Given that there was always, in Botkin's view, folklore in the making, there could be no fixed canon of American folklore. Not only was a canon of American folklore open-ended, but there was also no way for a diverse public to become familiar with it unless folklorists published the materials they recorded and studied. Furthermore, as scholars at the time acknowledged, Botkin's synthesis provided them with questions that called for continued research centering around issues such as how folklore was preserved, created, and functioned in a literate and industrial society, the interaction between folklore and popular culture, and the relationship between folk literature and written literature.

To a significant degree, Richard Dorson's attack on Botkin and his treasuries constituted a recognition that these volumes were works of synthesis that provided an agenda that Dorson found unacceptable. In his view, Botkin was offering a synthesis that, if accepted, would harm the study of folklore and make it difficult to develop folklore departments in universities—hence his vituperative denunciation of Botkin as a "fakelorist."

The time has long since passed when Dorson's attack on Botkin seemed the last word on the subject. Folklorists since Botkin have not been particularly successful at creating works of synthesis—Dorson tried and failed. His own *America in Legend: Folklore from the Colonial Period to the Present* (Dorson 1974) was a critical and commercial failure. Dorson, like Botkin, realized that humanistic studies like folklore, and perhaps especially folklore, needed works of synthesis that not only met the needs of other scholars and students but also justified the field's relevance and importance to a general public. In addition to its significance in the history of American folklore studies, *TAF* would repay renewed and humble reconsideration by American folklorists, who need to keep in mind that the book has never been out of print since it was first published more than sixty years ago.

Notes

1. B. A. Botkin to Herbert Halpert, January 21, 1952, Botkin Papers, University of Nebraska Archives, Lincoln (hereafter BPUNAL).

2. When Botkin was National Federal Writers' Project folklore editor, Richard Dorson (then a young student of American culture) visited Botkin in his Washington, D.C., office. The previously unexplored relationship between these two individuals is part of my ongoing research. After having first turned to Botkin as a mentor and friend who could teach him about American folklore, Dorson engaged in an almost thirty-year campaign against Botkin's work. His goal was to delegitimize Botkin's work among lay readers and in those academic disciplines that mattered most to Dorson. At the same time, Dorson used his attack on Botkin to help define the role of the folklorist and the material folklorists studied. See Dorson 1948, 1949, 1950a, 1950b, 1971b, and 1976.

3. See in particular Van Wyck Brooks's "America's Coming of Age" (1915) and "On Creating a Usable Past" (1918) in Brooks 1968: 79–158, 219–26.

4. As FWP folklore editor, Botkin created "Living Lore" units in Chicago, New York City, and New England, consisting of talented writers. He encouraged them not only to collect folklore but also to use what they had learned in their own writing.

5. Botkin to James Aswell, July 4, 1940, *TAF* correspondence, BPUNAL.

6. Robert Simon to Botkin, May 10, 1940, *TAF* correspondence, BPUNAL.

7. Botkin to Simon, May 13, 1940, *TAF* correspondence, BPUNAL.

8. Simon to Botkin, May 14, 1940, *TAF* correspondence, BPUNAL.

9. Full-page advertisements in the *New York Times Book Review*, February 4, 1945, and May 21, 1944, and undated publicity statement, all in *TAF* correspondence, BPUNAL.

10. Stewart Holbrook, review of *TAF*, ed. B. A. Botkin, *New York Herald Tribune*, May 7, 1944, clipping in *TAF* correspondence, BPUNAL.

11. Review of *TAF*, *Chicago News*, May 5, 1944, clipping in *TAF* correspondence, BPUNAL.

12. John Norcross, review of *TAF, New Masses,* n.d., clipping in *TAF* correspondence, BPUNAL.

13. Arthur Palmer Hudson, review of *TAF, Southern Folklore Quarterly,* n.d., 250.

14. Levette Davidson, review of *TAF,* ed. by B. A. Botkin, *California Folklore Quarterly* 3 (1944): 337.

Benjamin A. Botkin (1901–1975)

BRUCE JACKSON

Ben Botkin died July 30, 1975, after a long and disabling illness. He was seventy-four years old.

More than any other folklorist of his generation, he was content to let his sources tell their own stories. What set him off from his professional colleagues was his consistent refusal—often in the face of violent attack—to limit those sources to things academics could find more or less respectable. Ben was a scholar, not an academic, so he never suffered that limitation of apparent respectability and he was willing to admit equally the voice of someone he met on the road and the copy on the back of a cereal box. What got him in trouble with the academic folklorists was the simple and sadly elusive fact that his vision was so much broader than theirs: they were looking for texts that could be properly annotated and indexed; Ben was trying to document the soul of a land.

His quest was poetic at heart, as he was. He sensed that when, in 1940, he abandoned his university position to devote himself to writing about the things he loved. Few professors have nerve for such a leap.

University people are not awfully good at dealing with poets. They sometimes hire them for a while and give them jobs as pets in English departments, but they are always more than a little uncomfortable about them, and rarely very unhappy when they revert to form and move on. It's not just that those poets insist on dancing to their different drum, but that they have the arrogance of refusing to tell us how to interpret it. They just keep saying, *Listen, listen, listen.*

Ben's youth was spent in the Boston area. Scholarships and a variety of part-time jobs enabled him to do his undergraduate work at Harvard (B.A. magna

Reprinted from *Journal of American Folklore* 89 (January–March 1976): 1–6.

cum laude, 1920). He took his M.A. in English at Columbia in 1921, working under John Erskine, Clayton Hamilton, Brander Matthews, and Carl and Mark Van Doren; his thesis was on Thomas Edward Brown, the Manx poet. He taught English at the University of Oklahoma for two years, then in 1923 returned to New York, where he attended classes at Columbia University, worked in settlement houses, taught English to foreigners, and spent as much time as he could manage seeing plays. In 1925, while visiting Quincy, Massachusetts, he met and married Gertrude Fritz.

When he returned to Oklahoma, Ben began collecting folklore among students and townspeople and involved himself with the Southwest "renascence." He was founder and editor of the annual *Folk-Say* (1929–32) and a monthly, *Space* (1934–35); he was also contributing editor of the *Southwest Review* (1929–37) and book reviewer for the *Sunday Oklahoman*. He took his doctorate in English and anthropology in 1931 under Louise Pound and William Duncan Strong at the University of Nebraska. His association with the University of Oklahoma continued until 1940, but his turn from a local to a national approach to regionalism began when he went to Washington on a Julius Rosenwald Fellowship in 1937 to do research at the Library of Congress in southern folk and regional literature. From 1938 to 1941 he was successively national folklore editor of the Federal Writers' Project, co-founder and chairman of the Joint Committee on Folk Arts of the WPA, and chief editor of the Writers' Unit of the Library of Congress Project; in 1941 he became Library of Congress Fellow in Folklore (Honorary Fellow 1942–56). In 1942 he was named head of the Library's Archive of American Folk Song. *A Treasury of American Folklore* was published in 1944; the following year, while still president of the American Folklore Society, Ben resigned from the Library and moved to New York. About that time, his interest shifted from rural to urban folklore; that work was helped by a Guggenheim Fellowship in 1951.

The most important advance in my thinking [he wrote in 1970] came in the fifties through my work with the Workshop for Cultural Democracy in the field of intergroup understanding and community integration. This was the reaffirmation of my applied folklore concept (folklore for understanding and creating understanding), first enunciated in 1939 . . . and first published in 1953. . . . "Whereas," I wrote, "a pure folklorist might tend to think of folklore as an independent discipline, the applied folklorist prefers to think of it as ancillary to the study of culture, of history or literature—of people." Of all my folklore concepts this gives me the most satisfaction because of its multi-disciplinary broadening and deepening of my perspective and insight. If I have any further contribution to make, it will be by way of the integration and crystallization of all my folklore thinking, beginning with my interpretive work in progress, *American Social Myths and Symbols,* made possible by a Louis M. Rabinowitz Foundation grant (1965) and a National Endowment for the Humanities Senior Fellowship (1967).

Ben was concerned with folklore in its broadest and most social sense, and in that his work was something of a contradiction, for he was both quiet and shy. Though he taught for many years and sometimes gave lectures after he left teaching, the major role he chose was not that of public speaker but of writer, perhaps the loneliest job of all, one that involves locking oneself away from the world in order to make some sense of it.

The second floor of his Croton-on-Hudson house was a place visitors would leave awed and tantalized: when you told Ben what you were working on he would go to the shelves or piles or stacks and haul out copies (often signed) of the appropriate classics, a dozen other things you'd never heard of but knew immediately you needed absolutely, as well as sheets of ephemera no one but Ben knew about anymore, let alone owned. The floors and shelves bulged with scholarly treatises, fictions, fictions posing as fact, guidebooks, magazines, Sunday supplements, handbooks, manuscripts, pamphlets, reference works, and all the other printed forms that have served to document or present or analyze or eulogize or indict those verbal artifacts of the complex of high and low and mass and pop and folk culture we sometimes call the American Experience: Ben's field.

He was always interested in the ways people negotiated and documented their lives, and he refused to draw a line—when it seemed to him a certain kind of informing idea was involved—between something uttered in a traditional conversation and something locked in print. (That was a concept that didn't get a name until a folklorist wrote a paper a few years ago on "folk ideas," a folklorist's attempt to come to grips with the curious and annoying reality that there is a lot of stuff out there that fits no genre we know or permeates too many we know, but seems traditional nevertheless, beyond genre and beyond performance, a notion that would have been perfectly clear to Ben Botkin.)

His work covered a multitude of subjects; his focus was always on people and their genius of expression. *The American Play-Party Song* (1937), a revision of his doctoral thesis, is still a classic collection and analysis; *Lay My*

Burden Down (1945), one of the most moving demonstrations of slavery as an experience, is a work of verbal choreography more than history; the several treasuries—*American Folklore* (1944), *New England Folklore* (1947), *Southern Folklore* (1949), *Western Folklore* (1951), *Railroad Folklore* (1953, with Alvin F. Harlow), *Mississippi River Folklore* (1955), and *New York City Folklore* (1956)— have, because of Ben's enormous range of interest and his consistent belief in the virtue of inclusiveness rather than airy exclusiveness, taught millions about the legitimate place of folklore in the American cultural continuum. That those books were long eschewed by professional folklorists perhaps tells us more about the ideological tunnel vision inculcated by grim professionalism than it does about Ben's work.

He did not look lightly on the work of making books. Not long before he died, when he was very ill and very tired, he asked me what I was up to. I told him I'd recently had a couple of new books published and I was now at work on two others.

"*Why* are you still writing books?" he said.

It was, for me, a very spooky question, because I often think about the arrogance of putting things to print, and fear it. We'd never talked about that before, but I knew, in that winky moment, that he was fully aware of it, had more than once wrestled with it himself, and that he had, in that moment, done the sort of thing he always did: threw something out and by implication said, "Here's something you might think about if you want to. You should." Then he got very tired and we talked of it no more.

In 1966 I edited a Festschrift for him on the occasion of his sixty-fifth birthday. The preface concluded, "In presenting Ben with this small collection of essays, we acknowledge the work he has done for and in the field of folklore and, more personally, our pleasure in having him as colleague, teacher, and friend." I would add nothing to that now, because the one thing I would like to name—my sadness and the sadness of Ben's family and friends that all that must now be relegated to the past tense—is not expressible. The magnitude of absence is named only by the locus of what was.

Ben's last project was that book he called *American Social Myths and Symbols*. He saw it as the fulfillment of his long career as teacher, poet, critic, folklorist, and social historian. Ten years ago, he described the project this way:

> In nearly a score of volumes I have explored the relation of folklore to folksay (a word which I coined in 1928 to designate unwritten history and literature in particular and oral, linguistic, and floating material in general); the folklore of regions and cities—New England, the South,

the West, the Mississippi River region, New York City, "Sidewalks of America"; the folklore of occupations—railroading; the folklore of slavery and the Civil War; the folklore of play and leisure time. In *American Myths and Symbols* I intend to integrate and culminate my thinking on applied folklore in an analysis of folk and popular assumptions and their symbolic expression in heroes, idols, butts, scapegoats, archetypes, stereotypes, totemic creatures and objects, fictitious personalities, cliches, catchwords, shibboleths, slogans, phrases, historical traditions, legends, myths, fables, anecdotes, jests, codes and rituals.

The project had its inception in the present revival of folk singing and song-making (ballads, blues, Freedom songs) and folklore in literature and education. By centering attention on folklore utilization and folklore values, the revival has raised basic questions as to the relevance of the past to the present, the uses and abuses of tradition, and the relation of folklore to the folkways and mores.

My own conception of the reciprocity of folklore and the folkways in the diffusion of myths and symbols has a theoretical basis in Sumner's neglected but still pertinent theory of *Folkways*, which I have extended as follows:

Like folklore, the folkways rest on assumptions with the backing of tradition and group acceptance. Like all tacit assumptions, the folkways (and the mores growing out of them) can be harmful when used as a substitute for or an obstacle to thinking. As the strength of folklore lies in its imaginative appeal, so the folkways are reinforced by the "instrumentalities of suggestion," or myths, symbols, and tokens in which outmoded folkways and mores are embodied. In a changing society with concomitant rapid growth and mixture of disciplines, a folklore study of socio-historical myths and symbols should help us to reassess old and new values and to understand the present in the light of the past and *vice versa* by providing a new approach to the positive or negative role of myth and symbols in unifying or separating people and promoting social progress or reaction. In the last analysis we may discover that whatever affects our values has symbolic meaning and whatever has symbolic meaning affects our values.

It seems odd to read that now, for much of what Ben had to say has become part of the working vocabulary of folklorists, many of whom know or recognize or admit nothing of the legacy involved.

Ben never finished *American Social Myths and Symbols,* which is hardly surprising, since he intended it to be a descriptive and theoretical compendium of everything he'd learned in all those years. There is no way for one book to report all that. But there was another reason he couldn't finish it: he'd done it already, he'd been doing it for forty years, he'd got a lot of other people doing it too, and what was needed now was commentary. But commenting never interested Ben half so much as simply saying, *Listen, listen, listen.*

Obituary: Benjamin Albert Botkin, 1901–1975

ELLEN J. STEKERT

Ben Botkin was a quiet man; now that he is dead it might take us a while to realize the vast silence left by his absence. He never wrote "the" book on folklore theory which his knowledge and insight promised, but how many of us could or have tried? He used his mind carefully and honestly. Discussions with him were invariably revelations, for although he was shy his mind was quick and he often would finish your halting sentences by interjecting a word or phrase which rounded out what you were attempting to say, or even elaborated upon it. He had the quality of compassion which allowed him to enter your thinking process, and he had the force of intellect to help you develop and articulate your own ideas. He leaves behind many friends whom he enlightened and inspired.

The body of work which Ben Botkin left behind has yet to be assessed objectively by folklorists. When his contribution to the field is tabulated we will be able to recognize the magnitude of our loss. Few folklorists in the past decade have had as many storms rage about them as did this man; his work has been both violently attacked and staunchly defended. It is time we looked carefully at his accomplishments before we have any more controversies about his products. His "Treasuries" were the focal point of much objection, but no matter which opinion one held, one could not deny that B. A. Botkin's work helped gain public recognition and respect for the field of folklore. He served as a lightning rod, a focus for positive and negative energies; he played his part quietly and with conviction.

Ben Botkin was a scholar of the first order. If credentials matter, he had them: a Harvard B.A. in 1920 (at age nineteen), an M.A. from Columbia the

Reprinted from *Journal of Western Folklore* 34.4 (October 1975): 335–38.

following year, and a Ph.D. from the University of Nebraska in 1931. By the time he published his first "Treasury" (*A Treasury of American Folklore,* 1944) he was one of the most thoroughly and extensively educated folklorists in the country: he was schooled in the areas of literary criticism, fieldwork, teaching, archiving, and editing. In the 1920s and 1930s he taught at the University of Oklahoma, he was the editor of the folklore section of the Federal Writers' Project, and he had held the position of head of the Library of Congress Archive of American Folk Song.

Above all, Ben Botkin was a humanist. He was concerned that too much application of the social sciences to the study of folklore would rob the rich subject matter of its essential character. When his works are viewed in a historical perspective, no one can fault his scholarship or claim that he misrepresented what he was doing. A comprehensive bibliography of Ben Botkin's writings up to 1966 appears in the Festschrift edited by Bruce Jackson and published that year. Even a cursory glance at those titles reveals that Ben Botkin produced pioneering works as far back as the 1930s: articles, books, reviews, which treated questions folklorists today still are "discovering." Jackson's introduction to the Festschrift is splendid; Ben Botkin knew while he lived that he was appreciated for the many "treasures" he gave others. Jackson's own words capture much of the man:

> Ben has been concerned with folklore in its broadest and most social sense, and in that he may represent something of a contradiction, for he is himself quiet and rather shy. Though he taught for many years and still lectures on occasion, the major role he chose was not that of public speaker but of writer, that loneliest job of all that involves locking oneself away from the world in order to make some sense of it. It is always a little awesome to consider just how various and great a mass of material is being made sensible: scan the footnotes of almost any of his books and you find a splendidly catholic range of sources. (Jackson 1966: viii)

Ben Botkin's mind was not only keen, it was sensitive as well. His shyness did not make him a star performer at the annual meetings of the American Folklore Society, but as increasing numbers of folklore students met him in small groups they found a humble, reticent, gentle man of enormous learning and concern for human beings. Ben Botkin's writings never made him wealthy; he had better things than money to offer, and he unselfishly gave all that he could to students and scholars who often visited with him and his family in his modest home in Croton-on-Hudson, New York.

One of Ben Botkin's most engaging qualities was the maverick side of his intellect. He never took the path before him because it was easy. Just like his mentor, Louise Pound, he walked directly into the tangled and difficult questions about folklore. He dared work with ideas many folklorists still fear to recognize. The much discussed "Treasuries" themselves reflect his concerns with the subtle distinctions between popular and folk traditions, regionalism, applied folklore, folklore, and mass media. He was honest enough to know that he might not be able to give definitive answers, but that never stopped him from discussing the questions. What he produced, he did openly, describing exactly what he was about; his works were never fraudulent.

Few people had the opportunity to know the whimsical sense of humor Ben Botkin had. On the occasion of my presenting a rather prosaic Christmas present to his family in 1954—the latest and most "modern" of kitchen aides— he wrote a delightful mock ode thank-you note ("Owed to a Beautyware Beautycan"); he always did feel that garbage should be called just that.

Both his mind and his heart were large; perhaps it was his early "popular" success that made such an honest man and a fine scholar the person who was attacked by those who felt he did not meet the criteria of folklore as an academic discipline. It is ironic how times have changed and how now we sell our discipline on the merits of its popularity. Ben Botkin might have known that time was on his side and that it might take his ultimate silence to provide the atmosphere in which the true value of his work and his explorations would be recognized.

One of the most appealing things about Ben Botkin was that he approached both people and his work from a positive stance; he looked constantly for what was good and he built upon that rather than upon faults. He was courageous, but he disliked wasting energy on personal quarrels. He picked his battles with a deep sense of honor for his field of study. Once, in 1956, he wrote me a letter in reply to a concerned note I had sent him regarding my teacher and his friend, the late Professor Harold Thompson of Cornell University. I had been groping, as most of us still are, for a definition of folklore. Professor Thompson had dismissed my fretting by saying that folklore was "what one liked." Ben Botkin's reply to my distressed letter was full of far more wisdom than I could appreciate at the time:

> Harold may be right about your avoiding theoretical discussion. You recall how hard we tried to define folklore, especially with Mr. [Charles] Seeger, and how little we got beyond establishing a few criteria—none of them absolute. Harold has a point in saying that folklore is a matter of

taste. He means the art of folklore—the art that appreciates as well as the art that creates—as distinct from the science, which analyzes and classifies. But even taste must have some touchstones.

Ben Botkin never claimed to know the ultimate truth; he joined you in the search. Sooner or later folklorists and students of American civilization will have to reckon with the life work that he has left behind.

Growing Up in Folklore
A Conversation with Ben Botkin's Children

DOROTHY ROSENTHAL AND DANIEL BOTKIN

DOROTHY: The first thing I think of when I think of growing up as a child of Ben Botkin is the books. Even before we moved to the house at 45 Lexington Drive in Croton-on-Hudson, New York, the largest house we ever lived in, the books were like another member of the family, the most important member! I don't know which our father liked more—reading books or collecting them. He bought most of our children's books at secondhand bookstores. He made a notation on the first page of every book he bought—his initials, where he had purchased it, and how much he paid for it. If the book was a gift for us, he would write an amusing nonsense rhyme on the title page. The rhymes were one of the things I loved best about being Ben's daughter. In the 1920s and 1930s he had written a few hundred serious poems and published a number of them, but by the time I can remember, most of his poetry was what he called doggerel—written in books or on cards for special occasions, such as birthdays. He also made up poems on the spot when we lived in Washington. While he was shaving in the bathroom, which was at the head of the stairs, I would sit on the top step and he would spin off a short poem for me. He communicated to me a love for books that has been influential all of my life. And he helped me to pass this love on to my daughter. When she was little, he would take her to secondhand bookstores in nearby Ossining when we visited Croton. He had his first stroke in 1970 when she was ten and couldn't continue the visits to bookstores, but she never forgot sharing those trips with him.

DAN: Dorothy, your remembrances of collecting books remind me that after we moved to Croton from Washington, D.C., and had easy access to New York

This essay was originally published in *Voices: The Journal of New York Folklore* 27 (Fall–Winter 2001): 11–15.

City by train, I went to the city with our father on many occasions, and we always wandered around Fourth Street, which was then a famous center for used-book stores. He knew many of the book dealers, and looking at dusty books of all kinds, from old children's books to obscure scholarly books, seemed an ordinary and normal thing to do. It was his favorite hobby.

DOROTHY: Do you remember his "Vernal Equinox," which consists of four short poems about New York City? It was published in the *University of Oklahoma Magazine* in 1926. The first section is called "Fourth Avenue" and goes like this:

> Somehow it makes booksellers seem less hard
> To talk, not shop, but flowers in the yard.
>
> And bookstalls bloom like gardens at the door,
> Where dingy, browsing folk have wings and soar
>
> And hover—plundering bees and butterflies—
> With eager fluttering of their hands and eyes . . .
>
> Poor city grubs and drones and bookworms stand,
> And take their spring, like books, at second hand.

DAN: Actually, Dorothy, I never saw or heard that poem, but I'm glad to see it now. It certainly captures his attitude about books and bookstores. It's an interesting contrast to the direction that interest in books seems to be going today.

Once we moved to Croton, you remember, our parents converted the master bedroom—a very large room—into a beautiful study. They had a carpenter build floor-to-ceiling bookcases on every possible wall space and at one end of the living room. They also bought a beautiful wood desk. But by the time you went off to college, that study was filled not only with books on the shelves but with boxes of books and papers. The entire floor was covered with boxes one or two layers deep, except for a narrow path that led from the doorway to a small spot by the front window. At the end of that path was a typewriter on a foldup table, an office chair, and a small fluorescent lamp. The desk was piled two boxes deep with books and papers and could no longer be used, except as storage. Ben sat and worked there, surrounded by all the boxes.

DOROTHY: That's the way I remember it also. By the way, the wood desk you mention is now my husband Jerry's desk. The books and boxes of papers eventually invaded all parts of the house—the hallways, the dining room, the sun room—and after we went off to college, he began to fill *our* rooms and closets with books. By the time Dad died in 1975, there were books and boxes in every room except their bedroom, the kitchen, and the bathrooms. The attic was, of course, full of them, and half of the garage was piled waist-high with old newspapers and magazines. He always hoped to make use of them, but he never had the time and they just kept piling up.

DAN: This seemed normal and ordinary to me. My high school buddies, with whom I spent most of my time riding around in hotrods, lived in houses that did not have rooms like that, but I thought that was simply part of the variety of lifestyles, not that there was anything especially unusual about our house.

DOROTHY: I thought that was the way a house *ought* to be, and for most of my married life I had bookcases in the living room. It was a long time before I realized that it was OK to relegate books to a study or other room.

DAN: The study looked like chaos, but whenever anyone visited and asked Ben for a particular book or article, or just inquired about a topic, he knew immediately where to find it. I never understood his overall organization, except for a number of file drawers holding 3-by-5 index cards, which he explained to me. They held handwritten notes on every possible subject—he was always writing down new ideas, or what people said and he thought was a contribution to folksay. Those file drawers were very nicely organized by subject, and there were many subjects.

DOROTHY: That ability of his to find anything in his study continued even after he had his stroke. Even if he couldn't remember what had just happened a few minutes before, he could explain where to find a particular book, and he was always right!

DAN: I didn't know that, but it says something about his love of his library. I browsed through the books and read the ones I liked. I remember his copy of the Century dictionary, named because it was published at the beginning of the twentieth century. It was about ten volumes, each huge. I will never forget the time I looked up the word "on" and found four pages of the huge volume completely devoted to that word, giving examples of each of its meanings and usage from Old English to contemporary phrases. "On" has never seemed the same since.

And I have to admit that I took from his library and have kept as my favorite of all the books a little obscure volume titled *English Wayfaring Life in the Middle Ages*. This is a book that I still love to browse in and have quoted in my own writings. It demonstrates the "muddle through" theory of human behavior.

And then there were the books that he brought home as free copies from his publisher. Among those were two series by Crown: *The Ten Best Plays* of each decade and *The Best Science Fiction Stories* of each decade. I read all of these. Some of the best science fiction stories I have ever read were the early ones, from the 1940s, when the authors had to guess at technology of the future that is ordinary to us today. I became an instant sci-fi fan. I read and reread the plays, imagining the scenes from such plays as *Dead End*—famous in their time, little known today. Again, all this seemed to be part of ordinary life. It is only now, when I read in the paper that fewer and fewer people read books, that I realize how fortunate we were to grow up in this most unusual household.

DOROTHY: We had many unusual childhood experiences. I remember when I was in the upper elementary grades and Dad would decide that I should learn Chaucer, or sonnets. We would go out to the lawn next to our duplex apartment in Fairfax Village in Washington and sit on a blanket. He would read me the Prologue to *The Canterbury Tales* in Middle English and translate it for me, or read sonnets and explain their structure. He would talk about rhyme and unrhymed verse and read some poems by one of his favorite authors, W. B. Yeats. I remember more from those informal lessons than I do from my college English courses.

DAN: You were lucky. By the time I came along and reached that age, he no longer did that. I had to learn these things myself. But I did, and I guess it was because of the general mood of our household and the feeling we both got that books and learning were a normal but wonderful part of life.

DOROTHY: When I think of my childhood, I also think of the work that went on in the house, beginning in the early 1940s when Ben began working on the *Treasury of American Folklore*. He was still working full-time as head of the Archive of American Folk Song at the Library of Congress, so all of the work on the *Treasury* had to be done at night and on weekends. And it involved Mother as well as Dad. Our apartment had a kitchen, dining room, and living room on the first floor with two small bedrooms and a bathroom on the second floor. So the work ended up in the dining room and living room. In addition to taking care of us and the house, Mother typed the manuscript and read proof to Dad while he checked for errors. Often they were up until late at night and were worn out the next day.

DAN: Some of my earliest memories are of our parents reading proof. One would sit with the manuscript and the other with the galley or page proof, and one would read aloud. I would sit on the floor and listen. When a person reads all the punctuation as well as the words, there is a tendency for the voice to drop when it comes to the punctuation: "You know [comma] he said [period]. So it seemed to me, as a little boy idly listening, that they were telling the stories to two people named Comma and Period and occasionally their friends, Semicolon and Question Mark. I sat there imagining what the creatures Comma and Period looked like and what they were doing while they were being read to.

DOROTHY: That's very funny—being more literal, I would never have thought of that.

After the work on the *Treasury* was finished, Dad began gathering material from the slave narratives collected by the Federal Writers' Project, which eventually was published as *Lay My Burden Down*. Somehow he had been able to bring a microfilm reader home so that he could work on this after his day at the library. By then I was ten or eleven and there were times—as when Mother was fixing dinner—when he would ask me to read the stories from the microfilm while he checked the manuscript. I was very proud of being able to read well enough to help him, and reading these stories had a profound effect on me. Some were tragic and others were humorous, but all were deeply moving and I gained a feeling for the institution of slavery and the lives of these former slaves that few children my age were privileged to have.

DAN: I never knew you did that. And by the time I was old enough to do that sort of thing, I guess the technology had improved so it was easier to do those things, so I didn't get a chance to be part of the proofreading.

DOROTHY: Even after he left the Library of Congress in 1945 and we moved to Croton-on-Hudson, where he devoted his time to writing and editing, the work dominated the household routine. The same pattern that began with the work on the *Treasury of American Folklore* continued through all the other books—with him collecting and organizing the material and writing introductions to explain his ideas about folklore. Meanwhile, Mother typed—and retyped—the manuscripts and helped with the proofreading. And he revised everything he wrote many times, so her work was multiplied. It really makes me appreciate the advantages we have now with computers.

DAN: You're right that the work dominated the household routine, but that made it seem all the more normal and ordinary. Most nights I would go to sleep hearing the sound of a typewriter. If I woke up in the middle of the night, often I would see a light on and hear the sound of that typewriter. Our father had definite patterns in his work—early mornings, then after dinner and sometimes in the middle of the night. Most afternoons he did other things—puttering around in the garden, visiting with friends, that kind of thing. What seemed normal to me was living in a house where books were made, carefully checked and proofed, and books surrounded us and everything about our lives.

Another part of our growing up that seemed ordinary, but doesn't seem so now, was the stream of visitors to the house—folksingers who brought their instruments and played, Alan Lomax and Pete Seeger and others like them who came and talked. You must remember that when I was very little, we were often visited in Washington by an old man who called himself Pappy, who sang folksongs from Trinidad. Since both of our real grandfathers had died, Pappy was like a grandfather to me—telling me stories, talking and playing with me—I must have been four or five.

DOROTHY: Dad recorded Pappy for the Archives. I always thought of him as the Caribbean Leadbelly and loved to hear him sing. Washington was still segregated at that time and I remember that during one of his visits we all took him to see the Capitol. As we were walking up the stairs, Mother said to me, "If you look around, you'll see that we are the only white people walking with a Negro." On the one hand, I think she was proud of our family for not bowing to the segregationist mentality; on the other hand, being a fairly timid person, maybe she was afraid that someone would make trouble for us.

I think we were really blessed to know such talented and interesting people when we were growing up. I remember when there were guests like that I would sit upstairs and listen to the conversation long after I was supposed to have gone to bed. While we lived in Washington, Ben was very close to Charles and Ruth Seeger and I remember going to their house in Chevy Chase. Mike and Peggy were close to my age and I recall one time that they taught me to play Parcheesi. Our family wasn't much for playing games—except for word games—so this made a big impression on me. Another family whom we were close to was George and Rae Korson and their daughter, Betsy. George is known for collecting the songs and folklore of coal miners in Pennsylvania, and Rae Korson worked as Dad's assistant at the Archives and later became head of the Archives herself.

In addition to the out-of-town visitors, there were many intellectual people living in Fairfax Village whom we saw very often. Harold Rosenberg and his wife, May, lived nearby. I don't remember what Harold's job was then, but he went on to become a well-known art critic. Irv Silverman and his wife, Faye, were very dear friends. Irv was a lawyer with the Department of the Interior and worked on statehood bills for Alaska, Hawaii, and Puerto Rico. Sidney Forrest and his wife, Faith, lived almost across the street from us. Sidney played clarinet with the Marine Band at that time. After the war he became one of the country's most famous clarinet teachers. His students have played in all the major orchestras. Faith was a pianist and was my first piano teacher after Mother, who had started me off. Now in their eighties, the Forrests still keep up some teaching and attend concerts at the Library of Congress. Croton, where we moved in 1946, also had a large intellectual community and we knew many interesting people, as well as those who continued to visit.

DAN: But the visitors who impressed me the most were Woody Guthrie, Pete Seeger, and Alan Lomax. Once, when I was eight, Alan brought Woody to visit us in Croton, and he and I sat outside and played mumbley-peg. To me, he was a friendly, jovial, fatherly person, wiry, with curly hair. He had his instruments and played them after our game. That's a memory I'll never forget.

After you went to college, Pete Seeger would stop by now and again to visit with Ben, and once in a while Ben would persuade him to give a concert in Croton or nearby. At those concerts I watched Pete intently. He had this ability to get a crowd to do whatever he wanted, and I was fascinated by it. We call it charisma these days, but I didn't know the word. I just knew that he held an entire audience in his hand. If he wanted them to sing, they sang. If he wanted them to be quiet, they were quiet. I kept trying to figure out what it was that gave him that quality, but I never figured it out—I still haven't. He quickly became my hero and I would always sit shyly and listen to whatever he said when he visited. He was always full of wonderful ideas and very enthusiastic about them. Visitors like that changed my life.

When we lived in Fairfax Village, we had the most remarkable neighbors, but once again it all seemed ordinary. There was Ted Carr, his wife, and two daughters. You remember they were from Britain and he designed military amphibious landing craft and had been sent over to the U.S. to work with his counterparts.

And then there was Pick Temple, who sang folksongs as a hobby and would sing in the evenings to the neighbors, mostly cowboy songs. I remember that he worked in the newly built Pentagon, doing some kind of bureaucratic work. From that start, of sitting around singing to us kids, he soon became the singing cowboy of Washington radio, and had a long career doing that.

An influence on me equally strong as the books was phonograph records— seventy-eights. As far back as I can remember, we listened to folk music on the old phonograph. Some songs and groups were favorites, including the Carter Family. I didn't realize what an influence they had on me until people started to tell me that I was saying *worry* funny—I said "whery." I realized I had learned the pronunciation by listening over and over again to the Carter Family's record of "It Takes a Worried Man to Sing a Worried Song," and they sang "wheried."

DOROTHY: I don't have the musical ability to sing or play instruments, but I love music, especially folk music, and those evening songfests with Pick

Temple were very special to me. When we went to Camp Woodland in 1945, I was happiest during the singalongs after dinner. I remember playing and listening to records, such as calypso songs and the recordings of the Carter Family you mentioned when I was five. I knew all the words by heart then, although it was years before I realized the real meaning of some of the more risqué calypso songs. One of my favorites was "Hot Dog," about the time that President Roosevelt served hot dogs to the King and Queen of England when they visited Hyde Park in 1939.

DAN: I loved those songs too and made a tape of those records that I play often.

DOROTHY: One of the most unusual things that Dad did was to encourage me to write poetry when I was only four or five years old. He would take me for walks in the cemetery near our home. That may sound rather ghoulish, but it was a beautiful park, with a pond overhung by a weeping willow tree. There was a tiny island in the middle of the pond and a lovely Japanese bridge to the island. Ducks and minnows swam in the pond and I thought it was one of the most beautiful sights I had ever seen. For years afterward, I would draw that scene in my school art classes. Anyway, I made up little "poems," which he wrote down and eventually made into an album with photos. I am afraid that those poems were the height of my career as a poet, but it was a memorable experience.

DAN: Your story about writing poetry makes me think about how much folk music became part of my life. You remember that the Library of Congress had a professional recording studio—a recording booth where the performers stood and sang and looked out through a sound-proof glass at the people doing the recording, the whole works. I think I was six when Ben took me there and put me in that room and recorded me singing. We had planned what I would sing. I remember singing "Soldier, Oh Soldier, Won't You Marry Me." But then in the middle of the recording I changed my mind about what to sing next, and we got into an argument, all of which is on the record. Dad and Mother loved to take that record out and play it for my friends—they did this all the way through college, playing it for my college friends. It always embarrassed me—it wasn't one of my outstanding moments.

DOROTHY: I haven't heard that record in years and would love to . . . if it wouldn't embarrass you! This reminds me that when I was in college at the University of Rochester, Ellen Stekert, who was then at Cornell, would come to visit a friend at the U of R. Ellen played and sang folksongs and was, in fact, playing for Harold Thompson's folklore class at Cornell. Harold was a friend of Dad's through the New York Folklore Society. Ellen and I became friends and I asked her to visit us in Croton so that she could meet Dad. Because of their mutual interest, they soon became friends as well. I know that Dad was very pleased when Ellen went on to get her doctorate in folklore and become a professor.

DAN: I was in high school when you met Ellen. By then I was playing the piano, clarinet, saxophone, and oboe. She asked me why I didn't learn folksongs, gave me a guitar and a banjo and a quick lesson. I bought a book of guitar chords, taught myself to play and sing "Cool Water," and have never stopped playing since. I learned guitar and banjo strumming from other folksingers whenever I could. Although I'll never be a professional, it's so much a part of my life that I couldn't imagine a life without playing and singing folksongs.

PART TWO

Botkin and His Contemporaries

"Twistification"
Work and Friendship between Two Pioneers of the Folk Revival, Benjamin A. Botkin and Ruth Crawford Seeger

JUDITH TICK

In the typical party game . . . which is a swinging play, each player is a multiplier for a whole series of multiplicands, as neatly expressed in the multiplication stanza of "Twistification," often used to accompany the movements of the Virginia reel in "Weevily Wheat."

Benjamin A. Botkin

"Five times five is twenty-five, / And five times six is thirty. Five times seven is thirty-five, / And five times eight is forty."

So opens a text variant for the folksong "Weevily Wheat," which Benjamin Botkin published in his doctoral dissertation, *The American Play-Party Song* (1937b: 38). In this source Botkin supplied this chameleon text with a tune called "Charley" (reflecting yet another of its variants and its historic origins in legends around Bonnie Prince Charlie) (345–51). Around the same time, the composer Ruth Crawford Seeger created a piano arrangement related to the same text/tune family called "Charlie's Sweet" in her collection of *22 American Folk Songs Arranged for Elementary Piano*. This article begins here, taking "twistification" as a metaphor for the working friendship between Ben and Ruth. As we explore ways in which it illuminates the folk revival movement in its formative decades, we witness ideas and music changing hands, like figures weaving in and out of another kind of reel, based on the interplay between ideology and practice.

This dance takes place in the wings, so to speak, offstage in the substantive literature on the folk revival, where typically both Botkin and Crawford Seeger look on Leadbelly, Woody Guthrie, Pete Seeger, Alan Lomax, and even occasionally Charles Seeger, basking in the historical spotlight. And Crawford Seeger, lacking formal job titles in the WPA world, looks over Botkin's shoulder (see Filene 2000: 133ff. and Hirsch 2007). Furthermore, on the surface their collaborations do not appear that extensive, for Botkin hired Crawford Seeger as music consultant only for *A Treasury of Western Folklore.* In her own collections of folk song arrangements (*American Folk Songs for Children, Animal Folk Songs for Children,* and *American Folk Songs for Christmas*), Crawford Seeger borrows from Botkin's work for a few songs here and there. Yet outer signs belie inner ties, for in the foundations of their approaches—their shared rhetoric, their sense of mission in regard to music education, and even their professional ambitions—they contributed to a profoundly influential methodology of mediating folk materials.

The point of this chapter (which focuses on their projects between 1937 and 1950) is not so much to reiterate familiar revival analyses but rather to show how Botkin and Crawford Seeger both challenged the categories of "purist" and "popularizer" within folklore and folksong scholarship. Trained professionally in folklore and classical composition, respectively, they chose outlets where they understated their expertise and scholarship in order to reach a wider public.[1] Who would anticipate that the sophisticated cultural theorizing in Crawford Seeger's deceptively "homespun" introduction to *American Folk Songs for Children* would earn the reputation of being "one of the master texts of the expanding folk revival" (Cantwell 1996: 278)? Similarly, Botkin's unduly neglected *A Treasury of Western Folklore* (1951) contains an unusually fresh repertory of songs and ballads.

Ultramodernism

Some introductory remarks about the life and work of Ruth Crawford Seeger (1901–53) will help center the subsequent discussion.[2] Recently described as "one of the giants of the early American experimental period," she composed what she herself called modern dissonant music during the 1920s and early 1930s, standing between Charles Ives, whom she honored, and John Cage, who honored her (Ross 1994: 59). Born the same year as Botkin in East Liverpool, Ohio (just across from Pittsburgh), into a family of Methodist ministers, Crawford trained primarily in Chicago. Initially she was supposed to be a "lady pianist," heading back to Jacksonville, Florida, to rejoin her mother after one year at the American Conservatory of Music and to open a local teaching studio. As she discovered her gifts for composition, she won a place among the ultramodernist or radical composers of the 1920s and early 1930s. Her most famous work is the String Quartet 1931, and in the past decade or so there has been a revival of publications and recordings of her small but choice oeuvre.[3]

Too often classical music is regarded as an abstract art, removed from the dynamic ebb and flow of ideas and events that shape other forms of expressive culture like literature and painting. Such alleged autonomy can be historically deceptive. Among Crawford and her peers, who wrote "abstract" music, their search for artistic identity in the 1920s relied on national character. Composer Vivian Fine, who was Crawford Seeger's student, explained: "There was a sense of mission that people [classical composers] don't have nowadays." The new modernist music was to be "vital, original, and at the same time American. The American style was going to be brave, brash, and groundbreaking."[4]

Fine's prophetic description applies equally well to Crawford's second surname. Few would have suspected in 1931 that Ruth Crawford, experimental composer, would become the matriarch of the family that includes her stepson, Pete Seeger, a leading folk revival singer of his century, and her own two children: the multi-instrumentalist Mike and the singer-songwriter Peggy.

The chain of events leading to this connection began with Charles Seeger. In 1929, when Crawford left the security of Chicago to come to New York to study dissonant counterpoint with him, Charles Seeger was known mainly as a musicologist and theorist of new music (Pescatello 1992; Greer 1998; Yung and Rees 1999). Thus their remarkable creative partnership began. In 1932, at the time of their marriage, they tenaciously clung to modernist values.

Slowly their priorities shifted in tandem with crisis and change. Like so many other American artists and intellectuals, the Seegers watched the Great Depression erode the culture of modernism as they had understood it. We need only touch on a few corroborating details from their own lives during this turbulent period, about which so much has been written. The Seegers joined the Communist-driven movement for proletarian aesthetics centered in the New York–based Workers' Music League, whose logo was a hammer and sickle against the backdrop of a musical staff. While teaching music history at the Institute for Musical Art (the present-day Juilliard School), Charles worked as a critic for the *Daily Worker,* lambasting bourgeois composers in his music reviews and opinion pieces. Ruth set to radical music two militant texts about the Sacco-Vanzetti case and the plight of the Chinese immigrant-worker (Tick 1997; Hisama 2000). Much energy was devoted to a group known as the Composers Collective, whose members included Marc Blitzstein, Elie Siegmeister, and Earl Robinson. Their idealistic ambition was to forge links between radical style and radical social theory.[5]

In the mid-1930s Crawford Seeger suffered an unexpected artistic fallow period, which was compounded by the responsibilities of motherhood (three children in five years). She slipped into a still much-lamented silence as a modernist composer for the next twenty years. Perhaps the critique of so-called elitist individualist art by the Communist-influenced artistic Left undermined her resolve to compose classical music, as Aaron Copland once suggested to a colleague.[6] Equally unexpectedly, a new kind of music filled the vacuum.

"From the Roosevelts on Down"

In 1936 Charles Seeger took a job with the Resettlement Administration in Washington, D.C. Botkin arrived there one year later, on leave from the University of Oklahoma, supported by a Julius Rosenwald Fellowship. And it is here that the lives and careers of Ben Botkin and the Seegers began to intertwine. Botkin's Washington years would last until 1945; the Seegers remained through 1953, the year Ruth died.

Upon meeting the Seegers Botkin was impressed by their stature as professional musicians and their Popular Front politics, which he shared. His membership in the League of American Writers paralleled the Seegers' involvement with the Composers Collective (Denning 1996: 134). It is not clear how familiar he was with Crawford Seeger's actual music; nor does it seem likely that her expressionistic dissonance would have appealed to him.[7] Still, he told his wife, Gertrude, that both Charles Seeger and Ruth Crawford had chapters devoted to them in Henry Cowell's book *American Composers on American Music*. Leaving behind the urban goals of the Composers Collective, and exchanging New York "cultural front" artistic expression for more centrist political work, the Seegers discovered contemporary American traditional music. Alan Lomax would later write how "everybody in Washington from the Roosevelts on down was interested in folk music. . . . They were the first prominent Americans ever to take a position about it in public consistently and the first Washingtonians ever to spend any money on it" (Lomax 1982: 15).

"Thus began an important period of national collecting," D. K. Wilgus wrote in his classic study *Anglo American Folksong Scholarship since 1898* (1959: 186). Folk music projects initiated under the WPA grew with the onset of World War II, which ushered in a patriotic folk-music boom on the home front. The relationship between Botkin and Ruth Crawford Seeger was sustained by the various overlapping jobs that Botkin and her husband took with federal programs. After the demise of the Resettlement Administration in 1937, Seeger relocated to the Farm Security Administration. He soon moved again, serving between 1937 and 1941 as deputy director of the Federal Music Project, in charge of developing activities based on folk music (Pescatello 1992: 154). In 1938 Botkin was appointed national folklore editor of the Federal Writers' Project, succeeding Alan's father, John A. Lomax. As a coordinating tool for the agencies, in 1938 they co-founded the important Joint Committee on Folk Arts of the WPA, which Botkin chaired. Alan Lomax and Sidney Robertson were hired as assistants; Herbert Halpert, who directed the musical efforts of the Folksong and Folklore Department of the Music Division of the National Service Bureau in the Federal Theater Project, served as primary fieldworker. In letters to Charles from 1938 to 1939, Ruth often referred to the Joint Committee, learning about scholarly methods in folksong research from its various publications and collecting activities.

So many job titles, so many committee reports: yet the various federal programs, whether intentionally or not, supported a more organic pioneer community of like-minded cultural workers, flourishing amidst the bureaucracy. Botkin responded with enthusiasm. His wife, Gertrude, remembered the bonds that formed. "His work was the most important thing; getting together with these people was very important."[8] In 1936 Botkin was with the Seegers during a transforming journey to Bascom Lunsford's Mountain Dance and Folk Festival in Asheville, North Carolina, along with Pete and a Resettlement Administration folk music fieldworker, Sidney Robertson. Her work would later become important to Botkin as well.[9]

Botkin and Crawford Seeger also shared an enthusiasm and admiration for the poet Carl Sandburg. During her years in Chicago, Crawford Seeger was in and out of the Sandburg home as piano teacher to his daughters, close enough to the famous poet that he came to consider her an adopted daughter. Crawford Seeger greatly admired Sandburg as poet and folk troubadour. In 1927 she contributed piano settings of four folksongs to Sandburg's landmark collection *The American Songbag*. Crawford Seeger would later write about the initial impetus that Sandburg provided for her own work in folk traditions. In 1938 Botkin in turn wrote about *The American Songbag* as an example of "folk history" (Botkin 1940b: 308–309). Indeed, Sandburg provided useful endorsements for both of them in relation to their most successful books.[10]

Botkin and Crawford Seeger participated in the deliberate cultural strategizing for the revival. The result was what Charles Seeger would later describe as a "World View," dependent upon their ability to synthesize and learn from one another.[11] In this period a "World View" grew out of a "functional" approach to the field, which emphasized contemporary usage of the material and its social contexts.[12] One letter from Ruth Crawford Seeger to Charles reports a visit to the Botkins: "We got into such an interesting discussion last night on folk music and how it is functional now and how to collect etc. that we stayed until 10:30. I having thus missed my bus, Gertrude asked me to spend the night; I did. Just left Ben on the elevator. He says, hello, thanks you for your two letters."[13]

The musical conversation coalesced around a few basic principles: disproving the commonplace misperception that America had no folksongs of its own; educating the general populace in oral traditions; developing a national consciousness about its quality; parrying vestigial romantic notions about the alleged primal simplicity of folksong; using "recreational" tools to promote the singing and playing of folk music among an urban public; and maintaining its relevance to the contemporary composer in shaping an American musical identity for "fine-art" music.

Both Botkin and Crawford Seeger articulated these values in their own work, with varying degrees of emphasis and purpose according to the task at hand. Some particularly relevant statements clearly demonstrate their affinities.

Mission statements about cultural mediation occur frequently in Botkin's writing, often in eloquent formulations about giving "back to the people what we have taken from then and what rightfully belongs to them, in a form in which they can understand and use" (Botkin 1939e: 10). Metaphors of building bridges and striving for balance serve as signature goals in Crawford Seeger's work as well. Her comment about the task of turning field recordings into notation is a case in point:

> Music notations of folk songs serve, then, as a bridge between, mainly, two different types of singers. Over this bridge a vital heritage of culture can pass, from the rural people who, for the most part, have preserved it, to the urban people who have more or less lost it and wish to recapture it. A great deal depends upon just how this bridge is built. The best solution would be "to catch a just balance" between the "rich complexity" of rural singers and the ability of the urban "interested amateur." (Crawford Seeger 2001: 13)

Both Botkin and Crawford Seeger delighted in turning process into a symbol, filled with rich multiple meanings for their work. Finding and documenting variants making their way from one part of the country to another, mobile and fluid, lay at the heart of their enterprise. Crawford Seeger wrote that folk music "bears many fingermarks. It has been handled roughly and gently. It has been used. It has been sung and resung—molded and modified by generations of singers from Maine to Florida and across the country" (Crawford Seeger 1948: 22).

For both Crawford Seeger and Botkin, this endowed the "variant" with almost mythic qualities of ideological purpose. She detected democratic attitudes and values in folk music. It has meaning for "progressive and democratic society as a whole," Botkin argued while working with the WPA. He further showed this process in action in his first book, *The American Play-Party Song* (1937), where text variants form the core of the scholarship and informants are honored as links in the chain. For example, alongside the text variants for "Old Dan Tucker" is a list of names of thirty-three people who provided material he did not use (Botkin 1937b: 265–66).

Considering that there is no one definitive version of a folksong, the challenge posed by oral tradition is to decide which version or variant to put into print. Such decisions reflect musical taste and expertise as well as cultural politics. How could collectors find the best and most creative musical versions of a tune? Which one variant captured the live musical experience most thoroughly? At stake was a philosophy of inclusion and responsibility to the sources, the idea that contemporary performers "made their own songs," and the practice of discovering worthy variants. As Herbert Halpert recalled: "I stayed at their [the Seegers'] house, she fed me, and she listened to me sing songs. She laughed at me when I said my version was the best. She knew the idiosyncrasies of folksong collectors, knew their egos. . . . [She knew that we thought] our versions were the most artistically superior."[14]

American Folk Songs Go to School

An educational mandate flowed easily from such progressive cultural nationalism. Crawford Seeger wrote how folk music "belongs to our children—it is an integral part of their cultural heritage" that expresses "the realities of the culture" in which they live ("Introduction" in Crawford Seeger 1948: 21). Between 1936 and 1938 she composed teaching pieces for elementary piano, which she based on folk tunes. They shine with her vivid musical imagination. Crawford Seeger prefaced her collection with a manifesto for their collective beliefs. Espousing a progressive nationalism, she explained why "Charlie's Sweet," "Sweet Betsy from Pike," and "The Gray Goose" mattered. She described her goal:

> To acquaint the piano student with at least a small part of the traditional (i.e. "folk") music of his own country. . . . There are thousands more, just as good and just as alive. It is the belief of this composer that, just as

the child becomes acquainted with his own home environment before experiencing the more varied contacts of school and community, so should the music student be given the rich musical heritage of his own country as a basis upon which to build his experience of the folk and art music of other countries.[15]

Crawford Seeger borrowed the tune for "Charlie's Sweet" from Cecil Sharp's books.[16] Far removed from the dance world of "Weevily Wheat," she set it in a kind of dissonant counterpoint, designed to show affinities between modernist taste and old-time music. The relevance of past to present emerged in her practice of supplying these challenging accompaniments for modal tunes. Not unlike Botkin's insistence on the functional approach to the material, she stressed how the spare lean sounds of traditional music shared an aesthetic with contemporary taste.

From the folk revival community came the core of what would later become a movement. Its spirit evoked the American singing-school movement in the late eighteenth-century, which sustained the first repertory of indigenous song composed in an emerging new country. Just as colonial composers William Billings and Daniel Read changed the nature of church and hymn singing in their tunebooks, the folk revivalists attempted to reform the music curriculum in public education. As was typical of their group as a whole, both Botkin and Crawford Seeger railed against resistance from professionals and the academic elitism in their respective professions: Botkin against folklore orthodoxies, Crawford Seeger against Eurocentric snobbery. She wrote: "Perhaps some people don't know how little our American material has been known in our schools, by our teachers and by the parents. Not only have they not been known, but people have looked down their noses upon them" (quoted in Thompson 1953: 192). Working at a cooperative nursery school in 1941, she composed piano arrangements of folk tunes that she had transcribed for the collection *Our Singing Country* (see the discussion below), to be distributed among the families at the Silver Spring Nursery School. She titled the purple-dittoed song sheets "American Songs for American Children, Volume I."

Around the same time, the Washington folk revivalists launched an assault on the Eurocentrism of music textbooks in the early 1940s. The war and home front urgencies made the moment propitious, as organizations such as the Music Educators National Convention (MENC) and the Music Teachers National Association (MTNA) offered new opportunities. In response to a survey of music class books, which concluded that most of the songs in music books of the last fifty years came from Europe, they compiled a sample leaflet songbook of "American Songs for American Children" to contribute to the MENC program "American Unity through Music" and brought it to the 1942 biennial MENC convention.[17] Crawford Seeger provided transcriptions for the manuscript, Charles Seeger wrote the foreword, and Alan Lomax wrote headnotes for the ten songs (among them "Cindy," "Jenny Jenkins," "John Henry," "The Wabash Cannonball," and Woody Guthrie's "So Long, It's Been Good To Know You," described as a "contemporary folk song"). Charles Seeger and Ben Botkin wrote similarly titled articles, "American Music for American Children" (Seeger 1942) and "American Songs for American Children" (Botkin 1944a), in which they reiterated their belief that the one essential basis of a country's music education is its folk music.

Everyone's involvement in the MENC was helped along by its executive director, Vanett Lawler, who also worked for Charles Seeger in his post as head of the Music Division of the Pan American Union, to which he was appointed in 1941. An invaluable ally, Lawler arranged for Alan Lomax and Pete Seeger to perform at the convention. "They asked me to come and sing for the teachers, as inexperienced as I was," Pete remembered.[18] Not all school supervisors and music teachers wanted to switch their loyalties from classical music to Woody Guthrie. In an incident that foreshadows the cultural conflicts in our own time, Pete recalled: "In a hallway a teacher accosted Alan. He shook his fist. 'Mr. Lomax, you are tearing down everything we are trying to build up.' This music teacher was trying to build up the great music of Europe. He said we were teaching the kids trash."[19] Pete Seeger's success as a master-teacher, "lining out" words to songs, would become one of his most enduring legacies.

The MENC convention of 1942 remained a watershed in the history of the urban folk revival. It marks the moment that the organization's president, Lilla Belle Pitts, called "official recognition by music educators of the American folk song. Music educators, individually and collectively, are directly responsible for the furtherance of the American Songs for American Children Program, and as an outgrowth of that, indirectly, for the general dissemination of knowledge and appreciation of the indigenous songs of the American people" (Pitts 1942: 9). From this endorsement sprang the revisions of public-school music textbooks during these years.

Words and Music in a "Sound Library"

With the demise of various WPA cultural projects, in the 1940s the Archive of American Folk Song served as a main base of institutional support and legitimacy for the folksong revival collective. Both Botkin and Crawford Seeger based significant projects and activities on its considerable and expanding resources. In the 1930s John and Alan Lomax had deposited about 10,000 field recordings at the Archive of American Folk Song, shaping the heart of the collection. With the establishment of the archive's Recording Laboratory in 1940, Charles Seeger headed a cataloguing project of 4,000 recordings (Botkin 1945d: 62). By July 1940 the WPA, together with the National Youth Administration, had made possible the three-volume *Check-List of Recorded Songs in the English Language in the Archive of American Folk Song to July, 1940.*

With such a resource at hand, the archive made music an equal partner to text in folklore and folk music scholarship. Just at the time when recording technology was revolutionizing the field of folklore and thereby challenging the preeminence of text-based scholarship, Botkin became directly involved with the archive as both scholar and administrator. In 1941 he served as chief editor of the Writers' Unit of the Library of Congress Project, becoming a Library of Congress Fellow in Folklore. By 1942 he was appointed assistant in charge and then later served as chief of the Archive of American Folk Song until 1944 (Jackson 1976).

Botkin's perspective on the relative importance of words and music changed —in fact, had to change. He had already demonstrated sensitivity to problems of capturing singing style in print in *The American Play-Party Song*, which contains fifty-four songs with sixty-two tunes (because some have tune variants printed with them). For that volume he hired an assistant who recorded the tunes in the field in 1932.[20] (Given the rarity of tape equipment at that time, it seems possible that what Botkin meant by "recording" was immediate notation of the tune at hand rather than the use of technology.) In a later description of the process, Botkin acknowledged his own sensitivity to the complexities of notating the musical styles at hand, in this case a "Negro dancing song" (Botkin 1937b: 302).

> Those familiar with folk singing will recognize the impossibility of representing, in ordinary notation, the slurs, glides and other subtle variations in pitch which usually occur on the accented syllables. Thus, in the melody of "Sandy Land," the first note is recorded as a "g," whereas in actually the singer begins on a note less than a half-step below "g" and glides into it. Minor variations of the melody for succeeding stanzas have not been indicated. (Botkin 1937b: 138)

Now ensconced at the Archive of American Folk Song, Botkin described his new home as a "sound library" (Botkin 1945d: 62). There he witnessed the Lomaxes and Ruth Crawford Seeger hard at work on the "impossibility" of representing the sound of music, in which she would play a leading role. Little did John Lomax imagine when he hired Crawford Seeger to serve as the music consultant for *Our Singing Country* that work on this project would thrust her into the front ranks of composer-transcribers of the twentieth century.[21] So extensive were her contributions that her name as music editor was included on the cover. As she labored intensively over methods for transcribing music from the Lomaxes' extraordinary collection of field recordings into Western classical-music notation, she produced a lengthy analytic treatise on the issues surrounding transcription and performance practice (it would remain un-published for sixty years).[22] She contributed an elegant and concise "Music Preface" that stands as a primer for city folk. It suggested how applied folklore might operate in an atmosphere of artistic integrity. She instructed amateurs in ways to approach the performance practice issues around singing the songs:

> No-one who has studied these [field] or similar recordings can deny that the song and its singing are indissolubly connected—that the char-acter of a song depends to a great extent on *the manner of its singing*. It is often to be noticed that the city person, unacquainted with folk idioms, will endow a folk song with manners of fine-art, or popular perfor-mance which are foreign to it, and will tend to sentimentalize or to dramatize that which the folk performer presents in a simple straight-forward way.

This was followed by sixteen suggestions of dos and don'ts. The first and next-to-last can serve as examples of her balancing act between encourage-ment and caution—on the one hand, a total dedication to "the thing itself"; on the other, an embrace of city folk as worthy and indeed rightful practi-tioners of expanding tradition:

> 1. Do not hesitate to sing because you think your voice is "not good"—i.e., has not been "trained." These songs are better sung in the man-ner of the natural than the trained (bel canto) voice. Do not try to "smooth out" your voice. If it is reedy or nasal, so much the better.

> 16. Do not "sing down" to the songs. Theirs are old traditions, dignified by hundreds and thousands of singers over long periods of time. (*Our Singing Country*, xix and xxi)

From his vantage point as a folklorist, Botkin used *Our Singing Country* as a foundation for handling the music sections in his most important and most successful book, *A Treasury of American Folklore*. Redefining "functionalism" for his trade audience and using *Our Singing Country* as his evidence, Botkin explained:

Certain "traditionalist" folk-song authorities like Cecil J. Sharp tend to stress the "heritage" rather than the "participation" aspects of folk song and the passive rather than the active role of the folk singer, making him out to be a carrier of national culture, who sings to "forget himself and everything that reminds him of his everyday life" and thus, by escaping into an "imaginary world," to "enter into [his] racial inheritance." The "functionalists," on the other hand, such as Alan Lomax, stress the role of folk song in America as "an expression of its democratic, interracial, international character, as a function of its inchoate and turbulent many-sided development."[23]

Botkin responded to this vision by including a variety of songs and rhymes in "Part Six: Songs and Rhymes" (about 250 pages) in *A Treasury of American Folklore*. In contrast to *The American Play-Party Song*, here the music gained visual integrity, with music notation sufficiently readable to sing from. He divided this part into three sections: "Play Rhymes and Catch Colloquies," "Singing and Play-Party Games," and "Ballads and Songs" (the largest section). This final section begins with the classic Child ballads that for so long dominated the field, but Botkin moves quickly to his usual concern for occupational ballads (sailormen and fishermen, lumberjacks, cowboys, miners, farmers), songs of marginal groups ("Hobo" and "Jailhouse"), and finally songs from the ethnic margins ("Mountain Songs" and "Negro Songs," known commercially as "hillbilly" and "race" music).

Overseeing all of this, Charles Seeger as music consultant annotated the printed sources from which most of these melodies came. He also added a few of his favorites, recycling his "Resettlement Song Sheets" from the late 1930s, which had been produced in his community music recreation programs.[24] They borrowed "The Old Chisholm Trail" from the MENC booklet *American Songs for American Children*. Their most controversial choices brought contemporary commercial recordings and performers into the mix, using transcriptions rather than printed tunes. Charles Seeger transcribed the Carter Family's "Worried Man Blues" from a commercial recording and used Alan Lomax as his informant for "The Gray Goose" (Botkin 1944j: 907). Peter Seeger transcribed "The Roving Gambler" from a Champion record of Pie Plant Pete (p. 889) and "The Midnight Special" as sung by Huddie Ledbetter (Leadbelly). Crawford Seeger contributed a tidy version of "Take This Hammer," complete with notations for the "huh" sounds, "as sung by the Almanac Singers" (p. 913).

New Folk Communities in the City

In between *Our Singing Country* (1941) and Botkin's *A Treasury of American Folklore* (1944), Crawford Seeger had been at work at her own independent project, *American Folk Songs for Children.* Although this book did not get published until 1948, it began in the early 1940s. Botkin played a role in its evolution, both in terms of its conceptual framework and in its eventual publication. Details are sketchy, but some evidence suggests active involvement. As Gertrude Botkin recalled: "In addition to the music she [Ruth] composed, she was working on this children's book, and they [Ben and Ruth] would go in the other room and they would discuss it, and they did that several times. So he was close to her like that."[25] His own dissertation, *The American Play-Party Song* (published in 1937), included material overlapping with children's game songs, so he had expertise in a relevant repertory. A later formal letter from Botkin to Crawford Seeger on October 28, 1946, confirms his permission for her use of "Jim Along Josie" and "Walk Along John." Botkin's concept of contemporary folk communities contributed to Crawford Seeger's approach to the material.

Crawford Seeger's book began when a group of mothers in her own community decided to start a cooperative nursery school. Responsible for bringing music into the school twice a week, she decided to use American folksong exclusively in the classroom. She organized groups of women into what she called her "music mothers," a collective that passed judgment on texts and tunes. Just as Botkin would advocate the "modern dynamic conception of the folk as part of urban society" (Botkin 1938b: 129), so Crawford Seeger theorized her own participation in the most seemingly humble of social institutions: the nursery school.

The "music mothers" sang their way through Child ballads, field hollers, play-party songs, Bahaman songs, minstrel songs—a huge repertory of material adapted to the purpose at hand. For each of these tunes Crawford Seeger crafted deceptively simple arrangements for piano, easy enough for amateur parents to play at home but filled with absorbing musical detail. She encouraged children to change the words of the songs to fit the moment, calling the process "text improvisation." Here too theory played its part. In the 1940s she wrote that

> too early and too frequently music is brought to our attention as something for us to learn. It was made, we are told, by remarkable young

people like Beethoven and Mozart and Haydn, who when they were young were remarkable children. We are, we feel, not remarkable people. So we say "I can't" to the making of our own music, and sense ourselves growing smaller as we say it. Perhaps feeling comfortable enough and free enough with a song to add their own words to it can be for many children a first step toward feeling free enough with music itself to make their own music.[26]

Crawford Seeger turned to Botkin for advice when it came time to get *American Folk Songs for Children* published. In the aftermath of Botkin's enormous success with *A Treasury of American Folklore* in 1944, he had resigned from the archive and moved from Washington to New York. Several letters around 1945 testify to his intercessions on her behalf, as he wrote letters of introduction for her to various publishers.[27] One reads:

> June 11, 1945
> Dear Nat,
> . . . She has taken folk songs and adapted them for game use in nursery schools. Some of the songs are quite charming and effective, and she has a good idea. As the book stands now, it is more of an educational book than a grade book; but I think it could be made over without much trouble.

When *American Folk Songs for Children* was published, Botkin wrote this letter of congratulations:

> November 23, 1948
> Dear Ruth:
> The book came, and I sort of expected you to trail along after it. But no doubt you were up to your ears in appointments. Anyway, the book is a beauty, and you should feel mighty proud. I suppose you saw Virgil Thomson's rave notice in the Sunday *Herald Tribune*, which says about everything there is to be said. I can add only that a lifetime of work and thought has gone into the book, and the result is a book that will live.[28]

The Breath of a Singer

After the success of *American Folk Songs for Children*, Botkin hired Crawford Seeger as his music consultant for *A Treasury of Western Folklore*. Crawford Seeger treated field recordings and variants as the life force of tradition. Even when one variant for a favorite tune satisfied her musically, alternatives tempted her just for the sake of representing possibilities. A letter written during a collaboration with Botkin captures the flow of this experience in her own words: "I would so much as always have the breath of the singer as close to my books as possible."[29] Botkin felt the gentle persuasion of that breath as well. In contrast to his practice of borrowing songs from printed sources, which he had used in the first treasury, in this collection all but seven of the songs represent new variants taken from field recordings. He spent the summer of 1950, as he explained in a letter to Charles Seeger (January 2, 1951), "hard at work on *Western Folklore,* for which I traveled in eight Western states during eight weeks last summer." A letter to Crawford Seeger on June 22, 1951, discusses his efforts to secure good versions of fresh tunes:

> On May 30 I went up to Woodstock, N.Y., with Sam Eskin and copied some 40 songs from his tapes to mine. These include some very good versions of the following: The Sioux Indians, Texas Ranger, Cole Younger, Trail to Mexico (Buffalo Skinners). I also have copies of a few of Sidney Cowell's songs (I had dinner with her and Henry at Shady), especially Custer's last charge. I could send you these on tape, if you have a way to play them. please let me know. This would give us a good start on the music. How much time will it take to do 30 or 40 transcriptions if we work continuously and intensively? Could it be done in the last two weeks of July? I figure that we could accomplish more if I were to play the tapes and if we could talk things over as we work. Don't you? I mean I could furnish some of the motive power as well as the moral support. If we set ourselves August 1st deadline, I think we could do it.

Crawford Seeger transcribed thirty-three of the forty-four songs herself and occasionally assigned some to her daughter Peggy, whom she pressed into emergency service (see the chapter appendix for a list of the songs and sources).

All of this does not mean that Botkin changed his priorities in a dramatic way. For him music would always remain grist for the mill of his cultural approach, through which he could map the fascinating processes of acculturation and adaptation. How wonderful that a Stephen Foster tune might resurface as the gold-rush song "Sacramento" and that Woody Guthrie's lyric "Roll On, Columbia" was "fast becoming a regional song of the Pacific Northwest" (Botkin 1951g: 731). As always he linked repertory to historical national narratives with songs like "Custer's Last Charge" and "The Sioux Indians." Thus he introduced the section on "Western Songs and Ballads" with his priorities intact:

The appeal of Western folk songs and ballads is quite independent of their musical interest and value, which on the whole would seem to be inferior to that of the folk music of older regions like the South. Their appeal is largely a matter of mood and tone, idiom and style, a freshness and vigor, a native tang and flavor, the heroic and democratic spirit of "a man's a man for a' that," unsurpassed by the songs of any other American region.

After that kind of introduction, one would hardly expect to find much in the way of musical arcana. But nobody who worked with Ruth Crawford Seeger slighted quality. Thus in hiring her as the musical consultant for the volume, Botkin acknowledged quality as an issue.

The book included brief "Notes on the Music" by Crawford Seeger, his music editor, who was encouraging amateur performance. Metronome markings reflected tempos on field recordings. Chord suggestions indicated above the melody made singing easier "as an aid not only to players of traditional instruments like the guitar but also to pianists who may wish to make their own accompaniments." Never would she want to ossify the music unduly, so she added: "These chord letters, however, are intended only as suggestions and in many cases different chord patterns are possible." Readers were further referred to her more extensive notes in *American Folk Songs for Children* and *Our Singing Country* (Botkin 1951g: 731).

In its own way the list of songs included in *A Treasury of Western Folklore* charts the course of the folksong revival collective over two decades of activity. Some cowboy songs had already entered into the revival repertory at this point, among them "Streets of Laredo" and "Shenandoah," in a particularly lyrical version recorded in 1951. Here Crawford Seeger's perfection of detail shines through her transcription, showing the song's lyrical course through several meter changes and delicate vocal ornamentation. The old Washington gang was all represented, with some songs from the Lomax legacy (including a few from *Our Singing Country*), some Woody Guthrie songs, and even a song picked up by Charles Seeger. It also contained examples from WPA projects, including fieldwork by Sidney Robertson (Cowell) and a tune from a Farm Security Adminstration camp. Determined to document "living lore," Botkin's material spanned a period ranging from the earliest selection (1917) to his own fieldwork in the 1950s, dividing his choices almost equally among the 1930s, 1940s, and 1950s.

The repertory also has some special qualities that one could easily miss: in this quintessentially masculine world of cowboys and loggers Botkin included songs that express women's voices in "Don't You Marry Those Texan Boys" and "The Frozen Logger."

"Twistification"

In many ways this collection shows just how far Botkin had traveled from his dissertation on play-party songs, with its music examples in tiny script. As a case in point, let us return to the play-party song "Five Times Five." As presented in its most scholarly guise in *The American Play-Party Song* (1937b: 345–51), "Weevily Wheat" came with one modest tune and several pages of text variants. The text for "Five Times Five" appears under the intriguing name "Twistification" (1937b: 349), as culled from "Lacie and Kaspar Huff, Cleveland Country, from W.T. Huff":

> Five times five is twenty-five,
> And five times six is thirty,
> Five times seven is thirty-five,
> And five times eight is forty.
> Five times eleven is fifty-five,
> And five times twelve is sixty.
> Oh, I won't have none o your weevily wheat,
> An' I won't have none o' your barley.
> But give to me some good old rye,
> To make a cake for Charlie.

"Weevily Wheat" makes a second appearance in *A Treasury of American Folklore*. Here Charles Seeger provided a new tune with a more complicated melody, which begins on the sixth degree of the scale and has a modal quality to its shape. No text variants about "five times five" appear here, but this tune too came from Botkin's prior fieldwork for *The American Play-Party Song* (1937b: 814).

In *A Treasury of Western Folklore* "Weevily Wheat" resurfaces with yet another melody and with new text. At last the silly multiplication table text gets its own melody and even names the song. This variant of "twistification" was collected fourteen years later: "as sung by Lannis Sutton, Doxie, Oklahoma, at Palo Alto, California, January 14, 1951" (1951g: 787–88). Small but effective chromatic inflections enhance the charm of this melody with a modal or perhaps even "blue-note" quality. The playful alternations of major and minor thirds (A to F in the first line, E-flat to C in the second line) "twistify" the music in keeping with the words. Peggy Seeger, who transcribed "Five Times Five," along with some of the "simplest tunes" ("the ones she [Ruth Crawford

Seeger] gave me"), still sings it in concert because it is a "great song especially for adults."[30]

Ben and Ruth were pleased with the book, even speculating about new projects.

December 2, 1951
Dear Ben and Gertrude,
It's a fine book, and the music looks beautiful. I haven't written you sooner partly because the block about writing anything to or about anyone or anything still seems almost unbreakable, and partly because I hoped to get more time to read more into the book, and haven't found it. My teaching schedule is heavier than it ever has been; whether this is wise, is a question. I have a wonderful time at it, and am tired after it. Also we are still being spartan about permanent help. Also, I like that, but get no time or will for book making or composition. So where are we at? Tomorrow is something to chase, or to nostalgic about ahead of time. . . . Are you resting up, or at the book you were going to finish by Christmas? Are you thinking of cotton still? . . . If you are still thinking about our getting together on cotton around the first of the year, will you give me warning plenty in advance? . . . I haven't put much thought on it. But if I had to, I would. I would still put up a fight for plenty of music. Do you think Crown is still interested in the series idea? If they are, we really ought to make ourselves get heated up about it. I've lost a number of things by this procrastinating I do; one just this last year. . . . Let me know about cotton. . . . Gertrude would undoubtedly enjoy short books for a change, wouldn't she??? Please tell her I think she is quite wonderful, and many thanks a few months late for taking such good care of me in August. And again, congratulations on the book— with room for more when I've read into it more. Sidney remarked with extra special enthusiasm about the quality of the songs.

Ben responded quickly:

December 5, 1951
Dear Ruth:
I was very glad to hear from you and that you liked the book. I had been sort of looking for such a letter from Chevy Chase, but I figured that you were busy. The words in the music are a little smaller than I like, and there are some burs (extra bits of metal) and some lines due to paste-ins that should have been cleaned up. But otherwise I think we have suc-

ceeded in doing what you wanted, and I think the songs have what Sidney or you call "quality." Of course, I don't expect Dr. Dorson to like the book, but then I don't like Dr. Dorson. . . . It would be nice for you to get back to composing. But I'll be selfish and hope you do another book soon. . . . Thanks again for doing such a swell job on the music. I think our collaboration worked. Let's try it again.

"Dr. Dorson" symbolized the challenges that confronted both Botkin and Crawford Seeger in the 1950s. For even though its first print-run of 20,000 copies had nearly sold out by December 5 (as Botkin mentioned in unquoted parts of the letter above), *A Treasury of Western Folklore* elicited some of the worst reviews of his career. Reception of the book as a whole was tarnished by the polarizing atmosphere around the discipline of folklore scholarship at this time (Widner 1986: 1, 10–11).

Cold War Challenges

As is often noted, the humanistic disciplines struggled to become more "scientific" and professionalized in the 1950s, and the reshaping of folklore into an academic discipline had repercussions for the Washington folk revival collective. Populist enthusiasms of the 1940s were just what an emerging new generation of critics and intellectuals intended to discredit in the solemnities of Cold War culture and the attacks on the political and cultural Left. "Rae [Korson] tells me that you and Charles were upset over Dorson's latest attack on me. As I wrote her, it is time that some one stopped him," Botkin wrote in a letter to Crawford Seeger on April 23, 1951.

Crawford Seeger watched the space diminish for her own kind of work as well. Editorial neglect at Doubleday plagued the marketing of *Animal Folk Songs for Children* (1950). She asked Botkin if he could help in getting the book reviewed in the *Washington Post,* as Rae Korson suggested. "I haven't yet acquired ease and worldly knowledge in the book process after it's published and done," Crawford Seeger told him. But the book merited her intervention. "We like it," she added. "It has some music mistakes due to my not having a chance to see final proof. But even Charlie is pleased with the book as a whole."[31] In *Animal Folk Songs for Children* she praised the music's "epic objectivity, its refusal to act chameleon to word meanings or moods, its rough vitality, its monotony," and she captured these aesthetic values in spare, often dissonant, musically provocative and captivating arrangements. Downcast, Crawford Seeger complained to Botkin in a letter of January 16, 1951:

I am quite aggravated about the treatment of this second book. It came out too late for children's book week. . . . Then because it was so late, they did the opposite of what seems good sense to me: didn't treat it as a Christmas item, gave it very little publicity (or did I miss seeing it?) . . . I decided with this book not to have the luxury of a clipping agency. . . . But I find I am quite lonesome for a few nice words dribbling in.

Some positive reviews were printed in the *New York Times, Saturday Review,* and a variety of big and small trade journals.

Echoing the spirit of Botkin's ideals and his travails, with a dash of her own skepticism about academic professionalism, Crawford Seeger explained to a friend: "I was trying to straddle and talk to folklorists and also ordinary human beings (help the humans to see how a folklore book is made, help the folklorists to see how a book can be a really true folk-lore book and yet be made for humans)."[32]

In her final anthology, *American Folk Songs for Christmas,* Crawford Seeger adopted even more of Botkin's perspective on treating folk music as a medium of cultural and social history. No longer writing as a parent advisor to mothers of preschool children, she reached out to the audiences of his treasuries in an introductory essay about Christmas folklore and folkways, past and present. Her cultural politics shifted more publicly to the left, as she espoused the category of the "people" and the role of people's advocate during the era of the McCarthy investigations. Responding to its implicit critique of commercial Christmas, one reviewer noted how the music was "rooted deep in our past, in a time before America knew the Christmas tree and the Santa Claus on every corner."[33] A miniature folk revival manifesto concluded Crawford Seeger's folklore essay for this volume:

In this country our modern Christmas has been celebrated to a large extent, with songs gathered by other countries from their respective traditions. This is partly because we have not been aware of our own. They have been hidden away, hard to find, or crowded out by the more easily available published collections around us. To make more easily available some of these songs from American traditional Christmas, religious and festive, is to serve two ends: to give back to the people songs that belong to them, and to supplement the already rich inter-national store of Christmas song. (Crawford Seeger 1953: 11)

Also embedded in this volume was an acknowledgment of a black Christmas, not just a white one. Crawford Seeger and Botkin shared a special interest in African American music. Naturally, her work with Lomax songs had introduced her to the greatness of this music. Both Botkin and Crawford Seeger paid attention to the contributions unfolding within African American folklore. Crawford Seeger used her expertise in a review of John N. Work's *American Negro Songs for Mixed Voices.* Similarly, Botkin published *Lay My Burden Down* and also edited a recording of "Negro Religious Songs and Services" for the Archive of American Folk Song. Two songs from that recording found their way into Crawford Seeger's book as well: "Holy Babe" and "Shine Like a Star in the Morning."[34]

In offering alternatives to cherished European carols and commercial Christmas music, Crawford Seeger simultaneously created a musical rainbow. In *American Folk Songs for Christmas,* black church songs, including spirituals and gospel tunes, outnumber the white shape-note tunes by half. Many of them are gems, rich in details of phrasing, harmony, and syncopation that provide special delights. Composer/theorist Mark Nelson writes that "each of these songs seems to come from some profound source."[35] The arrangements show a great composer at the height of her form. Crawford Seeger made the potential race-relations implications of the repertory explicit by requesting that the book illustrator draw some nonwhite faces among the white children. The publisher refused. The Supreme Court decision against school segregation lay two years away.

Postlude

Our tale of two intellectuals ends here, for *American Folk Songs for Christmas* was Crawford Seeger's last project. Diagnosed with cancer in the winter of 1952, she had surgery that summer, rebounding fast enough to revive her hopes for a full recovery. In the midst of it all, Ben Botkin spent a month as the Seegers' house guest while he finished up a manuscript for a book. As the ever cordial hosts, they wrote him a comic letter of recommendation, certifying him as a duly proper "ideal guest . . . with the exception of his predilection for making a phun [*sic*] upon any occasion."[36]

Upon publication of *American Folk Songs for Christmas,* Botkin wrote his friend a congratulatory letter, still not knowing that she was dying:

November 9, 1953
Dear Ruth:
The book arrived last week, and it is beauty from kivver [*sic*] to kivver. Every page shows the loving care and labor of love that you lavished on it, and the result is the same experience of praise, worship, and festivity

that inspired the songs. I really believe it is your best book. Certainly it seems your lovingest book. There is so much of you in the book and so much of Christmas—and the lore as well as the song—that it is hard to tell where one (you) begins and the other (Christmas) leaves off. Congratulations and felicitations!

Dispel all your sorrows and banish your fears,
For Ruth a true angel in Yule songs appears.

On November 16, 1953, Crawford Seeger died at home. In a condolence letter to Charles three days later, Botkin wrote: "I heard the sad news from Vanett [Lawler] last night. It is hard to conceive of a world without Ruth. . . . There is no use in saying: why didn't you tell me when you were here? It is better to ask: What can I do now? Surely there is something. . . . Last night I held Ruth's three books in my hands and thought about the wonderful gift she has left us, and what wonderful gifts she had still to give."

Shortly afterward, Botkin wrote a formal obituary of Ruth Crawford Seeger for the *New York Folklore Quarterly.* He turned it into a partial review of *American Folk Songs for Christmas,* tacitly recognizing its indebtedness to his own work:

This, I believe, is her best book, because, almost as if by premonition, she put so of herself into it, and lavished on it all the love (of music, people, and children) and all the labor of love of which she was capable. There is more folklore in this book than in either of its predecessors in the series—*American Folk Songs for Children* (1948) and *Animal Folk Songs for Children* (1950). And I know there was enough material left over from the excellent introduction on Christmas lore and music to make another book, which I hope will be published, along with the revealing essay she showed me last summer on her problems as writer-mother-composer-wife, torn between the worlds of editing, teaching, composing, and home-making. I have before me an undated letter of 1951, in which she apologized for not writing me on business: "I'm sorry. This week has been such a precious thing. I have done a rare thing: turned off the feeling of weight and conscience about letters and deadline, and spent two solid days, and parts of others, just writing music. I don't know whether I'm a lost soul or a found one . . . I think I'll work much better for this orgy of vocal silence and pianistic noise."[37]

I like to think that she found herself in these children's books (the last of which, *Let's Build a Railroad,* is scheduled for spring), because she could let herself go in them and because they were social books, growing out of her own work with children. As her friends and pupils know, she was happiest when she was working with people and with music for and through people. The 54 songs in the recent book are arranged according to the two phases of Christmas. "There is worship," she writes, "and there is festivity. And in both there is music." And that was Ruth Seeger. (Botkin 1954m: 73–74)

In fact, Botkin had contributed to Crawford Seeger's own journeys more than he ever could or did acknowledge in print. Attending the Midcentury International Folklore Conference at Indiana University in the summer of 1950, Crawford Seeger reaffirmed her musical mission: "In publishing books I have thought it extremely important that what we might call the authentic, as we head it in traditional recordings or in the field, should be given to the public. They have a right to know the words as they are. Then if we want to suggest that things be done with it, that should be a separate thing. Somehow let them have a taste of the thing itself."

Then she added these words, where the cultural spirituality she shared with her old friend shines through: "In selecting material, we must also make it usable for the people who are going to use it. In other words, though we have love for the folk, we also have love for the people we are giving it to, and we must make it as usable by them as possible" (quoted in Thompson 1953: 194). And that was the spirit of Ben Botkin.

Appendix: List of Songs in *A Treasury of Western Folklore* (including date and field recording collector or printed source)

1. Rio Grande 1939, Sidney Robertson [Cowell].
2. The Girls around Cape Horn, 1938, from Colcord, *Songs of American Sailormen.*
3. Sacramento, 1918, *King's Book of Shanties.*
4. Shenandoah, 1951, Sam Eskin.
5. The Days of Forty-nine, 1939, Sidney Robertson [Cowell].
6. Mi Mulita, 1943, from Korson, *Coal Dust on the Fiddle.*
7. In Kansas, 1938, Sidney Robertson [Cowell].
8. The Little Old Sod Shanty, 1936, Sidney Robertson [Cowell].
9. The Sioux Indians, 1951, Sam Eskin.
10. 'Way Out in Idyho, 1932, from *Cowboy Songs, Folk Songs and Ballads from Green Grow the Lilacs* by Lynn Riggs.
11. Custer's Last Charge, 1938, Sidney Robertson [Cowell].
12. The Old Settler, 1950, Benjamin A. Botkin.
13. Root, Hog, or Die, 1936, Sidney Robertson [Cowell].

14. On the Road to California, 1947, Austin and Alta Fife.
15. Echo Canyon, 1946, the Fifes.
16. The Handcart Song, 1946, the Fifes.
17. Doney Gal, 1941 from Lomax, *Our Singing Country.*
18. The Strawberry Roan, dated incorrectly as 1959, Botkin.
19. Away High Up in the Mogliones (High Chin Bob), 1951, Botkin.
20. The Cowboy's Lament, 1950, Botkin.
21. Jim Porter's Shanty Song, 1926, from Franz Rickaby, *Ballads and Songs of the Shanty-Boy.*
22. Jack Haggerty, 1950, Botkin.
23. The Frozen Logger, 1949, from Stevens, "Bunk-Shanty Ballads and Tales," *Oregon Historical Quarterly.*
24. Jackhammer Blues, 1941, written and sung by Woody Guthrie.
25. Roll On, Columbia, 1950, Botkin.
26. The Dying Hobo, 1948, Eskin.
27. The Texas Rangers, 1948, Eskin.
28. Mustang Gray, 1932, from J. Frank Dobie, *Tone the Belt Easy.*
29. Cole Younger, 1936, Sidney Robertson [Cowell].
30. The Portland County Jail, 1950, Botkin.
31. Gambling on the Sabbath Day, 1951, Eskin.
32. The Santa Barbara Earthquake, 1940, recorded by Charles Todd and Robert Sonkin in an FSA camp, California.
33. The Sherman Cyclone, 1937, John A. Lomax.
34. The Great Dust Storm, n.d., written by Woody Guthrie, transcribed from the recording *Dust Bowl Ballads, Volume 2.*
35. Don't You Marry Those Texan Boys, n.d., recorded by Charles Seeger.
36. All Her Answers to Me Were No, 1951, Eskin.
37. The Gypsy Davy, 1940, as sung by Woody Guthrie and recorded by Alan Lomax.
38. Ay! Vienen Los Yankees, 1917, as notated and collected by Eleanor Hague, *Spanish-American Folk-Songs.*
39. Five Times Five Is Twenty-Five, 1951, Eskin.
40. Little Fight in Mexico, 1937, Botkin, *The American Play-Party Song.*
41. La Viudita de Santa Isabel, 1934, John and Alan Lomax.
42. Vibora de la Mar, 1942, from the WPA project *Spanish-American Song and Game Book.*
43. Señora Santa Ana, 1934–39, recorded by John A., Ruby T., and Alan Lomax. Transcribed in *14 Traditional Spanish Songs from Texas* by Gustavo Durán.
44. Fod, 1941, recorded by Charles Todd and Robert Sonkin.

Notes

1. This article relies on interpretations of Botkin's work by Jerrold Hirsch (1987) and Ronna Lee Widner (1986). Widner begins her article with the "purist/popularizer" dichotomy.

2. This account is drawn from my biography *Ruth Crawford Seeger: A Composer's Search for American Music* (1997) as well as my essay "Writing the Music of Ruth Crawford into Mainstream Music History," in Allen and Hisama 2007.

3. See in particular the compact disks *Ruth Crawford*, (American Masters Series, CRI, 1993) and *Ruth Crawford Seeger: Portrait* (Deutsche Gramophon, 1997). Dawn Upshaw has included Crawford Seeger's "White Moon" in the CD *White Moon: Songs to Morpheus (Warlock, Handel, Monteverdi, Crawford, Seeger, Schwantner, Dowland, Villa-Lobos, Crumb and Purcell)* (Nonesuch, CD 79364-2, 1996, and Deutsche Schallplatten Preisher DVD).

4. Excerpt from an interview with Vivian Fine by the author, November 29, 1984.

5. Blitzstein's *The Cradle Will Rock* came out of this milieu. In addition, the Composers Collective specialized in rounds with texts satirizing corporate executives. Three of these ("Poor Mister Morgan" and "Schwab, Schwab" by Elie Siegmeister under the pseudonym "L. E. Swift" and "Oh, Joy upon the Earth" by Charles Seeger under the pseudonym "Carl Sands") were later used in Waldemar Hille's *The People's Songbook* (New York: Boni and Gaer, 1948). Alan Lomax and Botkin contributed a foreword and a preface to this collection.

6. Allen Dwight Sapp, keynote address on April 9, 1987, for a symposium festival devoted to Ruth Crawford, organized by Karin Pendle for the University of Cincinnati in 1987. "I studied with Copland in the 1940s at the Hotel Empire, and I told him that I found Crawford to be an exciting composer and I asked him what had happened to her. He was pleased and confided that he had great admiration for her work and that her career had sort of foundered on radical politics. . . . We agreed that she was a truly wonderful composer."

7. Hirsch (1987: 11) describes Botkin's negative attitudes toward "rampantly subjective modern poetry" and expressionistic style. Crawford's music conveys this aesthetic as well.

8. Interview with Gertrude Botkin by the author, June 28, 1989.

9. Robertson is better known as Sidney Robertson Cowell. Her own WPA collection project, *California Gold: Northern California Folk Music from the Thirties*, can be accessed online at http: memory.loc.gov/ammem/afcchtml/cowhome.html.

10. Sandburg wrote endorsements for Botkin's *A Treasury of American Folklore* and for Crawford Seeger's *American Folk Songs for Children*.

11. In analyzing his own intellectual identity, Seeger wrote: "Strictly speaking, I do not regard myself as a scholar, I am a systematist. The two are very different. For one thing, the scholar is primarily interested in knowing everything he can of other people's work; the systematist, in appropriating everything he can lay his hands on in the continual task of fortifying his World View" (quoted in Pescatello 1992: 284). I am adapting this phrase to the ideology that marks a formative period in his life. Given the acceptance of "appropriation" at this point, it can sometimes be difficult to document who thought and expressed an idea first. Obviously, the writings of Charles Seeger and Alan Lomax overlap with issues discussed here as well. Botkin's influence on Seeger lasted throughout Seeger's life. One example from a set of interviews in 1972 reads like a summary of Botkin's values: "[Academic folklorists] neglect going out into the broad panorama of American life. They fail to realize that

there's a folklore not only of the most backward people in the Appalachian mountains, but there's a folklore of the local county boss and city boss, and a folklore of the businessman and the clerical workers and the workers in the factories" (Seeger 1972: 286–87). For an overview of Seeger's work in American folklore, including some discussion of Botkin, see Helen Rees, " 'Temporary Bypaths'?: Seeger and Folk Music Research," in Yung and Rees 1999: 84–108.

12. Rees, "Temporary Bypaths," 89, notes that, according to Botkin, the "functional" label for their approach was more or less accepted by the late 1930s.

13. Letter from Ruth Crawford Seeger to Charles Seeger, January 26, 1939. Quoted with permission from the Seeger Estate. Private Seeger Collection.

14. Telephone interview with Herbert Halpert by the author, September 26, 1989.

15. The set was published as *Nineteen American Folk Tunes for Piano* (New York: G. Schirmer, 1995).

16. Sources for tunes are listed in the typescript, where she cites "Sharpe II, 340" as the source. This most likely refers to Cecil J. Sharp's collection *Nursery Songs from the Appalachian Mountains* (London: Novello and Company, 1923). Botkin cites this source as well in *The American Play-Party Tune* (1937b: 346).

17. See Waters 1941. A letter from Charles Seeger to Ben Botkin (April 6, 1943) describes the booklet as "American Songs for American Children" and notes that it was "specially printed" for this convention.

18. Interview with Pete Seeger by the author, June 3, 1990.

19. Ibid.

20. Botkin 1937b: 8. "The tunes were recorded in the field by my assistant, Gerald Whitney, now of the music department of Hobart High School and Junior College."

21. John A. Lomax and Alan Lomax, collectors and compilers, *Our Singing Country: A Second Volume of American Ballads and Folksongs* (New York: Macmillan, 1941). It was reissued by Dover Publications, Inc., in 1999, with a new introduction by the author.

22. Although Crawford expected this treatise to be published as an appendix to *Our Singing Country,* it was published only recently (Seeger 2001). For Charles Seeger's reliance on this work, see Judith Tick, "Ruth Crawford, Charles Seeger, and 'The Music of American Folk Songs,' " in Yung and Rees 1999.

23. Botkin 1944j: 818. The quotation from Sharp as cited by Botkin comes from Olive Dame Campbell, *English Folk Songs from the Southern Appalachians* (London: G.P. Putnam's, 1917).

24. These songs were "Down in the Valley," "The Dodger," "Buffalo Skinners," "Young Man Who Wouldn't Hoe Corn," and "The Farmer Comes to Town."

25. Interview with Gertrude Botkin by the author, June 28, 1989.

26. Ruth Crawford Seeger, "Pre-School Children and American Folk Songs" (in Crawford Seeger 2001: 135). The exact date of this speech is not clear, but it was probably given in the late 1940s.

27. Unless otherwise indicated, quotations from correspondence between Botkin and Crawford Seeger come from the Benjamin A. Botkin Collection of Applied American Folklore in the Archives and Special Collections of the Library of the University of Nebraska.

28. Virgil Thomson was a distinguished composer and major music critic. Already respectful of Crawford as a composer, he gave her book high praise.

29. Letter from Ruth Crawford Seeger to Jean Ritchie, July 31, 1952. Private Seeger Collection.

30. Peggy Seeger in an e-mail communication to the author, November 17, 2001. She also sings other tunes such as the strangely named "Fod," "The Sioux Indians," "The Frozen Logger," and "Texan Boys."

31. Letter from Ruth Crawford Seeger to Benjamin Botkin, November 27, 1950. Botkin Collection.

32. Letter from Ruth Crawford Seeger to Rose Gregg, January 28, 1951 (in author's possession).

33. Ellen Lewis Buell, "New Christmas Books for Younger Readers," *New York Times,* December 6, 1953.

34. This tape is listed in the current online catalogue of the Archive of Folk Culture as "AFSL10, recorded in the southern U.S. by John and Alan Lomax, 1934–1942, edited by B.A. Botkin."

35. Letter to the author, May 23, 1994. Nelson is the author of an important article, "In Pursuit of Charles Seeger's Heterophonic Ideal: Three Palindromic Works by Ruth Crawford," *Musical Quarterly* 72.4 (1986): 458–75.

36. Letter from Charles and Ruth Seeger to Benjamin A. Botkin, September 2, 1953. Botkin Collection.

37. Crawford Seeger had just composed the Suite for Wind Quintet, the first new formal composition in about ten years.

Benjamin Botkin and Play-Party Scholarship in America

NANCY CASSELL MCENTIRE

Benjamin Botkin worked throughout his life to achieve a democratic plan for the study of folklore in a pluralistic society. Conflicting ideologies of his day, personal rivalries, and his own shyness distanced him from academic recognition, despite the continued success of his publications.[1] More than thirty years after his death, we are still recognizing his insights. Many of Botkin's ideas, such as celebration of cultural diversity and regionalism, acceptance of technology and urban lore, and a dynamic, functional approach to folklore studies, were adopted years later by folklorists who were unaware that Botkin was the first to promote them (Stekert 1975; Jackson 1976; Widner 1986; Hirsch 1987 and 1996).

Botkin's biography is covered in depth in other chapters in this volume, but it is worth emphasizing that he was the product of a range of often disparate intellectual traditions and influences that crossed many boundaries. He was an early-twentieth-century child in east Boston from a family of Lithuanian Jews. He was a Harvard student deeply influenced by the famous ballad scholar George Lyman Kittredge. He was a master's student at Columbia immersed in an assortment of poetic traditions. After answering the "call of the West" and leaving the East Coast for Oklahoma, he found his "Harvard accent and 'indifference' breaking down" in unexpected ways that made the Midwest a better source of "enlightened regional consciousness" (Hirsch 1987: 10; Botkin 1935b: 322–23). Becoming a doctoral student under Louise Pound at the University of Nebraska reinforced his connections to regional folklore

Portions of this chapter appeared in "The American Play-Party in Context," *Voices: The Journal of New York Folklore* 28.1–2 (2002): 30–33. I am grateful to be able to expand upon those ideas here. I also appreciate helpful suggestions from readers and from Larry Rodgers and Jerrold Hirsch.

studies that were worlds apart from his East Coast roots. Botkin and Pound agreed that the individual was more important than the folk group in the formation of folklore. (Pound's criticism of the communal theory was well known among folklorists of the day.) On issues of sources of cultural material, however, they did not agree. Pound still endorsed the idea of high culture "materials that had shifted down to the folk," whereas Botkin, while recognizing the movement of folklore, saw more of a shifting back and forth between high culture and folk culture (Hirsch 1987: 13).

It was within this climate of excitement, dissent, and heightened curiosity about folklore texts and their origins that Botkin undertook a dissertation on the play-party. His data came mainly from students at the University of Oklahoma. Although he had been—and continued to be—active as a promoter of poetry, he himself noted that along with his interest in the play-party came the professional conviction that poetry and folklore would go "hand in hand" (Botkin 1935b: 323–24). According to Botkin, there was nothing else in America quite like the play-party. It became, for him, the ideal topic for scholarly investigation, full of rich and spontaneous (if sometimes crude) lyrics that reflected an immature America, still grappling with its frontier identity. Writing in 1928, Botkin saw his topic as a testing ground for concepts he had learned from Louise Pound as well as an opportunity to express his own ideas about folklore and social history:

> This anomalous, hybrid, eclectic character of the play-party, which is thus dance, game, and song all in one and yet no one of them in particular, makes a fascinating study for the folk-lorist intent on tracing origins and development through all the changes and corruptions of oral tradition.
>
> But the significance of the play-party extends beyond its mere antiquarian or research interest to the collector and the scholar. Its value to the future social historian is inestimable. (Botkin 1928g: 9)

As well as providing historical benefits, Botkin's method in conducting and including extensive life-history interviews for his study was as innovative as it was effective. With Pound's guidance, Botkin received his doctorate in English in 1931. He published his dissertation as *The American Play-Party Song* in 1937 through the University of Nebraska. It met with favorable reviews and was quickly recognized as a classic. George Herzog praised Botkin's work as "one of the most solid treatments" of a specific genre of American folksong (Herzog 1937: 215). A year later Emelyn E. Gardner described it as having all the necessary components required of a "standard reference book on the subject" (Gardner 1938: 357). In 1963 the book was reprinted by New York publisher Frederick Ungar. Botkin dedicated the new edition to Pound, who had died in 1958:

> In dedicating this new edition to Louise Pound's memory I want to pay tribute to her stimulating guidance of the book through its later stages as acknowledged in my original preface, as well as to her continued, unstinting encouragement and assistance over three decades and the constant inspiration of her interdisciplinary, humanistic scholarship in the fields of literature, dialect, and folklore. (Botkin 1963a: 2)

Although twenty-six years had elapsed since the original publication of the book, Botkin decided to reprint it with only minor corrections, claiming in the preface to the 1963 edition that he had not changed his conclusions and that no important body of new material or theory had appeared to challenge them (Botkin 1963a: 1). Although the play-party had severely declined as a social institution in America since the first printing of *The American Play-Party Song*, the ideas that shaped it had not.

This chapter examines the play-party within the context of Botkin's enduring work, noting how his presentation and analysis of play-party songs created a solid foundation for the functional study of folksong in America. It discusses the work of subsequent folksong scholars Leah Wolford, Alan Lomax, and George List, who followed Botkin's lead in documentation and analysis of the songs, as well as Keith Cunningham, whose reassessments of the play-party shed new light on several of Botkin's ideas. The last part of the chapter (which includes transcriptions of conversations) gives a glimpse of how the play-party reflected a changing social and cultural climate in rural America.

As far as we know, the play-party originated in the final decades of the nineteenth century and lasted through the late 1920s and early 1930s.[2] The "play-party," "party," "party play," "jig play," "frolick," or "bounce around," as it was also called, was a specialized kind of dancing game for adolescents and young adults, held in local people's homes. It was sung, usually (but not always) unaccompanied by musical instruments. Often the verses were borrowed from existing children's songs and folksongs (Botkin 1963a: 16–17). This community-centered event was a living paradox: how could a rural pastime be a dance, yet not be called a dance? Why were these "dances" sung and not simply danced to the music of a fiddle? Why did the participants use children's songs as part of the dance repertoire?

The answers to these questions can be found, in part, through an examination of the social restrictions that forced the creation of the play-party. Like other genres of folklore (such as specialized, secret languages), the play-party grew in popularity because other forms of entertainment either were not accessible or were not allowed. At the time Botkin was conducting his research in Oklahoma, he was able to interview people who remembered attending play-parties when they were younger as well as those who were still attending play-parties. Therefore his understanding of the genre was derived from actual practice and not simply from the examination of surviving lyrics or melodies. Thanks to his attention to every detail of dances, texts, and their functions, we have a definitive understanding not only of the genre itself but also of a youthful, rural America at the end of the pioneer days—a society on the edge of irreversible change. In assessing Botkin's forward-looking view of folklore, Jerrold Hirsch wrote:

> In the 1930s most folklorists still perceived the modern world as a mortal threat to folklore and regarded isolated and homogeneous communities as the places in which a pure and uncontaminated folklore survived. Botkin took a different approach. In his view folklore was not only survivals from the past that were fast disappearing, but also something that was still being created. Botkin regarded much of the study of folklore as a study in acculturation—the process by which the folk group adapts itself to its environment and to change, assimilating new experiences and generating new forms. (Hirsch 1989: xix)

Much of the history of the play-party focuses on rural American communities and their attempts to create amusement and courtship opportunities when other sources of entertainment were not allowed or in some cases not available. Like a weed in a stone wall, the play-party grew and thrived, even alongside other established, more-complicated traditions, such as the square dance. According to Botkin, the play-party allowed "a combination of game and dance which possessed distinct advantages over either type singly." Part of the appeal of the play-party was that it was simple and accessible. He noted that it developed the "opportunity for human, humorous, and dramatic by-play" (Botkin 1963a: 53).

Certain social and cultural conditions nourished the play-party. One of these, according to Botkin and subsequent play-party researchers, was isolation. In the days before "railroads, highways, automobiles, mail-order houses, mail delivery, movies, phonograph, and radio, the play-party was . . . one solution of the amusement problem" (Botkin 1963a: 19). In her 1916 study of the play-party, Leah Wolford also had commented on how southern Indiana's rugged hills and hollows contributed to a sense of separation from the outside world: "The southern half of this county is cut up by swiftly flowing creeks and high hills, which have served to isolate the different communities and disconnect the whole district from the outside world" (Wolford 1959: 113).

In the decades preceding World War I, disconnected rural communities throughout America were dependent on their own resources for entertainment. When there were clusters of young people in these communities who wanted to get together, the play-party became a popular option. Isolation was not the only factor that prompted the play-party, however; if that had been the case, it would have been no different from a square dance, with music provided by a fiddle and other popular instruments of the time (such as the banjo or guitar). The play-party was like the square dance (or hoedown), yet it was not that dance; and although some of the tunes performed for the play-party were indeed fiddle tunes, they were usually sung.

For the play-party participant, entertainment options were often limited by religious and social practices. Throughout rural America, the pervasive religious view of the time was one of distrust and, in many cases, repudiation of dancing. Leah Wolford noted that even though many religions (Quakers, Disciples, Methodists, Baptists, and Presbyterians) were represented in southern Indiana, where she witnessed the play-party, "they were one in opposing the dance as a wicked sport" (Wolford 1959: 114). Religious opposition to dance was especially obvious to musicians, who were aware of their power to move people to dance. Documenting a musical family from Norman, Oklahoma, Botkin obtained the following statement in 1929 from W. L. Wilkerson, who had been playing the five-string banjo (as well as the fiddle and the guitar) at entertainments and square dances since the age of twelve. At the time of the interview, Wilkerson was fifty-eight years old:

> The church's attitude was against dancing. . . . How could a man reconcile religious scruples and dancing? He didn't. Active church members didn't go to dances. If a boy or girl belonging to any church danced, the saying went round that they had danced themselves out of the church, and that was made a moment of history. The reference was made that at such and such a dance a boy or a girl danced themselves out of the church. For there seemed no ground of justification from the church standpoint for a boy [or girl] to dance. (Botkin 1963a: 21)

Here Botkin's findings are particularly valuable. He not only recognized the importance of contextual information surrounding the practice of the play-party but also used field research to obtain recollections from actual participants in the dances. Botkin went on to describe an incident in

Headrick, Oklahoma, that further confirms a negative attitude toward dancing at the time:

> The convictions or prejudices of the community may further be gauged by the incident of the Sunday school superintendent who one Sunday got up and actually wept because he had heard that his daughter had gone to a dance. He offered to resign because he didn't feel fit for the place, but the people wouldn't hear of it. His daughter, a graduate of Oklahoma Agricultural and Mechanical College, was teaching school and had accidentally mentioned the dance in a letter. (Botkin 1963a: 22)

In addition to their reservations about dancing, many churchgoers were opposed to the fiddle, as Wilkerson recounted: "I can't understand why it was but in my boyhood days—I don't know how to express it—but the fiddle was the instrument of Satan. The Devil was in the fiddle—that's the saying exactly" (Botkin 1963a:, 21; see also Lomax 1966: n. 66; Adams 2000: 190–91).[3]

Folklorist Herbert Halpert cites a story, collected by Helen White Charles, about the son of a strict Quaker father in Indiana. The son secretly acquired a fiddle and took to practicing it in the hay loft. One day his father overheard him and investigated.

> Father said to me, "What is that thing with which thee is making such unearthly noises?" I answered, "It is a fiddle." He said, "Whoever thought thee would bring that instrument of the Devil here, give it to me," which of course I did. He then ordered me to follow him and we marched up to the house where a good fire was burning in the large fireplace. He directed me to a chair while he placed the fiddle and bow in the roaring flames. We watched them burn and listened for the strings to break. The E string broke first and the others in order, and as the bass string broke I seemed to feel my heart break too. (Halpert 1995: 48, citing Helen White Charles, *Quaker Chuckles, and Other True Stories about Friends*)

Despite this kind of prejudice, the fiddle gradually became an acceptable instrument. Community debates shifted from whether fiddles should be played at all to *how* they should be played. In one New Hampshire case, the fiddle was acceptable only if its tones were "stretched out in prolonged notes": lively, short notes, such as would be found in a reel, were unacceptable (Halpert 1995: 47). The location of the musical performance was also important. While the fiddle was gaining ground as an instrument for home entertainment, it was still strictly forbidden in the church. Even the sweetest, most stretched-out tones were not to be brought into the Lord's house (Halpert 1995: 48).

Within the prevailing climate of widespread distrust of dancing and lively fiddle playing, the play-party thrived. Although it contained elements of older, mostly English children's singing games, it was not merely a survival from that period. The play-party was a vibrant and spontaneous event that borrowed widely from existing traditions to create a new form that would meet the needs of its participants. In 1928 Botkin offered this description of play-party lyrics in Oklahoma:

> The fertility of invention is no less astonishing than the length of these productions. Surprise and novelty abound in the language, which is full of picturesque dialect and racy colloquialism, new combinations and formations, *galimatias,* and plays on words. Images and allusions, drawn from country life, are piled pell-mell on each other, in a breathless hodge-podge, playing variations on a theme or ringing the changes on a rhyme with remarkable ingenuity. Irrelevance and impropriety reign supreme. (Botkin 1928g: 20)[4]

Thriving amid repressive mores of the time, the play-party offered amusement and courtship opportunities within a familiar, community-sanctioned setting. Adolescents and young adults took part in a dance that was not given the name "dance," yet followed dance steps, moving in time to tunes that were products of their own voices. The function of the play-party, as Botkin first described it, was to allow rhythmic dance movement, melody (often sung), and companionship to flourish in the face of geographic, social, or religious constraints. The play-party included dance movements but was regarded essentially as a game; it included vocal music (but not exclusively), and singing was not always performed because of a ban on fiddle playing. Botkin saw this genre of folklore as a "natural development" of traditional games that were performed under conditions that created a variety of constraints, not just one. He summarized his views of natural development with the following observation:

> That the play-party game was not truly a substitute for the dance but a parallel and supplementary form is borne out by the fact that play-party games frequently made use of instrumental accompaniment; that dances had in themselves the seeds of vocal accompaniment in the words that went with many dance tunes (especially those derived from popular songs), which were often sung in the absence of fiddle or to reinforce it; and that play-parties sometimes came under the ban of the Church along with dances. (Botkin 1963a: 18)

Keith Cunningham cited the use of the fiddle at play-parties in Arizona in the 1920s and 1930s, confirming that the absence of a fiddle at these events was not necessarily due to religious objections. For example, singing could have resulted simply from an absence of instruments (Cunningham 1972: 13; see also Richmond and Tillson 1959: 244). Cunningham also points out that some play-party melodies became part of the repertoire of folk instrumentalists, supplying further evidence that singers and instrumentalists did not operate independently—they were bound to influence each other (1972: 19).

Play-party activities did overlap with other traditional dances and with other musical settings, as Botkin, Wolford, Cunningham, and others have observed.[5] In some communities, a more liberal religious worldview allowed fiddlers to play for local play-parties. Sometimes a fiddle player who was expected to show up at a dance might not arrive or a fiddle player might be too intoxicated to play coherently. In such cases singing would fill the gap, as it had in the past (Botkin 1963a: 18, 40 n. 11; see also Lomax 1966: 71 n.; Sandburg 1927: 136–38). Sentiment against the fiddle remained strong, however, and ventures of combining fiddle playing with play-party steps could lead to social discomfort. Botkin cites this Oklahoma example: "Many of the girls of the pre-Statehood days believed it a sin to dance but not to go to a play-party. Consequently they would do the regulation square dances as long as the accompaniment was sung, but if the fiddle was sounded they would stop immediately" (Botkin 1963a: 23, from informant Cora Frances Starritt, Pontotoc County, Oklahoma).

Similarly, in documenting the Kansas play-party, S. J. Sackett reports this dramatic reaction to the fiddle at a play-party: "A group of young people were playing play-party games in the barn when one of the young men present took out his fiddle and joined in the same tune which the players were singing. Immediately the outraged parents rushed in and broke up the party, sending the guests home" (Sackett 1961: 5; see also Lomax 1966: 67 n.).

Within the boundaries of play-party dance definition, further infractions were noted both by observers and by the dancers themselves. For example, one play-party standard, "Weevily Wheat," offended dancers, who found it too close to the square dance movements of the Virginia reel (Wolford 1959: 116; see also List 1991: 152). Here the issue was how partners would accomplish a swing. The play-party differed from the square dance in using the arm swing instead of the waist swing. In the arm swing, partners joined right hands or locked right arms. In the waist swing, the man actually held his partner around the waist as they danced, thus presumably inviting seductive or licentious activity. If play-party "dancing" was to be tolerated at all, swinging had to involve only the hands or arms. Botkin notes that in its most extreme form of propriety the swing could also be accomplished as the "entirely blameless" do-si-do, back-to-back dancing (Botkin 1963a:, 24). A Tulsa County, Oklahoma, text collected by Botkin reveals in a mocking tone the connection between dance steps and religious beliefs:

> Do-ce, ladies, ain't you old enough to know,
> That you'll never get to heaven till you do-ce-do [do-si-do]?
> (Botkin 1963a: 24, from Mary E. Vaughn)

If the do-si-do brought the dancer closer to heaven, then the offending waist swing was surely the path to hell. Botkin cited a commentary on the waist swing in Lynn Riggs's Oklahoma play *Big Lake*, produced in 1927 (Riggs is the author of the 1931 *Green Grow the Lilacs*, which became the basis of the famous Broadway musical *Oklahoma!*). Miss Meredith, the strait-laced teacher, interrupts a play-party in a tone of righteous indignation:

> MISS MEREDITH: Stop it, Bud Bickel! *(She crosses over right, angrily.)* We won't play any more.
> BUD *(following her over)*: Whut is it, whut've I done?
> MISS MEREDITH: You're swinging the Waist Swing, Bud Bickel!
> BUD: Well, o' course.
> MISS MEREDITH: It's wrong, it's wicked. I'm ashamed of you. I'm surprised at you. . . . Don't you ever do it again, you hear me? And don't you girls ever let me catch you letting a boy swing you by the waist instead of by the arms.
> (Botkin 1963a: 23–24, n. 27)

In actual texts of play-party stanzas, allusions to the waist swing are numerous. Sometimes the message takes the form of a playful family dispute:

> Paw says swing them, Maw says no.
> Sis says the waist swing or it don't go.
> (Botkin 1963a: 23)

The message was also subtly delivered, concealed in folk metaphor:

> Meet your lady, pat her on the head,
> If she don't like biscuits, feed her cornbread.
> (Botkin 1963a: 24; see also 1928g: 12–13)

Referring to competing types of swings, a "biscuit" is the contested waist swing and "cornbread" is the arm swing—the more reserved style, presumably suitable for the play-party. Similarly, "hoecake" also refers to the waist swing:

Meet your pardner, pat her on the head,
If she want to eat hoecake, feed her cornbread.
(Botkin 1963a: 24)

Much like a dance, yet not a square dance, the play-party was a distinctive genre of folklore, both in form and in function. In a "make-it-yourself-or-do-without" culture, the play-party filled an important social need. Play-parties could be "jumped up" on short notice or could be announced beforehand through word of mouth. If the area had a telephone line, those who were on the same party line could be informed through a general call. Otherwise, the news could be carried by messengers on horseback. The setting was usually the front room of someone's home. On summer evenings the "dancing" might be held outside. Indoor preparation included removal of all the furniture, sometimes even the stove. Chairs and benches were placed around the walls. Entire families came as far as ten miles, regardless of the condition of the roads or the weather. Most people arrived around dark to socialize and eat refreshments, which could include several kinds of meat, vegetables in season, jelly and preserves, pickles, and a generous supply of cakes and ice cream. Once the children had been taken into a separate room and put to bed, the fun began. Those dancing could be as few as four or as many as fifty.

At times the dancers all sang together, drawing from children's games, folksongs, and square dances for their material. Occasionally the play-party had a leader, chosen for his or her strong voice and high energy, who would guide the dancers through their steps. A good leader could improvise new stanzas to fill in lapses of memory or to introduce humor into the party by making jokes about those in attendance (Botkin 1963a: 26; see also Wolford 1959: 117).

Once underway, the dances had their own spontaneous and individualistic style:

There was a rhythm to the whole thing, a certain keeping time to the music, but this rhythm was almost as much of the arms, head, and body, as of the feet. The players bowed, they knelt, they kissed, they promenaded, they swung, each keeping time to the singing in whatever way his innate sense of dance directed. The walking, the running, the skipping, and the promenade steps could all be recognized, but the players did not all use the same. The impression which a visitor would get from the dance was that of a jumble of old dance steps, all in time, yet related in no other way. . . .

What did they sing? The only requirement was that the words indicate, or at least conform to the movements of the dance. Since the refrain alone usually accomplished this, the singers were at liberty to use the traditional stanzas or to improvise others to suit the occasion. (Wolford 1959: 116–17)

The party might not break up until well after midnight. It was not unusual for men to return home in the early morning, just in time to start their chores. "During a siege of parties, one would think nothing of going without a wink of sleep for several nights in a row" (Botkin 1963a: 19, 24–27). Wolford confirms this practice in her documentation of the Indiana play-party: "From such a party the boys seldom reach home before 3 or 4 o'clock. Yet the lateness of the hour is not allowed to interfere with work the next day. The husky country lad oftentimes merely changes from his Sunday clothes to overalls and goes out to do the feeding, ignoring till the next night his loss of sleep" (Wolford 1959: 119).

We now turn to actual dances and the lyrics that were sung to them, for most play-party pieces contained within their lyrics instructions on how they were to be danced. The first type of play-party piece is sung to an existing square-dance tune and contains nothing more than directions for the dancers. Consider, for example, the following lyrics, sung to the tune of "The Irish Washerwoman":[6]

> Gents to the centre and back to the bar,
> Ladies to the centre and form in a star.
> Gents to the centre and form in a ring,
> Oh, when you do form, oh, then you do swing.
> When you do swing, remember my call,
> Bow to your partner and promenade all.
> Promenade all, promenade all,
> Bow to your partner and promenade all.
> (Botkin 1963a, 41; played in Custer County, Oklahoma)

A second type of play-party piece adapts a portion of an existing folksong to the play-party setting. Consider, for example, "The Girl I Left Behind Me" (also known as "Brighton Camp"), a lively tune dating from the late 1700s that was sung. The song depicted the plight of a young Englishman assigned to military duty in Brighton. He laments having to leave his lover and prays for safe return to her (Chappell 1965: vol. 2, 708–11).

> I'm lonesome since I cross'd the hill,
> And o'er the moor and valley,
> Such heavy thought my heart do fill,

Since parting with my Sally.
I seek no more the fine or gay,
For each does but remind me
How swift the hours did pass away,
With the girl I've left behind me.

Oh, ne'er shall I forget the night,
The stairs were bright above me,
And gently lent their silv'ry light,
When first she vow'd to love me.
But now I'm bound to Brighton camp,
Kind Heaven then, pray guide me,
And send me safely back again
To the girl I've left behind me.

The play-party song retains the line "the girl I left behind me" and the melody, originally a march.[7] It creates a game that turns this phrase into an instruction for the dancers. Botkin collected the following stanza from Oklahoma City:

Same old boy and brand new girl,
Swing her by the right hand.
Now your partner by the left,
And promenade the girl behind you.
(Botkin 1963a: 49; also Owens 1936: 29–30; McIntosh 1974: 3)

According to Botkin, "the refrain line is taken over to fit the movement in which each boy swings the girl *behind* him, with or without additional lines describing the girl and her effect on the singer (Botkin 1963a: 49). An example of this additional description is found in a play-party song collected in Nebraska by Edwin F. Pipe. In this version, the young man's military duty is fighting in the Civil War:

I'm lonesome since I crossed the hills,
And come over the hills and valleys;
I think I'd better go back and see
The girl I left behind me.

Chorus
O swing that girl, that pretty little girl,
The girl I left behind me;
O swing that girl, that pretty little girl,
The girl I left behind me.

If ever I again go near that place,
And the tears don't fall and blind me,
I'll take my way straight home again,
To the girl I left behind me.

Chorus
And when this cruel war is o'er,
And the Lincoln boys unbind me,
I'll seek my love, and part no more,
From the girl I left behind me.

Chorus
(Piper 1915: 286)[8]

A third type of play-party song addresses not only the steps of the dance but stages of courtship. In "I'm a Poor Old Chimney Sweeper," the instructions for the dancers include a kiss. Its gestures recall the African American wedding custom of jumping over a broom to signify the transition from single to married life:

I'm a poor old chimney sweeper
I have but one daughter and cannot keep her.

Since she has resolved to marry,
Go choose your lover and do not tarry.

Now you have one of your own choosing,
Hasten away, no time for losing.

Join your right hands, this broom-stick step over,
And kiss the lips of your true lover.
(Wolford 1959: 172–73)

In this dance, all join hands and form a circle around one boy, who stands in the center and sweeps the ground with a large broom. At the singing of the line "go choose your lover," the boy circles right inside the ring, looking for a partner. He carries the broom like a gun in his right arm. At the line "now you have one of your own choosing," he places the broom on the ground between himself and his chosen partner. Then, with the line "this broom-stick step over," the couple step over the broom from opposite sides, each leading with the right foot. As they meet, they kiss (Wolford 1959: 173).

Kissing, an obvious bonus in the courtship function of the play-party, is often mentioned both in the descriptions of the dances and in the lyrics themselves.[9] Alton Morris's *Folksongs of Florida* contains these stanzas of the play-party song "When I Was a Young Girl":

> Pretty soon we quarrelled, we quarrelled, we quarrelled:
> Pretty soon we quarrelled; we quarrelled, oh then.
> It was shut your mouth this way, and mash your mouth that way;
> It was shut your mouth this way, and mash your mouth that way;
> Pretty soon we quarrelled; we quarrelled, oh then.
>
> Pretty soon we made it up, we made it up, we made it up,
> Pretty soon we made it up; we made it up then.
> It was (sound of a kiss) this way and (sound of a kiss) that way;
> It was (sound of a kiss) this way and (sound of a kiss) that way;
> Pretty soon we made it up; we made it up then.
> (Morris 1990: 205; see also Tolman 1916: 189; Davis 1929: 169–70;
>   Harbison 1938: 151; Brewster 1939: 221–22; Newell 1963: 88)

Another play-party standard, "Old Sister Phoebe," contains this stanza:

> Put a hat on her head to keep her head warm,
> And two or three kisses will do her no harm.
> (Morris 1990: 218)

The note for this dance contains kissing instructions: "At the beginning of the second stanza, one of the boys puts a hat on Sister Phoebe's head, and at the conclusion of the stanza, the boys kiss her" (see also Hudson 1936: 298–99; List 1991: 71–72, 138–39, Randolph 1946: vol. 3, 322–23). Sometimes kissing games unconnected to dance were used to "break the ice" at the beginning of a play-party evening or to set a mood at the end of several hours of dancing.[10] References to kissing and directions for kissing were often part of play-party lyrics, as in the examples cited above. Botkin noted that the arrangement of the rooms for play-parties could invite kissing games: "In at least one case that has come to my notice it was the custom for the young people to occupy the front-room and the older folk the dining-room and kitchen, an arrangement that favored kissing games behind closed doors when the young folk went in for that sort of thing" (Botkin 1963a: 25)

One might wonder at this point how the play-party tradition could develop out of a widespread condemnation of something seemingly as innocent as the waist swing and yet could contain explicit commands for kissing within its lyrics. Part of the answer may lie in recognition of the fashions of the time. In the 1959 edition of Leah Wolford's book, editors W. Edson Richmond and

William Tillson make this observation: "Oddly enough, before 1890 kissing was proper, waist swinging never—after that the custom gradually reversed itself.... The play-party served many functions ... but always more than mere dance, song, or music" (Wolford 1959: 260).

In his book about southern Indiana folksong (*Singing about It*), George List transcribes part of an interview that Herbert Halpert conducted in 1941 while he was a graduate student at Indiana University.[11] His informant, Abraham Lincoln Gary, of Rushville, Indiana, was seventy-four years old at the time.[12] Gary referred to play-parties, which he had attended, as "parties" but also called them "gum sucks" or kissing parties. According to him, kissing was appropriate at the play-party, but playing the fiddle was not. The following excerpt not only offers an interesting account of play-party conventions but also brings up the touchy subject of how "Methodists" viewed the fiddle.

HALPERT: What was the name of this?
GARY: "Weevily Wheat."
HALPERT: And what is it or what is it like?
GARY: Well, it's something like ... it's a game, a young people's game and it was played something like they did the square dance.
HALPERT: What was that? Did they have any kind of a name?
GARY: Well, they ...
HALPERT: Like "play-party"?
GARY: Well, this was "parties." Sometimes they said they were "gum sucks."
HALPERT: They were what?
GARY: Gum sucks. [Laughter.]
HALPERT: What does that mean?
GARY: A kissing party. [Laughter.]
HALPERT: And ... does "Weevily Wheat" have kissing in it?
GARY: No, it doesn't, but it was played at those parties.
HALPERT: Well, suppose you sing it and then tell about it.

[Mr. Gary sings.]

> I will have none of your weevil in my wheat,
> I will have none of your barley;
> But I'll take some of your good old rye
> To make a cake for Charlie.
> *Chorus*
> Oh, Charlie he's a fine young man,
> Charlie he's a dandy;

> He can hug and kiss the girls,
> And give them lots of candy.
> Oh, Dear, if you love me as I love you,
> We won't have long to tarry.
> We'll keep the old folks hustling about
> To fix for us to marry.[13]

GARY: That's about all.

HALPERT: You just repeat that?

GARY: Just repeating. Just repeating. [He sings the first stanza again.]

> I will have none of your weevil in my wheat,
> I will have none of your barley;
> I'll take some more of your good old rye
> To make a cake for Charlie.

Just repeating, just repeating, it's a round like . . . running after, all the time. While the couples were dancing across the floor, a good deal the same as the old square dance.

HALPERT: Well, now how was it? Was it in two lines?

GARY: Two lines. The boys on one side and the girls on the other. And then they'd skip across and take their girl and waltz up and down the floor with her.

HALPERT: Well now, did they have any music with it?

GARY: Only the singing, everybody singing.

HALPERT: Everybody singing together?

GARY: Singing together and it was astonishing sometimes. Some in monotones and some singing all bass but it was—it was entertaining. They kept the time.

HALPERT: Well, why did they sing? Why didn't they have, say, a fiddle or a banjo?

GARY: Well, we had no musical instruments in the neighborhood and the singing was to keep step to the music, to keep in time to the music as they sang it. They furnished it themselves.

HALPERT: How about—if you had had a fiddler, let's say, would people have not objected to your playing, having a fiddle at your parties?

GARY: Usually. Well, it was the Devil was in the fiddle. In our community there were Methodists and Campbellites.[14] The Methodists were all sure the Devil was in the fiddle. The Campbellites didn't object so much, but if the Methodist preacher, if he found anyone had a fiddle in his house or had been playing it, why that person was called before the Church.

HALPERT: What happened to him when he was?

GARY: Well he'd remonstrate. If he wouldn't agree not to commit that sin again why he would be put out or put on probation again. You see the Methodists had six months' probation for anyone that joined the Church, and he wasn't taken into full membership for six months. After he had behaved himself for six months, then he was taken in full membership. But after that if he committed a sin like playing a fiddle, or going to the circus, or racing horses, he was brought before the Church and he had to either apologize and promise not to do it again or he would be put out. They took their religion very seriously in those days. (List 1991: 153–55)

In the midst of a climate of hostility toward "sinful" activities such as dancing and fiddle playing, the play-party had indeed become an important part of courtship for the young. This was its essential function. At the end of the evening, after the dancing and singing and kissing, came a flurry of offers and exchanges regarding the journey home, deciding who would be an escort for the walk or the trip on horseback. Wolford offers this description:

In the spare room the dancers continued their games until the boys without "girls" had each summoned enough courage to ask his partner if he might "see her home safe" or until the head of the house, in a rough voice called out the hour. Hasty departure was a relief in that awkward moment. While the boys fetched the horses, the girls slipped on their riding skirts. In an incredibly short time each girl was mounted sidewise behind her partner, and all were riding away, some talking about the party, others singing old time ballads, several couples enjoying a lively horse race. (Wolford 1959: 117; see also Botkin 1963a: 380)

For young people struggling to start a romantic acquaintance, this would be a crucial part of the evening.

The play-party continues to shed light on social and cultural practices in America in the early decades of the twentieth century. Following Botkin's lead, we find within this genre of folksong the evidence of a changing society. The play-party represented conflicting views about music, dance, religion, and courtship. By analyzing its function and its context in a changing American society, Botkin was far ahead of his time. While many of his contemporaries were viewing folklore as something apart from the world outside, he was viewing it as a dynamic presence. According to Bruce Jackson, Botkin's primary interest was in people, "in seeing folklore as part of the fabric they construct with which to face the world" (Jackson 1966: xii). Botkin recognized the play-party as part of that fabric, created during a time of shifting values in American life.

Notes

1. See Jackson (1966: viii); Stekert (1975: 335–36).

2. Revivals of the play-party have been reported after the play-party was supposed to have died out (Cunningham 1972). In a reassessment of the play-party, Keith Cunningham recalls that Altha Lea McLendon reported in 1944 that play-parties had been collected in Missouri, North Carolina, Connecticut, Idaho, Maine, Oklahoma, Indiana, Tennessee, Virginia, Georgia, Southern Carolina, Michigan, Ohio, Mississippi, Kentucky, Arkansas, Wisconsin, and Illinois (Cunningham 1972: 13). See also Spurgeon 2005: 57.

3. Motifs linking the Devil and the fiddle are common in folk literature. Note, for example, the following: the Devil takes a violinist when he needs a good fiddler in hell (G303.9.5.8), the Devil appears to a fiddler (G303.25.23.1), the Devil engages a fiddler in fiddling contest (G303.25.23.1.1), and the Devil guides the bow of a violin player (G303.25.23.3). In one North Dakota narrative, collected by Barbara Woods in a Norwegian community, a fiddler gives up his playing (as do his cousins in Norway) after perceiving the Devil among the dancers for whom they are playing (Halpert 1995: 47).

Alan Lomax gives the following summary of opposition to the fiddle and to the use of the swing in dancing (recorded from Jean Ritchie in 1948): "The strict religious folk of the frontier regarded the fiddle as an instrument of the devil, and the square dance as a stepping stone on the road to hell. Barred from dancing, the young people held play parties where the courtly children's games of the past were played and sung by adults, and where other sung-dances, called play-party games, were invented. Although they closely resembled the forbidden square dances, they were held to be innocent so long as all the music was vocal and the dancers didn't cross their feet or swing the girls while dancing" (Lomax 1966: 66 n.).

4. Writing in the 1970s, folklorist and editor of the Arizona publication *AFFword* Keith Cunningham took Botkin to task for not going far enough in celebrating the poetic freshness of the play-party lyrics. To prove his point, he studied the poetics of the lyrics of "Miller Boy," following the analytical methods of John Ciardi, showing how the lyrics perfectly matched the actions of the game itself (Cunningham 1972: 15–20).

5. In an article on the play-party, L.D. Ames offered the following observation: "These play parties were really dances. The players did not dance, however, to the music of instruments, but kept time with various steps to their own singing. But they were not called dances: they were called simply parties. The better class of people in the country did not believe in dancing. Regular dances, where the music was furnished by a 'fiddler,' were held, for the most part, only in the homes of the

rough element. They were generally accompanied by card-playing, and frequently by drunkenness and fighting. The better class ranked dancing, in the moral scale, along with gambling and fishing on Sunday" (Ames 1911: 295).

6. This tune is usually played very quickly. It would have to be slowed considerably to be sung.

7. According to folk music scholar Samuel Bayard, "The Girl I Left Behind Me" had a vigorous life as an instrumental march. "Indeed," he writes, "the tune seems to have been set to words rather often, though its instrumental role predominates because of its popularity as a military march" (Bayard 1982: 325). See also Spaeth 1927: 16–17.

8. Leah Wolford collected a version of "The Girl I Left Behind Me" that retained the original tune, yet the text focused on the theme of a jilted lover, not a man bound for military duty. This second plot is similar to that of an American ballad of the same name but containing a completely different melody and rhythmic style.

> Oh the girl, the girl, the pretty little girl,
> The girl I left behind me.
> She stole my heart and away she ran,
> Away down in South Carolina.
> (Wolford 1959: 156; see also Lomax 1960: 318–19)

9. Even when references to kissing do not appear in actual play-party texts, they can be found in the instructions for the dancers, as in "Here Come Three Dukes A-Riding" (List 1991: 72).

10. See Conn 1978. Conn mentions kissing games being played after work, along with dancing, music, and other games. "Kissing games were favorites," he writes, "particularly spin-the-bottle (in which the fellow spins the bottle and kisses the girl toward whom it points) and post office" (36).

11. The original acetate disk recording is housed in the Indiana University Archives of Traditional Music, Bloomington, Indiana, Accession No. 54-215-F; ATL 171.

12. According to George List, Abraham Lincoln Gary was born in 1868 in a log cabin and raised on his family's farm in Rush County, Indiana. His father was a minister of the Methodist Episcopal church and a circuit rider. He was the fifth of nine children. Gary became a superintendent of schools in Rush County. He earned a degree from the Indiana Law School and took up the practice of law in Rushville, Indiana, where he resided until his death in 1953 (List 1991: 26–27).

13. Some variants of "Weevily Wheat" contain instructions for the dancers:

> Step or two with your weevily wheat,
> Step or two with your barley.
> Step or two with your weevily wheat
> And gather in some barley.
>
> [The facing rows step out and back.]
> (Botkin 1963a: 350)

14. List notes that "Campbellite" was another name given to the Disciples of Christ. "It arose," he says, "on the basis of a desire to develop unity among all Christians and the belief that all should be allowed to worship together as they wished. Its founders were Presbyterian ministers, Martin W. Stone of Kentucky and Thomas Campbell, who came from Ireland seeking a better home for his family" (List 1991: 156–57).

Of Philosophy and the Folk

Intersections in the Thought of Charles Seeger and Benjamin Botkin

Taylor Greer

In the autumn of 1920 Charles Seeger and his first wife, Constance Edson, set out on a self-styled concert tour as a violin-piano duo, beginning in New York, swinging south into Appalachian country, and finally returning home via Washington, D.C. Highlights of their inaugural visit to Washington included performances at the National Theatre in Lafayette Square and a series of outdoor concerts in Rock Creek Park. Their plan was to make enough money playing at small concert venues and private parties to be able to perform for free in school, churches, and fraternal meetings. Promotional arrangements were usually improvised, but the repertoire they played was not: Bach, Mozart, Beethoven, and Brahms (Pescatello 1992: 81–85). They must have been quite a spectacle: a Model T Ford pulling a homemade seventeen-foot trailer with three young children inside.[1] During the rainy season when they could go no further, they settled down for the winter in Pinehurst, North Carolina. Seeger recalled:

> One morning there was a knock at the door again and Jess said they had a job unloading a freight-car . . . and so-and-so was sick and they needed [another] pair of hands, and would I come down. He said, "You'll get paid." So I said of course I'd go, and I unloaded roof tiles for a day, passing them from hand to hand: two in the car, as I remember, one outside on the ground and another one in the truck that was to take them to the place where they were to be put on someone's garage.
>
> At the end of the day I got my pay . . . and [I] asked to whose house the tiles were destined to go. it turned out that they were destined to go to the house [where] I was going to have supper that night. So after getting

home and washing down (it was hard work—I used gloves, but the others didn't; they had rough hands), I put on my black tie and my wife put on her pretty evening dress, and we went in and had a nice supper in the house. I turned the conversation onto the garage, but didn't mention that I had earned I think it was three dollars passing tiles that day. (Seeger 1972: 157–58)

It is appropriate to begin with a story about being on the outside and the inside. During the 1930s Charles Seeger and Benjamin Botkin were pivotal figures in the discovery, transmission, and interpretation of American folk traditions. More important, both were mediators who could live in two different worlds at the same time and still reconcile any differences between them. Both questioned prevailing social attitudes that strictly separated high and low art, literature and folklore, classical music and folk music.

Both believed that popular culture should be given the same respect and recognition as the fine arts and letters: field hollers alongside Homeric odes, blues, bluegrass, and folksong alongside passions, preludes, and plainsong. The story of Botkin's and Seeger's collective efforts to preserve and disseminate American folklore and folksong is too long and rich for this short space. Indeed, the shared commitment of Botkin and Ruth Crawford Seeger (Charles's second wife) to making folk traditions more accessible to a wider audience deserves a chapter in itself. My goal in this chapter is to provide an introduction to Seeger's and Botkin's thought by showing where their intellectual ideals and philosophical ambitions intersect.

Before beginning this comparison, it will be useful to sketch out brief biographical portraits of Botkin and Seeger. Both men turned to the study and preservation of folk traditions after having pursued careers as practicing artists. Born in Boston in 1901 to Jewish immigrants from Lithuania, Benjamin Botkin received his B.A. from Harvard in 1920 and one year later completed a master's degree in English at Columbia University. His new vision of folklore only began to emerge, however, when he accepted his first job teaching English at the University of Oklahoma. Through a series of columns in the *Daily Oklahoman* and later in formal published essays, he developed a view of culture in which cosmopolitanism and provincialism complemented each other. Eager to introduce modern literature to Oklahoma natives, Botkin tried to honor their midwestern tastes and at the same time expand them—or, as he quipped, "to make Oklahoma culture-conscious and Oklahoma-conscious (a two fold pioneering)" (quoted in Hirsch 1987: 11). He also began writing poetry in which he reacted against the aesthetic vision of one of the leading modernists of the period, T. S. Eliot. According to Jerrold Hirsch, where "Eliot saw fragmentation and the threat of cultural decay, Botkin saw pluralism and the opportunity for creating a new revitalized culture" (Hirsch 1987: 12). Botkin eventually brought to fruition his ideal of folklore as literature in his ongoing project celebrating regionalism, which he called *Folk-Say: A Regional Miscellany.*

Eventually Botkin moved to Washington, D.C., and took a leading role in shaping government support of folk culture in organizations such as the Federal Writers' Project. He rejected the notion of the folklorist as specialist, an antiquarian writing for the pleasure of other antiquarians. In short, by preserving and popularizing folklore of the past, he hoped to enrich the present. His audience was the general public, and his subject matter was as eclectic as it was expansive. Between 1944 and 1957 he compiled anthologies on American, southern, western, New England, New York, railroad, and even "sidewalk" lore. Viewed as a whole, the series of anthologies amounted to a political vision of national identity, a folk literature that all Americans could celebrate. For Botkin, the series reflected one of his overarching ideals: to balance the anthologist with the anthropologist. Echoing Carl Sandburg, he described his ideal as "a history in which the people are the historians as well as the history, telling their own story in their own words—Everyman's history, for Everyman to read" (Botkin 1940b: 308).

Born into a middle-class family with strong New England roots, Charles Louis Seeger was nearly a generation older than Botkin. Seeger's artistic aspirations first appeared at Harvard, where he earned his B.A. in music 1908. As an undergraduate, he scorned most of his professors, instead preferring to attend rehearsals and concerts of the Boston Symphony, where he could hear the contemporary music of composers such as Debussy, Strauss, and Mahler. After a short stint in Germany, in 1912 he received an appointment as professor of music at the University of California, Berkeley. He decided to initiate a regimen of self-tutoring in a wide range of fields such as history, anthropology, political theory, and philosophy. In the process, he discovered not only that he loved the life of the mind but that he hoped somehow to reconcile two opposite ways of understanding musical experience: the intellectual and the intuitive or the rational and the practical.

When Seeger moved to New York in the early 1920s he undertook a creative journey that can be divided into several stages. The first stage was to renew the birthright of American experimental composers, which for him meant developing a systematic approach to music composition. In the course of his private teaching, initially with Henry Cowell in California and later with Ruth

Crawford in New York, Seeger developed a technical regimen that preserved and at the same time adapted traditional approaches to music pedagogy, which he called "dissonant counterpoint." These exercises were understood as a prelude to acquiring a new sensibility, which he described as follows: "So it becomes necessary to cultivate 'sounding apart' rather than 'sounding together'—diaphony rather than symphony" (Seeger 1930: 28). Composers such as Cowell, Crawford, and Carl Ruggles became associated with American experimentalism during this period and were dubbed "ultramodernists." Yet Seeger's ultimate goal was not merely to expand a composer's musical technique but rather to broaden the entire inquiry so as to include philosophical questions of consciousness, aesthetic judgment, and human creativity in general. Neglecting his own creative life, Seeger instead focused most of his energy on compositional theory and aesthetics, and in 1931 with Crawford's help, he assembled his diverse teachings into a single volume entitled "Tradition and Experiment in the New Music,"[2] which was published posthumously (Seeger 1994). In a recent article Nancy Rao has explored the question of joint authorship, that is, what role each played in the genesis of the treatise (Rao 1997).

The second stage of Seeger's artistic journey coincided with several dramatic personal and political events. Ruth Crawford, already a successful composer and his constant intellectual and musical companion, became his second wife. In addition, the onset of the Great Depression reawakened their social conscience, and they immersed themselves in the world of radical politics. Charles joined the Composers Collective, a group of passionate New York composers who shared a common idea of fusing avant-garde music and political protest.[3] He also tried his hand at music criticism, writing occasional reviews and commentaries under the pseudonym "Carl Sands" for the *Daily Worker*.

In the third stage of Seeger's journey he and Ruth focused on a particular musical tradition that they had previously either ignored or rejected outright: folk music. When he moved to Washington, D.C., in 1935, Seeger began working for the federal government, initially in the Resettlement Administration and later with the Federal Music Project. Seeger met and befriended Ben Botkin during the late 1930s, when they served on several government agencies together, such as the Joint Committee on Folk Arts (Tick 1997: 256). Hirsch argues that all three shared a common "cultural strategy" to secure a foundation for folklore research in the government and, in the process, foster a more expansive vision of national identity (Hirsch 2007: 196). Many years later Seeger enshrined a playful tribute to Botkin's writings in the title of one of his articles, "The Folkness of the Non-Folk vs. the Non-Folkness of the

Folk" (Jackson 1966). Following his years in Washington, D.C., Seeger returned to academia, teaching for nine years in the Institute of Ethnomusicology at the University of California at Los Angeles.

Despite these dramatic shifts in musical taste and political orientation, during the 1920s and early 1930s Seeger formulated his basic philosophical views about art and human understanding, which would stay constant throughout the rest of his life. His conception of philosophy was based on discovering ways of mediating between extremes—art and science, intuition and logic.

Although Botkin's philosophical aspirations may have been less grandiose than Seeger's, it is fair to say that they were in no way less innovative. His early essays were abstract and speculative, addressing the definition of terms as though he were unveiling a new discipline. In his 1937 essay "The Folkness of the Folk" he focuses on the assumptions bound up in the traditional vocabulary of anthropological debate, arguing that the "mystery and misunderstanding surrounding the terms 'folk' and 'folklore' constitute a species of folklore in itself." In his mind these two terms have a paradoxical relationship: "folk" is more ambiguous; "lore" is more definite "as the homely native word for learning . . . [it] implies knowledge, erudition, doctrine, in custom and belief" (Botkin 1937c: 461–62). In reaction to this terminological confusion, he coined the term "folk-say," to place the emphasis on "*folklore as literature* rather than as science"; this term serves as a double lens, embracing "*literature about the folk as well as literature of the folk*" (Botkin 1931c: 405–6; emphasis in original). Botkin's love of paradox in his theories of folklore reveals a deep kinship with Seeger's approach to music criticism and aesthetic judgment.

Later in the same essay Botkin rejects the physical sciences as a framework for the study of folk traditions, especially any analytical method that treats human beings as mere empirical data. In so doing, he reenacts some of the same arguments for "life philosophy" that the German philosopher Wilhelm Dilthey had proposed in the late nineteenth century. Botkin also rebelled against the prevailing anthropological models of the early twentieth century, in which the folktale was regarded as a "surviving" or vestigial glimpse of the past, frozen in time like a photograph. In its place he proposed a "functional" approach inspired by the writings of Franz Boas, Paul Radin, and Lewis Mumford. Botkin believed that folklore should be considered the "germ plasm rather than the fossils of culture . . . and the study of folklore becomes a study in acculturation—the process by which the folk group adapts to its environment . . . assimilating new experience and generating fresh forms" (Botkin 1937c: 465).

Like Botkin, Seeger became interested in philosophical speculation as an outgrowth of this frustration with the prevailing methods of describing, interpreting, and, indeed, understanding art. In the composition treatise he argues that artists and scientists conceive of musical experience in opposite ways and therefore should have different terms to describe it. In all, he enumerates six fundamental elements of music: pitch, dynamics, timbre, proportion (or rhythm), accent, and tempo. To the artist, they are known as "resources"—all interdependent and understood as a single gestalt. By contrast, to the scientist, these elements are called "functions" and, most important, each is separate and measurable.[4] Ultimately, Seeger imagined a way of blending these two opposing orientations, the artistic and the scientific, into a new, more balanced perspective that he believed belonged to the realm of the music critic. Seeger's theory of music criticism reflects the influence of three contemporary philosophers, two of which I briefly summarize below: Henri Bergson and Bertrand Russell.[5]

It is hard to overestimate the significance of Henri Bergson on the European intellectual landscape at the turn of the century: "In the eyes of Europe's educated public he was clearly THE philosopher, the intellectual spokesman par excellence of the era" (Kolakowski 1985: 1). Bergson drew a sharp distinction between two human faculties, the intuition and the intellect. Intuition was an immediate and apparently infallible activity by which "one places oneself within an object in order to coincide with what is unique in it and consequently inexpressible" (Bergson 1949: 23–24). Reason, by contrast, perceived all things as a means to a practical end; efficiency and simplicity were its watchwords. Bergson also applied this dichotomy to the aesthetic realm: the artist's sensibility was purely intuitive; the nonartist's sensibility, purely rational. For the vast majority it is as if an "opaque veil" blocks our view of nature and ourselves. The artist's mission is not to reveal some statement of universal or mystical truth but rather to begin lifting the veil, to capture some finite, utterly unique aspect of nature or the inner world of the artist. Beginning in the treatise and for the remainder of his life, Seeger shared this passion for intuition, arguing that, above all, artists view their work from an intuitive perspective.

Considering that Bertrand Russell wrote little about the field of aesthetics, he is an unlikely source of inspiration for a new approach to art. Although infamous for his inflammatory attacks on organized religion during the 1920s (such as "Why I Am Not a Christian" and "What I Believe"), Russell was fascinated with mysticism in his earlier writings. In his essay "Mysticism and Logic," written for an American lecture tour in 1914 and published the same year, he offered a sympathetic critique of mystical thought that was to have an enormous influence on Seeger.[6] Russell developed a philosophical model of mediation in which two opposing human faculties or styles of thought were balanced against one another. He describes their interdependence as follows:

> It is common to speak of an opposition between instinct and reason. . . . But in fact the opposition is mainly illusory. Instinct, intuition or insight is what first leads to the beliefs which subsequent reason confirms and confutes; but the confirmation, where it is possible, consists of agreement with other beliefs not less instinctive. Reason is a harmonizing, controlling force rather than a creative one. Even in the most purely logical realm, it is insight that first arrives at what is new. (Russell 1985: 165)

Seeger directly applied this notion of mediating between extremes to his theory of musical criticism, which he developed in a series of articles, culminating in the treatise. In Seeger's view the first phase of understanding is the individual's intuition of beauty, which cannot be qualified or analyzed into parts; either it is present as a whole or it is not. The second and more complex phase is the process by which the two faculties work together; in particular, the initial intuition is examined, questioned, and tested by the faculty of reason. This process is open-ended, without any predetermined goal or conclusion. In a curious passage Seeger describes intuition and reason as though they were two characters in a drama—the mystic and the scientist—who ultimately must be reconciled by the critic: "The mystic may roar down his opposition with eloquence or silence it with enigmas. The scientist may bear it down with incontestable argument. But the critic can do none of these. Relativity is his subject matter and relative, his results—relatively beautiful, relatively true" (Seeger 1994: 65).

Yet there is something paradoxical about Seeger's ideal of music criticism. On the one hand, in some writings he argues that musical experience is ultimately ineffable, beyond description or schematization. No matter how detailed the chart, how precise the diagram, it can never re-create each one's intuitive experience. In that sense, he was thoroughly Bergsonian, never tiring of preaching an intuitionist creed. On the other hand, beginning in his writings during the 1920s Seeger assumes that all of human experience is based on oppositions—art versus science; intuition versus logic; and historical analysis versus study of current practice. Once we become aware of these oppositions, we can then begin the process of balancing or of mediating between them. Ultimately, Seeger's philosophical legacy is for each musician to reenact the critical process that he described and then to measure its success for himself or herself.

In conclusion, let us return to the opening anecdote about passing roofing tiles by day and hors d'oeuvres by night. To dramatize the differences between Seeger's and Botkin's philosophical approaches, let us imagine that they had formed a traveling duo during the late 1930s—a latter-day version of Lewis and Clark; but instead of performing their own music, they had collected and studied examples of folk music and folklore sprinkled around various corners of the country.[7] Seeger would have been the cartographer par excellence, passionate about retracing the sum of their individual journeys in order to map the regions, provinces, and even currents of folk music practice. After completing a series of musical maps, he would have considered what properties all these maps had in common, aiming for a comprehensive theory of cartography. His ultimate goal would have been to develop a general model of the cognitive faculties involved in making music.

Botkin, by contrast, would have been the consummate chronicler. Passionate about collecting stories, he would have compiled an exhaustive record of the folklore that they had encountered in hopes of capturing the rich diversity of human experience. Less interested in human cognition per se, he would have focused more on historical transmission as well as the differences in tone and in language among the individual storytellers. His theoretical interests would have centered on how folklore often unites two opposing temporalities within a single framework: what elements of the past are preserved in a given tale and what new elements from the present are added.

In short, each "folk explorer" would have been inspired by different aspects of their discoveries. Seeger was by nature a generalist, always in search of systematic explanations even if they sometimes led to paradoxes or contradictions. Botkin was part historian, part historiographer, always trying to preserve the integrity of regional traditions and still integrate them within a broader cultural context. Both were humanists who borrowed the methods of science to make sense of artistic experience, whether musical or literary, and yet both were skeptical about the assumptions underlying these methods. Their unique fusion of scientific precision and artistic integrity played a vital role in the preservation and transmission of American folk culture during the mid-twentieth century.

Notes

1. The children were Charles III, John, and Peter Seeger.
2. Ann M. Pescatello, the editor of the second collection of Seeger's works, which

includes the treatise, prefers a slightly different title: "Tradition and Experiment in (the New) Music."

3. For more information about the turbulent years in the Collective, see Dunaway 1980.

4. For more information about Seeger's theories of composition, see Greer 1998: 121–84.

5. The third is Ralph B. Perry. For a detailed overview of his theory of value or axiology and its influence on Seeger's thought, see ibid., 67–77.

6. The original version of Russell's essay "Mysticism and Logic" appeared in *Hibbert Journal* 12 (July 1914): 780–803.

7. There is something ironic about such an imaginary journey: in their original tour, Charles and Constance considered themselves musical missionaries, enlightening their rural audiences with superior music.

No *"urbanized fake folk thing"*
Benjamin Botkin, Sterling Brown, and "Ma Rainey"

Steven B. Shively

In a letter dated May 17, 1929, Charles S. Johnson, founder of *Opportunity* and then-head of the Department of Social Research at Fisk University, suggested that Benjamin Botkin contact Sterling Brown, who was "well-versed in Negro Folklore," especially "Negro music" (Johnson 1929).[1] Johnson's letter was in response to a query from Botkin seeking contributors to *Folk-Say,* the annual collection of folk material (subtitled a "regional miscellany") that he published from 1929 to 1932. And so began the collaboration between Benjamin Botkin and Sterling Brown, which was marked by the commitment of both men to a vision of folklore as the vital, created expression of people "living a life close to the earth" (Brown 1930: 339). Among the first fruits of their joint work was the publication of what is perhaps Brown's best-known poem, "Ma Rainey," in the 1930 issue of *Folk-Say.* Frequently anthologized and often quoted, Brown's poem has long been recognized as a classic of African American folk poetics. Correspondence between Botkin and Brown reveals the lesser-known yet significant contributions that Botkin made to the creation and publication of Brown's poem.[2] "Ma Rainey" represents a landmark expression of African American folk modernism, and a study of the unique partnership between poet and editor offers a view of the creative and political forces seeking to relocate the locus of the New Negro movement in the rural South rather than in Harlem.

Houston Baker, Jr., argued in *Modernism and the Harlem Renaissance* that "[t]he indisputably modern moment in Afro-American discourse arrives, I believe, when the *intellectual* poet [Sterling] Brown, masterfully mantled in the wisdom of his Williams College Phi Beta Kappa education, gives forth the deformative sounds of Ma Rainey" (Baker 1987: 92–93). Brown's poem "Ma

Rainey," Baker says, with its "blending . . . of class and mass . . . constitutes the
essence of black discursive modernism" (93). There is considerable irony in
Baker's selection of a Sterling Brown poem as the pinnacle of the African
American modernism that he suggests found its strongest expression in the
culture of Harlem: Brown never considered himself part of the Harlem movement, explicitly removed himself from that movement, and argued for a
different source for the African American aesthetic. While Baker acknowledges that "there was no Harlem Renaissance . . . until *after* the event" (xvii;
his emphasis), his title, his frequent placement of the world of the New Negro
in an urban setting, and his designation of Harlem as a premier site of the
African American modernist strategy that he calls "mastery of form" and
"deformation of mastery" posit a different aesthetic and political credo than
that of Sterling Brown.[3]

Early in his career as a poet, Brown found an ally in the folklorist Benjamin
Botkin. Botkin was the first to publish several of Brown's finest poems, and
their relationship became mutually beneficial. They formed a lifelong friendship, later working together on various activities of the Federal Writers' Project, especially the collecting of slave narratives later published as *Lay My
Burden Down.*

In 1929 Botkin, a professor of English at the University of Oklahoma, was
still early in his lifework of broadening existing conceptions of the folk, folk
culture, and folk literature; creating and celebrating American diversity and
cultural pluralism; and advocating for the power of a vibrant folk culture to
combat the decay and fragmentation expressed by many literary and cultural
critics of the time. *Folk-Say* was an early expression of this work. Its four
annual issues contained a mixture (at least one some reviewer called it "an
unholy jumble") of poetry, fiction, drama, and nonfiction; original material
as well as retold items; and critical and descriptive articles.[4] The first volume
contained Botkin's manifesto on folklore: "The Folk in Literature: An Introduction to the New Regionalism." Bringing a sense of what was modern to
folklore, Botkin argued in this groundbreaking essay that "the [contempo-
rary] folk artist [was] not content to remain an observer" (Botkin 1929b: 15) or
a chronicler; instead, Botkin advocated the use of folk material to break the
traditional boundaries of the field. His task (and he invited others to do the
same) was not to collect folk material but to *use* folk material to create art.
Botkin did not limit his material to the oral tradition, finding it not in isolated
pockets of rural life where old traditions still hung on but in the work and play
lives of many people.[5] "Realizing that one needs more than observation in
order to interpret," he wrote, the New Regionalism "is bringing to native

materials the maturity of sensitive, civilized minds, supplementing first-hand acquaintance with research and sympathy, getting beneath mere physical sensations to causes and meanings, back of rhapsody and rhetoric to objective expression, and beyond crude mimicry or grand gestures to intelligent attitudes" (1929b: 15).

In 1937, five years after the president of the University of Oklahoma pulled the plug on *Folk-Say*,[6] Botkin drew on his *Folk-Say* experience: "Contemporary and realistic regional literature . . . can create new forms, styles, and modes of literature by drawing upon place, work, and folk for motifs, images, symbols, slogans, and idioms. And more than a mold of literature it can serve as an organizer as well as an interpreter of social thought . . . by showing the failure and breakdown of old patterns and the growth of and hope for new ones" (Botkin 1937f: 157). Botkin's faith in the artistic and humanist value of folk material appealed to Brown, who made a career as both poet and cultural critic.

Excerpts from Botkin's philosophical treatises sound remarkably like comments made by reviewers and critics of Brown's first book of poetry, *Southern Road*. Louis Untermeyer noted that "the book is suffused with the extreme color, the deep suffering and high laughter of workers in cabins and cottonfields, of gangs and gutters, but it vibrates with a less obvious glow—the glow which however variously it may be defined, is immediately perceived and recognized as poetry" (Untermeyer 1932: 250). The *New York Times* reviewer claimed that in Brown's poems "there is everywhere art" ("A Notable New Book" 1932). More recently, Henry Louis Gates, Jr., has argued that "[Brown's] language, densely symbolic, ironical, and naturally indirect, draws upon the idioms, figures, and tones of both the sacred and the profane vernacular traditions, mediating between these in a manner unmatched before or since" (Gates 1987: 227–28). Certainly Brown, who used folk observations to create new poetic forms (like the blues-ballad) and avoided mimicry to create new renditions of folk speech, found a sympathetic note of understanding in Botkin's approach to folklore.

Benjamin Botkin and Sterling Brown would appear at first glance to have little in common. Botkin was white, Jewish, the son of Lithuanian immigrants; Brown was black, the son of a former slave who pastored Lincoln Temple Congregational Church in Washington, D.C. Yet in important ways the two men shared similar experiences and impulses beyond their common birth year of 1901. Botkin learned from his family's artistic and cultural connections: his brother Harry was an accomplished painter with a New York studio, and George and Ira Gershwin were cousins. Brown, too, responded to the cultural heritage of his parents: his mother graduated from Fisk University and participated actively in Washington's African American arts community, and his father directed the School of Theology at Howard University. Brown benefited from the vibrant and varied intellectual atmosphere provided by Dunbar High School, Howard University, and his father's church. Nevertheless, both Botkin and Brown were undoubtedly outsiders when they studied at Harvard: Botkin for his Jewish immigrant heritage, Brown for his skin color.[7] Both men also found their first professional jobs away from the eastern cities in places where they could participate in colorful and authentic folk cultures.

In 1921 Botkin joined the faculty of the English Department at the University of Oklahoma, where he would stay for sixteen years and, according to Jerrold Hirsch, "promote the idea that the allegedly crude life of the provinces was as culturally significant as the culture . . . of the Victorian poet Matthew Arnold" (Hirsch 2003b: 22). Brown spent the six years between earning a master's degree from Harvard and joining the English faculty at Howard working as a teacher at Virginia Seminary and College in Lynchburg, at Lincoln University in Jefferson City, Missouri, and at Nashville's Fisk University.

These important interludes shaped the work of both men, putting them in familiar contact with a lively folk culture. Botkin encountered cowboys (working cowboys, not performers in a Wild West Show), oil-field workers, dirt farmers, and Native Americans, all with unique modes of dress, music, and speech as well as colorful ways of living. He discovered multiple examples of folk groups that illustrated the definition of folk that he would borrow from J. Frank Dobie: "any group of people not cosmopolitan who, independent of academic means, preserve a body of tradition peculiar to themselves" (quoted in Botkin 1929b: 12). Botkin wrote that in Oklahoma he "encounter[ed] a different and more vital variety of word and deed" (quoted in Hirsch 2003b: 22). Brown seems to have been intentional in completing his education by getting out of his university office to meet the folk: "Brown often went out into the surrounding counties, embracing African American folk culture, speech, and lore. He encountered Slim Greer, Mrs. Bibby, and Calvin 'Big Boy' Davis, all of whom would become heroes in his mythmaking projects. On farms, in bars, and in juke joints, he interacted with the rural folk" (Tidwell and Sanders 2007: 6). Brown pursued what Mark Sanders calls a "self-conscious cultivation of an outsider status" that brought him into "intimate contact with the folk art and culture that would serve as a cornerstone of his artistry" (Sanders 1999: 35). The successful alliance between Botkin and Brown might have been predicted due to their shared intellectual backgrounds, their common interests in folklore and experimental poetry, and their commitment to empowering the proletariat through the celebration of folk cultures.

By 1930 Sterling Brown and Benjamin Botkin were undoubtedly aware of each other's work. In the late 1920s both men were contributing regularly to the African American journal *Opportunity*, both publishing reviews, articles, and original poetry. In 1927 Botkin contributed the review essay "Self-Portraiture and Social Criticism in Negro Folk-Song," in which he praised the work of Howard Odum and Guy Johnson, two scholars also admired by Brown. In this essay Botkin commended folk art for its "natural vigor," the "directness of its pathos," "its beauty," and its ability to achieve "emotional release from the sweat and grime of backbreaking soil" (Botkin 1927w: 39). Such qualities are hallmarks of Brown's *Opportunity* poems, including "When de Saints Go Ma'ching Home," which won the magazine's 1929 prize for poetry, and "Riverbank Blues" (1929).

In 1927 *Opportunity* published one of Botkin's poems, "Spectacle," which has little in common with Brown's poetic style but much in common with his aesthetic and thematic impulses:

> Down by the river, where the storm clouds lift,
> I watch the curtain rising on a play.
> The hills grow light, and slowly through the rift
> Of sky unfolds the drama of the day.
>
> Behold the spectacle! as huge as fate
> And silent, for here language plays no part.
> For shame, you poets! who can only prate
> Of beauty, while dumb nature shames your art.
> (Botkin 1927x)

The rhythm of the first line and its details from nature (the river, the storm clouds) would be at home in a poem by Sterling Brown. Botkin's emphasis on performance—the unfolding of the drama of the day—and his recognition that something larger than language is a source of power match some of Brown's ideas. Though it is milder and more subtle than the irony that characterizes much of Brown's writing, Botkin's ironic use of a poem to put down poets likely drew an appreciative glance from Brown, who was publishing similar material at the same time in the same journal.

It is not surprising that Botkin actively sought African American contributions for his folk collection; indeed, Botkin's attention to African American material in *Folk-Say* is remarkable for its day. Botkin signaled his surprising and impressive knowledge of the state of African American literature by recommending at the end of his 1929 prefatory essay a bibliography of eight African American periodicals and twenty-nine books by seventeen black writers. In *Folk-Say* Botkin published poems by Langston Hughes, Waring Cuney, and Lewis Alexander and gave the most extensive treatment to date of Brown: eighteen poems in three issues. In addition to this creative work, Botkin also included in the 1930 *Folk-Say* several critical and interpretive articles and reviews on African American topics. Brown's "The Blues as Folk Poetry" remains a classic early commentary and has been reprinted several times. Brown and Alain Locke collaborated on "Folk Values in a New Medium," a review of two early African American talking movies (*Hallelujah* and *Hearts in Dixie*). Guy Johnson contributed two articles, "The Speech of the Negro" and "Folk Values in Recent Literature on the Negro," and Lowry Wimberly provided a review of Johnson's book on the African American folk hero John Henry.

Botkin signaled his belief that African American literature should not be consigned exclusively to the black magazines like *Crisis* and *Opportunity;* that African American critics should have their opinions presented beside those of luminaries like Mary Austin, Louise Pound, Carl Sandburg, and J. Frank Dobie; and, most significantly, that "Negro Folk Values," to use his phrase, did not exist only in memories of plantation life or on mythic chain gangs or in backwoods hamlets. When given sympathetic voice, "folk values" could become a meaningful presence in contemporary life, could be found in the most innovative forms of expression, and, in the words of Brown and Locke, could "have the highest artistic potentialities" (Brown and Locke 1930: 340).

Correspondence between Botkin and Brown reveals Botkin's substantial editorial contributions to the poems Brown submitted, the intricacies of the poet/editor relationship, and a strong mutual respect. Only a month after their correspondence began, Botkin wrote: "I expect much good to come out our cooperation" (February 5, 1930). For his part, Brown thanked Botkin for his comments on his poems: "I am grateful for your sensitive criticisms." He continued: "My wife is enthusiastic about your changes—An' de ole woman knows—" (February 17, 1930). In the same letter Brown told Botkin that "this is one of the very infrequent times I've ever got criticism that helped." Brown repeatedly indicated a trust in Botkin's judgment, writing that he leaves certain changes "willingly to your editorial blue penciling" (letter dated "Monday Night," but internal evidence points to late February 1930). Brown was particularly deferential in acknowledging Botkin's editorial help: "Am I not responsible to you for some of the best hits in these [poems]—I hate to call them mine." Botkin quickly responded to Brown's submissions, praising his work and the way his poems fit his vision for the project: "Your own poems are just what I want. They couldn't have been any better if they had been written to order" (February 5, 1930). Later Botkin began a letter to Brown: "Yours is just the kind of letter I like to receive. I, too, write to you as friend to friend" (February 21, 1930). Of Brown's article on the blues, Botkin wrote: "I have perfect confidence in [you]."

Despite their obvious respect for each other, neither man blindly or impetuously catered to the other. Responding to some of Botkin's requests for revisions in "Ma Rainey," Brown wrote, "About the Ma Rainey changes: I see your weak places. I need some time to think them over. The difficulties you see, I did struggle with" (February 17, 1930). Faced with a deadline and unable to get Brown's approval of one significant change to "Ma Rainey," Botkin left the second stanza of the poem out of the *Folk-Say* publication, hoping that Brown did not feel too much "violence" had been done to the poem (December 12, 1930). While Brown did not agree with the deletion—he restored the second stanza when "Ma Rainey" appeared in his 1932 book *Southern Road*—the incident did not harm their relationship. (The importance of the *Folk-Say* publication, however, is indicated by the fact that Langston Hughes and Arna Bontemps included the three-stanza version in their 1958 anthology, *The Book of Negro Folklore*.) The Botkin-Brown correspondence reveals the give-and-take of two artists, treating each other with respect but also engaged in the hard work of making a statement, of creating art that makes a difference.

Early in their correspondence Botkin asks Brown: "How is it that such good stuff goes unpublished? Haven't you been sending out? What about *Opportunity*?" (February 5, 1930). At this point in his career, Brown did not want his "stuff," especially "Ma Rainey," published in *Opportunity*, a magazine published in New York City, which was increasingly caught up in what Saunders Redding calls the "obsession" of black writers with Harlem. Redding writes: "The Negro writers' mistake lay in the assumption that what they saw was Negro life, when in reality it was just Harlem life. . . . For literary purposes . . . Harlem became a sort of disease" (Redding 1973: 28). Brown's antipathy toward the idea of an urban locus for African American literary artistry is well known; he frequently stated that he was no Harlemite, that "the whole business of Harlem has been blown out of proportion" (Brown 1996: 185). Mark Sanders notes that "Brown made extensive efforts to place himself outside standard definitions assigned the black arts scene," including Harlem (Sanders 1999: 34). In his *Folk-Say* article on the blues, Brown complains about "urbanized fake folk things" and condemns the renditions of the blues on Broadway, on phonograph records, and in cabarets. Brown's correspondence in the Howard University collection includes a request for poems from Elmer A. Canter, an editor at *Opportunity,* with the words "Hell, No!!!!!" scrawled upon it (July 30, 1931). In addition, he declined Langston Hughes's offer to introduce him to Alfred and Blanche Knopf.

Gates goes so far as to say that *Southern Road* "truly ended the Harlem Renaissance, primarily because it contained a new and distinctly black poetic diction and not merely the vapid and pathetic claim for one" (Gates 1987: 227). Such a statement, while ignoring economic and political forces that diminished the Harlem Renaissance, nevertheless indicates the power of Brown's new direction. While it might have been notably brazen to present his new vision for black aesthetics in an established journal, Brown wanted to go in a different direction. Twice Brown sent Botkin copies of articles he wrote for *Opportunity*—and both times he communicated concerns about the black literary establishment. On February 17, 1930, he writes: "I think the article is explanatory—I am sorrier than you imagine to state that the Southern scene is being neglected by our writers. I do not know any poets who are dealing with it"; and on March 9, 1930, he explains: "I felt [my article] was needed—though I'm not so sure it will avail much."

By contrast, multiple letters reveal that Brown was an active promoter of *Folk-Say,* purchasing copies for gifts, recommending it to libraries and friends, and soliciting contributors, including Langston Hughes, Waring Cuney, James Weldon Johnson, Alain Locke, his students, and others. Hughes responded to Brown: "Thank you for your letter about *Folk-Say.* I've sent them two poems of mine" (April 30, 1930). One of Brown's signature poems (the poem from which he drew the title of his first book, *Southern Road*) was among the first group of his poems to appear in *Folk-Say;* James E. Smethurst points out that "[t]he very title *Southern Road* is a declaration of independence from the 'Harlem Renaissance,' specifically set in opposition to the poem 'Bound No'th Blues' by Langston Hughes" (Smethurst 2003: 70). Furthermore, "Southern Road" and the other *Folk-Say* poems illustrate Brown's revolutionary approach to dialect in poetry. James Weldon Johnson, who had earlier condemned dialect poetry, recognizes in his introduction to *Southern Road* that Brown's poems are "unique" precisely because he writes of "the common, racy, living speech of the Negro in certain phases of *real* life" at a time when most "Negro poets had generally discarded conventionalized dialect" (Johnson 1996: 16–17). To the extent that there was an African American poetry "establishment," Brown clearly disagreed with it and preferred to publish his work with Botkin, to whom he wrote: "You have an inerrancy about folk speech recognition" (February 17, 1930).[8]

Newly ensconced at Howard University and with a solid record of publication in New York–based *Opportunity*, *Crisis*, and Countee Cullen's important anthology *Caroling Dusk*, Brown no doubt could have placed his poems in such outlets, had that been his wish. Instead, he found a fresh, sympathetic editor in Botkin.[9] Publishing his poems in *Folk-Say*, an Oklahoma-based journal far removed not only from the eastern urban centers but also from recognized centers of African American life, reinforced Brown's folk aesthetic. The poem from this group that was destined to earn the most fame was "Ma Rainey." Brown recognized its importance; he wrote to Botkin: "Ma Rainey is my favorite of the lot, and I should like so much for it to be approved. . . . [I]t illustrates some of my ideas better than my prose can" (March 9, 1930). A retrospective examination of "Ma Rainey" reveals those ideas, which would dominate Brown's writing and critical work for the rest of his career.[10]

Ma Rainey

I

When Ma Rainey
Comes to town,
Folks from anyplace
Miles aroun'
From Cape Girardeau,
Poplar Bluff,
Flocks to hear
Ma do her stuff;
Comes flivverin' in,
Or ridin' mules,
Or packed in trains,
Picknickin' fools. . . .
That's what it's like,
Fo' miles on down,
To New Orleans delta
An' Mobile town,

When Ma hits
Anywheres aroun'.

II

Dey comes to hear Ma Rainey from de little river settlements,
From blackbottom cornrows and from lumber camps;
Dey stumble in de hall, jes a-laughin' an' a-cacklin',
Cheerin' lak roarin' water, lak wind in river swamps.

An' some jokers keeps deir laughs a-goin' in de crowded aisles,
An' some folks sits dere waitin' wid deir aches an' miseries,
Till Ma Comes out before dem, a-smilin' gold-toofed smiles
An' Long Boy ripples minors on de black an' yellow keys.

III

O Ma Rainey,
Sing yo' song;
Now you's back
Whah you belong,
Git way inside us,
Keep us strong. . . .

O Ma Rainey,
Li'l an' low;
Sing us 'bout de hard luck
Roun' our do';
Sing us 'bout de lonesome road
We mus' go. . . .

IV

I talked to a fellow, an' the fellow say,
"She jes' catch hold of us, somekindaway.
She sang Backwater Blues one day:
  It rained fo' days an' de skies was dark as night,
  Trouble taken place in de lowlands at night.

  Thundered an' lightened an' the storm begin to roll
  Thousan's of people ain't got no place to go.

  'Den I went an' stood upon some high ol' lonesome hill,
  An looked down on the place where I used to live.

An' den de folks, dey natchally bowed dey heads an' cried,
Bowed dey heavy heads, shet dey moufs up tight an' cried,
An' Ma lef' de stage, an' followed some de folks outside."

Dere wasn't much more de fellow say;
She jes' gits hold of us dataway.
(Brown 1980: 62–63)

The regional folk grounding of the poem is obvious: the location is the rural
South of Missouri and the Mississippi Delta; the people are from the river
bottoms, from the cornrows, from the lumber camps. Cape Girardeau and
Poplar Bluff are near the Bootheel of Missouri, locations Brown came to know
when he explored the region while teaching at Lincoln University in Jefferson
City, Missouri, and at Fisk University in Nashville. The diction of the poem
is rural, southern, and African American. The poem speaks of real people
(jokers, folks, Ma and her accompanist) from real places (the towns and cities
named but also lumber camps and little river settlements) doing the things of
real life (laughing and stumbling and crying). The specific details of picnic
trains and mule-riding farmers contrast with the streetlights, jazzy crowds,
and smoky cabaret clubs evoked by Harlem writers of the time.

Brown's selection of Ma Rainey as his subject is itself a powerful statement
for the proletariat of the rural South. Gertrude "Ma" Rainey and Bessie Smith
today are often grouped together when they are celebrated as the early "black
pearls" of the blues, but in the twenties they were rivals. Both women claimed
the label "Mother of the Blues." Rainey was from Georgia, always maintained
her residence in the South, and returned there in retirement. Her performances were largely in southern tent shows, and when she did northern
engagements they were more often in Chicago, Cleveland, and Cincinnati;
there are only two documented performances in Harlem. She recorded her
records in Chicago. In a 1941 essay on "Folk Literature" in *The Negro Caravan,* Brown praised Rainey's "deep husky voice" and noted her ability to
keep southern audiences "spell-bound" as she "gave them back their songs"
(Brown, Davis, and Lee 1969: 427).

Bessie Smith, in contrast, while she was born and grew up in Tennessee,
lived in Pennsylvania. Angela Davis writes that "[w]hen Harlem emerged as
the cultural capital of black America, Bessie Smith became the quintessential
Harlem blues woman" (Davis 1998: 152). Even when she traveled, Smith's
touring show was often billed as the "Harlem Frolics" or "Harlem Follies"
(Evans 2007: 106). Francis Davis, in *The History of the Blues,* documents that
"Smith had a larger following than Rainey in the North, and a much larger

white audience" (Davis 1995: 77). Unlike Rainey, Smith appeared on Broadway and in one movie; Davis argues that it was "chiefly through the efforts of Carl Van Vechten, a white novelist, photographer, and *Vanity Fair* opinion maker," that she "became a darling of café society and a goddess of the Harlem Renaissance" (Davis 1995: 77). Other blues commentators note the "personal animosity" between Smith and Rainey and label them "formidable rivals."[11] The rivalry became legendary when August Wilson included it in his 1984 play *Ma Rainey's Black Bottom;* he gives Ma this speech: "Bessie what? Ain't nobody thinking about Bessie. I taught Bessie. She ain't doing nothing but imitating me. What I care about Bessie?" (Wilson 1985: 78).

Brown did not shy away from the fray. By selecting Rainey rather than Smith as his blues performer *par excellence* he was sticking it to Van Vechten, whom he later condemned as "one of the worst things that ever happened to people in Harlem" (quoted in Sanders 1999: 99). While Brown sometimes praised Smith, in *Southern Road* his preference for Ma rather than Bessie as the more authentic, more folk-grounded singer is clear. Compare the celebratory poem "Ma Rainey" with "Bessie," in which Brown presents Bessie as a tragic figure and offers his damning judgment on the Harlem that took her down:

> Who will know Bessie now of those who loved her;
> Who of her gawky pals could recognize
> Bess in this woman, gaunt of flesh and painted,
> Despair deep bitten in her soft brown eyes?

> Would the lads who walked with her in dusk-cooled byways
> Know Bessie now should they meet her again?
> Would knowing men of Fifth St. think that Bessie ever
> Was happy-hearted, brave-eyed as she was then?

> Bessie with her plaited hair, Bessie in her gingham,
> Bessie with her bird voice, and laughter like the sun,
> Bess who left behind the stupid, stifling shanties,
> And took her to the cities to get her share of fun. . . .

> Her mammy and her dad for whom she was a darling,
> Who talked of her at night, and dreamt dreams so—
> They wouldn't know her now, even if they were knowing,
> And it's well for them they went just as soon as they did go.

Brown is sympathetic to Bessie's decline, but he characterizes her as a diminished figure, virtually unrecognizable, unhappy, and alone; Ma, in contrast, is powerful, even majestic. "Ma Rainey" has moments of humor—happy, laughing people—but "Bessie" is completely void of comic balance. Significantly, in "Ma Rainey" both Ma and the crowd are vocally alive, whereas in "Bessie" there is neither performance nor audience. Ma is "back whah you belong," but Bessie is hopelessly out of place. Even without the comparison to "Ma Rainey," "Bessie" shows Brown's preference for the rural South over the city: back home she "laugh[ed] like the sun," had parents who worshiped her, and was "happy-hearted" and "brave-eyed." Even the "gawky" and "stupid" folk are preferable to the leering men of the city.

In "Ma Rainey" Brown further heightens the tension between Rainey and Smith—and thus the two aesthetic worlds they represent—by having Rainey sing "Backwater Blues," a song that Angela Davis labels "one of Bessie Smith's greatest compositions" (Davis 1998: 108). Smith's recording was extraordinarily successful from both a popular and sales perspective. Ma Rainey never recorded "Backwater Blues"; while she may very well have sung it in live performances, in critical and popular opinion the song was Bessie's. Brown was well aware of the authorial reality; in *The Negro Caravan*, an anthology he co-edited, he includes a transcription of "Backwater Blues" and credits Smith as the author (Brown, Davis, and Lee 1969: 478).

"Backwater Blues" came to be known as a song about racism and racial victimization, thus lending racial and political overtones to "Ma Rainey." Undoubtedly taking a cue from popular opinion of the time, scholars have long believed the song memorializes the devastating 1927 flood of the Mississippi River, the resultant displacement of thousands of black people, and their subsequent victimization by relief programs (see Davis 1998: 108–109; Oliver 1961: 216–25). David Evans has recently provided careful documentation that Smith wrote "Backwater Blues" two months before the worst of the Mississippi flooding; by examining Smith's touring schedule and recollections of her companions, he concludes that the song was inspired by a Cumberland River flood at Nashville (Evans 2007). While this flood caused significant problems for many people—especially blacks, who tended to live in substandard housing—the actions of Nashville city officials were more helpful than the inhumane and discriminatory response to the more destructive Mississippi River flood.

In the case of Smith's song, popular opinion mattered more than the truth. Because "Backwater Blues" was written such a short time before the Mississippi River flood, which affected more people and got much more publicity than the Cumberland River flood, people linked Smith's song to the "wrong" flood. The terrible aftermath of the Mississippi River flood lingered for many months and coincided with Smith's performances and recording of "Backwater Blues." Evans reports that "by the middle of 1927, 'Back-Water Blues' was well on its way to becoming permanently associated with the flood of the Mississippi River" (Evans 2007: 101). With his close connections to Nashville's Fisk University (he would serve on the faculty there a year after the flood), his residence at the time in Jefferson City, Missouri, and his keen following of African American affairs, Brown undoubtedly knew the truth about the prompt for Bessie's song, just as he knew that it was her song and not Ma Rainey's. When he embeds "Backwater Blues" into "Ma Rainey," Brown subtly selects particular stanzas from Smith's song that emphasized the problems for the folk (the "trouble taken place," the "thousan's" of homeless people, and the destruction of homes) as he makes the proclaimer of the people's trouble and their comforter Ma Rainey instead of Bessie Smith. He further casts Rainey in the role of sustainer of the community, implying that survival of the community itself becomes an act of resistance. Brown's manipulations allow his poem to transcend history and biography to achieve a high degree of universality.

"Ma Rainey," of course, is more than a political or social statement; it is a triumph of Brown's aesthetic craftsmanship. The poem's arrangement reinforces its messages. Joanne Gabbin has noted that the entire poem suggests the performance of a blues singer, emphasizing the symbiotic relationship between the performer and the audience (Gabbin 1985: 160). The first stanza is the gathering of the crowd, the second stanza is the building of anticipation of the performer, the third stanza is the appearance of the artist, and the fourth stanza is the performance itself. Take away either half of the equation—performer or audience—and the poem would be empty indeed. Brown also embeds the classic blues formula in the last grouping of three lines. There is a leading line (its twelve syllables mirroring the twelve-bar musical formula), which is repeated with slight variation, followed by a rhyming third line. These lines are given to "a fellow," a representative of the folk, so that the blues, the "artistry," belongs to both the singer and this representative of the audience as well as, presumably, the poet who narrates the incident. The effect is to bring people together, to unite rather than separate.

Brown further suggests the improvisational nature of the blues in his formulation of the poem's stanzas. In terms of subject, the second stanza improvises on the first (the coming together), and the fourth improvises on the third (the singing). But in terms of line length and voice, the first and third stanzas are linked, as are the second and fourth. Similarly, the second stanza is tied to the fourth with the imagery of line four: the "roarin' water" and the "wind in river swamps" foreground the storm that comes in the performance in stanza four. Brown experimented with bringing together disparate forms—work songs, spirituals, protest songs, and, in the case of "Ma Rainey," the ballad and the blues. Brown creates here what has been called the blues-ballad. In the tradition of the ballad, "Ma Rainey" emphasizes episode and narrative as it tells a story; Brown uses plenty of action verbs to present an event. But the heart of the poem is not in its omniscient, objective telling; it is found, rather, in the emotional, lyric performance of the blues. In "Ma Rainey" Brown put into practice one of Botkin's key principles: folklore is as much about the creation of art as it is about the reporting of art.

Brown continues his emphasis on unity by bringing together in this poem the different participants in the artistic event. This is not just a poem *about* Ma Rainey; she actually sings in the poem. The poet/narrator, the singer, and the audience are not only present but are given voice in the poem. Singer and audience come together not just spiritually, as kindred spirits, but literally when Ma leaves the stage and goes out with the people at the end of the poem. The poem, then, can be read as an indictment of those singers and dancers of the city who stuck to the stage, who appeared in films, who separated themselves from the people. The direction of the poem becomes more personal and more intimate as the third-person narration of the first and second stanzas becomes first-person in stanzas three and four; stanza two speaks of "Dey," but stanza three speaks for "us." Everything builds to the climactic resolution of the poem, the mystical uniting of performer and audience—"she jes' catch hold of us, somekindaway"—that acknowledges the charismatic, transforming, healing power of the true artist fully connecting with her audience.

Of course, "Ma Rainey" is a poem about race, and Brown subtly uses language, setting, people, and events to thread racial implications throughout the poem. The second stanza offers some wonderful examples. The twin puns of "blackbottom cornrows" add authentic humor; one of Ma's trademark lines was "You've seen the rest, now I'm gonna show you the best; Ma's gonna show you her black bottom." The double entendre referred to a popular, jazzy dance of the twenties, thus making "black bottom" a triple pun. The rich, black soil of the bottomlands is linked to Ma's earthiness and sensuality. "Cornrows" is a pun evoking the image of rows of green corn as well as the braided hairstyle common among rural southern black women; prior to the 1960s unstraightened, braided hair occurred more in rural areas than in cities, as expressed in Brown's description of "Bessie with her plaited hair" in "Bessie."[12] The "black an' yellow keys" at the end of the second stanza are also rich with multiple meanings. Readers expect black and white piano keys: Brown avoids the overtly self-conscious placement of black and white together while still calling the contrast to the attention of readers. "Yellow" nicely suggests a mood and scene and echoes the "gold" in Ma's smile in the previous line, but "yellow" also allows a pejorative connotation for whiteness through its suggestion of cowardice. "Yellow" further signifies color differences in the audience, for the word was often used as a label for mixed-race, "yellow" people. The audience that gathered to hear Ma was undoubtedly composed of a mixture of "black an' yellow" folks.

In the hands of a lesser artist, "Ma Rainey" could have become a sad example of the negative stereotyping and even buffoonery that James Weldon Johnson had condemned and that black writers were trying to leave behind. Brown's use of dialect was particularly daring, given the artistic pressures of the time. Images of black people riding mules and stumbling around a performance hall and of Ma and her gold tooth could have been caricatures. Instead, Brown captured the genuineness and spontaneity common to all people who seek a respite from a troubled world. He dignified his folks by giving them authentic emotional responses: the joy of coming to the party, sympathy for those who face troubles, the fear that those troubles might happen to you, and the hope for strength to face the difficulties of life. Readers laugh *with* the revelers, which makes it impossible to laugh *at* them, and Brown gives their blended gaiety the power of roaring water and the wind. Readers bow their heads in respect with the rest of the folks, making it impossible to pity their humbleness, and Brown touches their souls.

"Ma Rainey," then, is a remarkable blend of racial, political, and artistic statements cloaked in genuine humanity. As such, it struck a sympathetic chord with Botkin, whose "interest in questions about poetic language and modern life was tied up from the beginning with the politics of cultural representation" (Hirsch 2003b: 18). Brown's concerns and method in this poem fit what Botkin was trying to accomplish with *Folk-Say*. "Ma Rainey" demonstrates precisely what Botkin believed folklore could do:

> These are the values that folklore can restore to the individual and that the individual should seek to recover for literature—a sense of the continuity of human nature; a sense of art as a response instead of a commodity; a sense of social structure, based on social intelligence and good will; and a sense of pattern, in its primitive use as a model and guide rather than a limit.[13]

When he submitted "Ma Rainey" to Botkin, Brown not only was distancing himself from the more common outlets for explicitly African American poems but also was establishing a relationship with a sympathetic intellectual.

Brown was accurate in his intimation that he was indebted to Botkin for "some of the best hits" in his poem. Responding to Brown's draft, Botkin suggested that Brown change the lines "In picnic trains / Packed tight lak fools" in stanza one to "Or packed in trains, / Picknickin' fools," a change Brown readily accepted. Most significant, however, is Botkin's complaint that stanza three was "dithyrambic." He suggested that Brown recast this section in "folk-speech." Brown took the advice to heart, and the result is one of the more remarkable and memorable passages from Brown's entire poetic canon:

Original	Revised
Ma Rainey	O Ma Rainey
Sing it for your people	Sing yo' song;
You who are of them,	Now you's back
Who know so well the darkness	Whah you belong,
Of their lowland days:	Git way inside us,
Gather from the Yazoo, the Red	Keep us strong. . . .
River Delta,	
From cottonfields of Mississippi,	O Ma Rainey
And Louisiana canebrakes,	Li'l an' low,
And then give them back	Sing us 'bout de hard luck
Their songs,	Roun' our do';
Give back what you have learned	Sing us 'bout de lonesome road
Of their joys and sorrow;	We mus' go. . . .
Give back their unflagging humor	
and the irony,	
That keeps their back up in their	
pressing days.	
O strongvoiced woman,	
Brown and solid planted	
So much still one of them.	
Oh staunch daughter of the low-	
lands,	
So much a daughter that they herd	
to hear you sing,	
Give to them words;	
Teach them to bear.[14]	

Brown's original version, stiff and tedious, speaks of Ma Rainey from the perspective of an outsider, an observer; the revised stanza speaks from the point of view of an insider who directly addresses the singer. The original reads like a catalog, while the revision celebrates that which is mystical about the performer rather than trying to explain all the details of her artistry. The drawn-out vowel sounds and alliteration make the new stanza a song itself. The lazy pace—it is impossible to read the stanza rapidly—contrasts suggestively with the message of power the words proclaim. "Ma Rainey" is Sterling Brown's poem, certainly, but Benjamin Botkin's contributions to its creation and its publication are significant. The fact that the "indisputably modern moment in Afro-American discourse" (Gates 1987: 92) was the blended creation of an eastern Jew and the son of a slave suggests a new vision of multiculturalism and a renewed hope for the power of art.

If some of his fellow travelers would not push the experiment of modernist racial expression as far as he might like, Brown did not waver. In "Ma Rainey" and in other poems and essays, he attacked the Harlem-worship he so disliked as he celebrated the power of the folk artist and the folk people. Always, Brown offered his own brand of African American modernism. He found an unlikely ally in Benjamin Botkin. Together they found—and created—a modernist African American aesthetic based not on artifice or fragmentation but on an essentially democratic impulse that celebrates a plurality of voices: authentic voices, voices of the folk.

Notes

1. The chapter title comes from Brown's complaint about the "urbanized fake folk things" that too often were classified as "The Blues." In contrast to the urban blues, he claimed, blues singers such as Ma Rainey were "of the folk, earthy and genuine" (Brown 1930: 324). Brown's essay "The Blues as Folk Poetry" was published in Botkin's *Folk-Say* in 1930, which also included Brown's poem "Ma Rainey."

2. Brown's letters to Botkin, along with some manuscript drafts of Brown's poems, are housed in the Benjamin A. Botkin collection of Applied Folklore, Archives and Special Collections, University of Nebraska–Lincoln Libraries. Botkin's letters to Brown are housed in the Sterling Brown Papers, Manuscript Division, Moorland-Spingarn Research Center, Howard University, Washington, D.C.

3. I do not know if Baker approved the photo of Ma Rainey that appears on the cover of the paperback edition of his book, but the placement of this photo directly beneath the words "Harlem Renaissance" in the book's title suggests a connection that did not exist. The photo does, however, emphasize the centrality of Brown's poem.

4. Botkin quotes the phrase "an unholy jumble" without identifying the reviewers (Botkin 1935b: 327).

5. Although Botkin included much folklore of the city in the folklore collections he published in the 1950s, *Folk-Say* has a decidedly rural flavor.

6. W.B. Bizzell, concerned about *Folk-Say*'s finances and unhappy about what he considered morally indecent and Communist-leaning selections in the 1932 edition, pronounced the death sentence.

7. Botkin and Brown did not know each other at Harvard. Botkin was an undergraduate from 1916 to 1920, and Brown completed a master's degree in 1923.

8. See Harper 1996 for a fuller discussion of Brown's use of dialect and Johnson's response to it.

9. Botkin, however, seems proud that *Opportunity* praised *Folk-Say*. He wrote to Joseph Brandt, director of the University of Oklahoma Press: "The February *Opportunity*, in an article by Alain Locke on Negro literature of the year, lists *Folk-Say* among the outstanding books on the Negro for 1930 and comments on the new attitude revealed by it toward the Negro as part of American life" (February 9, 1931).

10. The transcription here includes stanza two, omitted by Botkin in *Folk-Say* but restored by Brown in *Southern Road*.

11. See Davis 1995: 71–75.

12. Most dictionaries do not document the use of "cornrow" for a hairstyle until long after Brown wrote the poem; the *Dictionary of American Regional English* (Cambridge, Mass.: Belknap Press of Harvard University Press, 1985), however, notes its use in North Carolina "as of 1900–1910."

13. These remarks are on a single typed sheet of paper under the heading "Folk Values" (1938) in the Botkin Collection at the University of Nebraska–Lincoln.

14. The original wording was included in the version of the poem that Brown sent to Botkin with a letter dated January 26, 1930.

Reading Sterling A. Brown through the Alembic of Benjamin A. Botkin and Folk-Say

JOHN EDGAR TIDWELL

I became interested in folklore because of my desire to write poetry and prose fiction. I was first attracted by certain qualities that I thought the speech of the people had, and I wanted to get for my own writing a flavor, a color, a pungency of speech. Then later I came to something more important—I wanted to get an understanding of people, to acquire an accuracy in the portrayal of their lives.

Sterling A. Brown, "The Approach of the
Creative Writer" ("Conference" 1946)

Folklore is not something far away and long ago, but real and living among us and something from which the writer has more than materials, idiom and forms to gain. He gains a perspective.

Benjamin A. Botkin (1940c)

Impelled by the middle-age predisposition toward self-reflection and stock-taking, Sterling A. Brown, in a 1942 retrospective, looked within himself and offered a succinct but revealing summary of the aesthetic vision that under-girded his career as poet, folklorist, and scholar. Black vernacular speech was, he shared with an audience at the Conference on the Character and State of Studies in Folklore, a portal not just to the way black people talked but, more importantly, to their philosophical vision of the world. A bit self-effacing, Brown reiterated that he did not see himself as a "scientist" but merely an amateur in folklore matters. What attracted him to the field, he said, was a desire to find for his poetry and prose fiction "certain qualities that [he] thought the speech of the people had, and [he] wanted to get for [his] own writing a flavor, a color, pungency of speech."[1] That Brown was able to achieve such a remarkable understanding of the efficacy of the black vernacular is itself a major achievement, given the somewhat genteel circumstances of his birth. En route to forming a folk-based racial identity and view of art, Brown had to divest himself of the rather comfortable status enjoyed by the group into which he was born: what one writer described as "the smug gentility" of Washington's black upper middle class. Of the several venues that made his escape from a confining middle-class ethos possible, too little has been said about Brown's intellectual and personal relationship with Benjamin A. Botkin.

The evolution of a personal relationship is often more easily traced than the evolution of an intellectual one. The claims for intellect can get messy because of the arguments for "influence," usually understood to be a precursor-imitator relationship (as in the imposition of thoughts on a less-informed person). It cannot be said that Brown or Botkin predominated in their relationship, because each one came to an understanding of folklore differently. Under the careful tutelage of Louise Pound and William Duncan Strong at the University of Nebraska, Botkin, armed with an undergraduate degree from Harvard, earned a doctorate in anthropology in 1931. Brown came to the field via his discovery of the New American Poetry of Edwin Arlington Robinson, Robert Frost, Carl Sandburg, Edgar Lee Masters, and Vachel Lindsay; his reconsideration of the poetic significance of Paul Laurence Dunbar and others for whom black orality was important; his careful study of Mark Twain's storytelling; and the teachings of Harvard's George Lyman Kittredge, under whom Brown studied Shakespeare "line by line" and possibly gained insight on Scottish folksongs.

While the intellectual coalescing of these two Harvard graduates might have been happenstance, their personal meeting now seems fortuitous. They were brought together in May of 1929 by Charles S. Johnson, who by this time had organized and assumed the directorship of Fisk's Department of Social Science. He replied to Botkin's letter soliciting contributors to Botkin's new annual publication called *Folk-Say: A Regional Miscellany* by enthusiastically endorsing the marvelous folkloric work being done by both Brown and musicologist John Work. With this introduction, a professional relationship and a friendship of nearly thirty-five years began.[2]

The foundation was firmly laid when Brown contributed eighteen poems and two essays to the 1930, 1931, and 1932 editions of *Folk-Say.* The prospect of finding a place to publish his work certainly recommended *Folk-Say* to Brown; however, an even greater attraction lay in Botkin's formulation of the concept of "folk-say." In 1928, after pondering the efficacy of finding new directions within traditional folklore, Botkin radically altered his own vision of folkloric studies by coining the phrase "folk-say."[3] Against the academic exercise of collecting, collating, cataloguing, and naming types, Botkin came to see with a poet's vision that folklore was something more than a "scientific" exercise. For him, folklore was people saying, doing, talking, and being.

While the term "folk-say" did not dramatically shift the normative grounds of folklore, it clearly positioned Botkin's revisionism against received ideas. The norm, in Bruce Jackson's summary of the opposition that Botkin encountered, was proper annotations and indexes, which Botkin jettisoned. "More than any other folklorist of his generation," Jackson continues, "he was content to let his sources tell their own stories" (Jackson 1976: 1). This conceptual mode engendered a form of validation, a trust, if you will. It affirmed the power and competence of the folk to relate the details and meaning of their own lives. Having left behind a grounding in the aesthetics of a latter-day Victorian sensibility, Brown himself had moved to a similar understanding of the importance of the folk. In part, Brown clarified his thinking about black folk orality/aurality in the intellectual exchanges he had with Botkin. The two young men were teaching each other, in an unusual collaboration, what it meant to realize a folkloristics foregrounded in the lives of people telling their own stories, virtually unmediated by a collector or cataloguer. Part of the learning experience was rooted in their several exchanges over the representation of dialect in print.

Brown was certainly aware of James Weldon Johnson's valedictory about the passing of African American dialect as a viable means of poetic expression. Johnson's observation that black vernacular speech had become overwhelmingly freighted with racial stereotypes forced him to conclude that it had devolved into "two full stops: humor and pathos."[4] But Johnson had written with Paul Laurence Dunbar and his "school" of writers in mind. For him, the use of dialect no longer signaled connections to local colorism or expressed racial consciousness; instead, it reflected the language fostered in minstrelsy, vaudeville, and even the lingering plantation tradition in American expressive culture. It came to represent the denigration associated with racial difference and its stereotypical representation of black people in American literature. Undeterred by Johnson's wide reputation and influence, Brown persisted in seeking to make the living speech of African Americans come alive in print. Botkin contributed to his effort in ways that we have only a few records to substantiate. He accepted Brown's request for assistance with the folk speech in three of his poems: "Southern Road," "Ma Rainey," and "Dark of the Moon."

"Southern Road" was Botkin's favorite, in part because the reliance on the work song signaled a poem that derived from impeccable folk sources. Although he had some problems with the syntax, he felt that "Dark of the Moon," as rooted in folk belief, was also excellent. He viewed "Ma Rainey" as the least successful of the poems, in part, because each verse was rendered in a different stanzaic pattern. So adamant was Botkin in his belief that the poem contained glaring weaknesses that he deliberately omitted the contested second verse when the poem was actually published. The record does not tell us Brown's response to this exercise of editorial license. Brown was self-effacing and referred to himself as "a hopeless amateur [in folklore matters]," who was "not an equipped sociologist" and whose "approach [was] literary rather than scientific," so perhaps he either deferred to Botkin or, more likely, accepted it as a fait accompli since the poem was already published.[5] In this exchange, Brown had the last word. For *Southern Road* (1932), he considerably improved the verse without further assistance from Botkin and restored it to the poem, making "Ma Rainey" one of the finest poems in the collection.[6]

Instead of ending in an irreparable rift, the relationship between Brown and Botkin seems to have deepened. In theory and practice, their understanding of folklore shifted rather dramatically in 1937 to a broader, more flexible description of folk-based activity. In that year Botkin won a Julius Rosenwald Fellowship, which enabled him to leave Oklahoma for Washington to conduct research in southern folk and regional literatures at the Library of Congress. From 1938 to 1941 he occupied a number of positions that permitted him to rethink and refine his theories of folklore: as national folklore editor for the Federal Writers' Project; as co-founder and chairman of the Joint Committee on Folk Arts; and as chief editor when the FWP dissolved into the Writers' Unit of the Library of Congress Project.

The change of venue encouraged Botkin's folkloristic interest to shift, this time from rural life to urban life. Botkin, a self-described "regionalist," became interested in "the neighborhood as a metropolitan region" in the late 1930s (Botkin 1958j: 193). In part, this was a response to the persistence of the "antiquarians," who, as he described them, found value in "only what can be traced back to a past for which they have a nostalgia" (Botkin 1958j: 194). This approach relied heavily upon methods and definitions captured primarily in questionnaires, subject indexes, classifications, instructions on interviewing, and so forth. What probably attracted Brown to this newest paradigm shift was Botkin's effort to make living lore "effect a compromise between folklore as a creative expression and folklore as a cultural record"

(Botkin 1958j: 195). This approach, Botkin further argued, was particularly inviting for the creative writer:

> Folklore, especially living lore, had a special appeal for the creative writer, just as it had a special importance for the Guides. To both it supplied imaginative color and flavor, human interest and human fantasy. It also gave the writer a social and cultural consciousness too often lacking in ivory-tower writing. Finally, it also gave the writer a new subject matter and a new technique. (Botkin 1958j: 196)[7]

Thus "living lore" can be distinguished from "folk-say" in a very important way. For Botkin, the earlier coinage was intended to capture "what the folk-sayer has to say for himself in his own way and in his own words" (Botkin 1958j: 197). But, as a result of his work on the Federal Writers' Project, Botkin "moved away from folk-say as folk literature to folk-say as folk history" (Botkin 1958j: 197). In other words, he now sought to encourage people, in a creative interview, to talk freely about their experiences instead of merely responding to questions. And the narrative would then form part of a bridge between the individual and the group or its community history. For Botkin this imaginative approach in "living lore" encouraged the collection of "folk fantasy" and "idiom." It required the folklorist to be equipped for "creative listening"—to see, to hear, and to be silent (Botkin 1958j: 200, 201).

Botkin's relocation, both physical and ideational, placed him in closer proximity to Brown, who already lived in Washington and taught at Howard University. Brown accepted an appointment as "Editor on Negro Affairs" for the FWP in April 1936. He served intermittently in this half-time position until August 1940. In between, he took time out for a Guggenheim Fellowship from October 1937 to April 1938. As editor, his principal job was to read all copy written by the various local, state, and regional project guidebooks for possible racial misrepresentation and to recommend improvements. This task alone would have been all-consuming, since he received manuscripts from thirty-seven cities and states. But Brown saw his task more broadly than FWP director Henry G. Alsberg and other officials intended. Brown felt that America was poised, for the first time, to take a searching look at African Americans and their place in the social fabric of American life and culture. To do so required a reorienting of vision. White Americans needed to understand not just the contributions that blacks had made to shaping a distinctly American culture but the *centrality* of black people in this cultural production. Persisting in furthering black racial stereotypes would do little to promote an improved vision of blacks' primacy in American cultural expression. It was time, Brown felt, to offer a radical revision of images of African Americans and to demonstrate the composite character of the American experience. It meant situating the experiences of blacks within the central purpose of the FWP.

Like Botkin, then, Brown redefined his folkloric vision. Spurred on by an abiding interest in capturing the flavor, ethos, character, personality, and fidelity of actual people, Brown saw virtue in the Writers' Project's efforts "to document real people telling their own stories in their own words" (Banks 1980: xiii). These accounts, as cultural historian Ann Banks tells us, were variously designated as "life histories, living lore, industrial lore, occupational lore, and narratives" (Banks 1980: xiv). What makes this effort significant for Brown's work is the purpose for collecting these life histories. The Writers' Project had committed itself to publishing a number of life-history collections that, when taken together, "would form a *composite portrait* of America through the storytelling of people from various occupations, regions, and ethnic groups" (Banks 1980: xiv).

The FWP had in mind a foundation in cultural diversity or pluralism. Unlike cultural difference, cultural diversity (couched especially in the description of immigrant experiences) led to wholeness not marginalization. In this case, difference was not being dissolved into a cultural blend, sameness, or "otherness." In effect, cultural pluralism would lead not to an alloy but to a mosaic (Banks 1980: xvi). For Brown, the metaphor of "composite America" posed a dual problem: how could blacks' experiences be convincingly shown to be inherently valuable and how could the portrait of America be shown to be demonstrably incomplete without those experiences? American literary history, he had demonstrated, sagged under the burden of black racial stereotyping, thus suggesting an uninformed effort to devalue black experiences. If the record misrepresented black Americans, then it logically followed that the portrait of America was incomplete. Brown used his editorial position as a corrective for both of these problems.

First, Brown wrote one of the most scathing denunciations of the American creed by showing black life in the shadow of the nation's capitol. Second, using his innovative scholarship on racial stereotypes in American literature, he proffered a life history that refuted the fallacious representation of blacks in the American Guide Series. Third, he proposed a number of writing projects that, if completed, would considerably enlarge the narrative of the black presence in constructing American history. While Botkin, with two exceptions, does not figure directly in Brown's Writers' Project undertakings, an implicitly shared sensibility is revealed.

"The Negro in Washington," the essay that Brown contributed to that enormous guidebook entitled *Washington: City and Capital*, seems to rebuke the urbane, cosmopolitan air of the rest of the tome. "The history of Washington so far sketched," he writes, "has been a chronicle . . . concerning itself mainly with the white population. But the story would be *incomplete* without a discussion of the Negro in Washington" (Brown 1937: 68; emphasis added). Brown sketches a portrait of the famous "Alley System," where people managed to construct homes out of cardboard, galvanized tin, and whatever else they could muster. Moreover, Brown had the temerity to mention, albeit in passing, that "several hundred former slaves . . . were settled in Arlington in a place known as 'Freedmen's Village,' *very near a tract of land left by George Washington Parke Custis to his colored daughter, Maria Syphax*" (Brown 1937: 75; emphasis added). Instead of provoking moral outrage at the horrifying living conditions, the reference to the indiscretion of George Washington's stepgrandson, whom he later adopted, resulted in a firestorm of criticism of Brown and the WPA. Robert Reynolds, a U.S. senator from North Carolina, found this reference to be Communist-inspired and called for proof.[8] When Brown and others returned to the Library of Congress to look for the documents containing this information, they discovered that their sources had "disappeared." Thus they were deprived of the opportunity to exonerate themselves by showing that George Custis had not only fathered a black daughter but also bequeathed her a tract of land.

Less controversial was Brown's participation in *The Negro in Virginia* (1940). From his editor's chair at the FWP, Brown assisted in bringing this pioneering foray into the history of American slavery into print. Roscoe E. Lewis, the Virginia Project's senior researcher for this book, sought Brown's assistance in devising a strategy to refute the renowned historian U. B. Phillips's inscribed notion of blacks as contented servitors and of slavery as educationally beneficial. By judiciously combining historical discussions of Virginia slave law with ex-slave personal testimony, Lewis and Brown avoided mere sagas or sensationalized accounts. As personal and written accounts coalesced, the Virginia story deepened into a collective history, remarkably candid in its revelation of actual slave life.

In his primary function as editor, though, Brown confronted considerable opposition from southern sources when it came to commenting on the representation of blacks in their guidebooks. The many editorial conflicts with state and regional project directors demonstrate how editorial decisions became tests of wills in determining accuracy, comprehensiveness, and omissions of blacks from guidebook material. For instance, Myrtle Miles, Alabama state project director, resented what she called the "Washington attitude," which would not allow the observation that "the Negro, in three or four decades before the Civil War, was economically and spiritually better off than in the twenty years after the War."[9] And South Carolina's state director, Mable Montgomery, rather angrily expressed her resentment that the Beaufort County Guidebook could not say: "A picturesque group, these Negroes are a happy people, primitive, indolent, unmoral, philosophical and deeply religious. For all their seventy odd years of freedom, they have never really learned to stand alone. Without the white man to furnish part-time employment, to lend them money and give them advice, it is doubtful if they could exist."[10]

Similarly, in an early draft of the manuscript titled "Studies of Negro Survival Types in Coastal Georgia" (ca. 1937), Mary Granger, director of the Savannah Unit of the Federal Writers' Project, compiled a body of material, as she said, in an effort "to preserve customs, habits, superstitions, beliefs, songs, and typical expressions of a generation closely linked to its native African origin."[11] What Granger proposed to preserve proved to be shopworn representations of African survivals in American culture:

> The reception following a wedding is the scene of unrestrained enjoyment. The host has killed no bullock as his forefathers did in Africa, but the delicacies of his adopted land are abundantly provided. Feasting and dancing loosen the thin veneer of civilization, and to the music of a Negro band the young people dance untiringly. As the musicians cast off the borrowed beat of the white man's music and pour out strange rhythms [*sic*] from the past, the dancers create barbaric steps, jerking their bodies and clapping their hands with hilarity. The older ones who have "got religion" do not lend themselves to this frivolity. They sit and keep time with their feet, being cautious not to lift the heel, for to do so would be sin.[12]

Brown cogently challenged the representations of "unrestrained enjoyment," "the thin veneer of civilization" loosened by feasting and dancing, and "barbaric steps" and received support from both Botkin and Alsberg.

> [They] respected the provincial sense of place and understood that every place possesses its own unique qualities and heritage, but they did not believe a sense of place was incompatible with a more cosmopolitan perspective informed by knowledge of other traditions. They saw American culture as pluralistic, a mosaic of different traditions, each contributing to the whole. But they found it difficult to communicate such a vision to state and local units. (quoted in Joyner 1940: xiii)

The struggle between cosmopolitanism and provincialism deepened into ideological differences about the focus of folkloric directions. As Charles Joyner summarizes it, "the Savannah Unit's concentration on African survivals rather than on Blacks' acculturation found itself in conflict with the vision of the national office, which felt that *Drums and Shadows* promoted a racist theory of cultural evolution in which cultural traits might 'survive' from earlier, more 'primitive' stages of culture but would eventually disappear under contact with more 'advanced' cultures" (Joyner 1940: xiii–xiv).

Brown, less theoretical in his analysis, soundly refuted the shallow connection that Granger used to link Africa with Afro-America: (1) the tracing of survivals was not completely proven in this study; (2) the author lacked requisite training in anthropology, sociology, or folklore; (3) stereotypes were used as explanatory concepts; (4) no attempt was made to analyze the American context of the coastal black Americans by comparing them with poor white Americans and with Europeans; and (5) the study derived its supportive evidence from the untrustworthy authority of travelers' reports, missionaries' diaries, and so forth.[13] Brown urged fieldworkers to avoid the white southern opinion of black folklore and to allow blacks to speak for themselves. Only in this way, he argued, would the representation of black Americans be extricated from the hopeless mire of stereotyping. That alone, Brown believed, "could ultimately bring about a revitalization of American culture" (Joyner 1940: xxiii).

In this expected editorial task, Brown was accused of encroaching upon southern hegemony. Cloaked in the conservative rhetoric of southern protectionism, the directors of projects in the South fought determinedly to keep "outsiders" from dictating their business. Undaunted by their carping criticism, Brown set forth an ambitious series of studies that would further refute the fallacious representation of black Americans by these "unreconstructed Confederates": "Portrait of the Negro as American," "Go Down, Moses: The Struggle against Slavery," "A Selective Bibliography on the Negro," "A Book on Negro Folklore," and "A Book of Narratives by Ex-Slaves." The common thread connecting these proposals was the folk-say idea of sources telling their own stories. Botkin was to be a collaborator on the last two projects, and his *Lay My Burden Down: A Folk History of Slavery* (1945) leaned on Brown for language to use in explaining the authenticity of the narratives he assembled.

Brown was instrumental in reformulating the questions that interviewers (most of whom were white) asked the ex-slaves about the conditions under which they had lived and worked. The "simple and 'homely' instructions and questions" issued to interviewers failed in their purpose: "When and where

were you born?" and "What kind of work did you do?" elicited mainly routine, predictably truncated responses (Botkin 1945h: xi). The most telling
example of Brown's revisionism is the memo that Charles T. Davis and Henry
Louis Gates reprinted in *The Slave's Narrative,* under the title "On Dialect
Usage" (Gates and Davis 1985). Although here Brown was concerned with
simplifying the recording of black speech in print, he restated a principle that
had become fundamental to understanding the revisionist view of language:
"truth to idiom is more important . . . than truth to pronunciation" (Gates
and Davis 1985: 37), This expressed Brown's belief that people speaking for
themselves present the most authentic self-portrait. Orthographic gymnastics
had led to distortions of images, circumscribing the representation of blacks
as a bevy of racial stereotypes. The way out of this illogic was to listen to the
voices of the folk.

After idiom, the most important feature was to encourage the ex-slaves to
reveal the perspectives that they would not otherwise share with white interviewers under many circumstances. Questions about what ex-slaves expected
after emancipation could lead to "nothing" or to long, discursive responses
about wandering, searching, and hoping. The principal way to encourage the
ex-slaves' to speak freely was to get out of the way and let them talk. And
Brown's questions paved the way for such openness and candor.

Brown's self-described role in the collecting of ex-slave narratives reveals
how he, like Botkin, participated in a folkloristics that had implications for
social history. The common denominator was language. In narrating the
stories of their lives and their careers, these survivors of a national policy that
viewed them as chattel were revealing themselves as human beings. As in his
studies of African Americans in literature and culture, Brown felt that he had
to deal at least somewhat with their folksongs, folk tales, folk sayings, and folk
speech. But even these cultural expressions had undergone change since their
origins in slavery. Not to be left behind in the shifting parameters defining
folklore, he confessed to being influenced by the recent trend "toward the
collecting and the using of a living folklore—the living speech of the people"
("Conference" 1946: 506). This trend extended folklore into what he termed
"living-people-lore, [into an analysis] of groups that couldn't be considered
folk except by a very wide extension of the word" (506). In this category, he
listed specifically "the urban group of jazz musicians whose language is fascinating, whose music is fascinating, and whose way of life is fascinating"
(506). Armed with these expectations for a new, more malleable concept of
folklore, Brown continued in 1942 a quest actually begun earlier. He sought to
capture the sounds, the moods, the distinctiveness of southern black life—a

journey (funded by the Rosenwald Foundation) to collect materials for *A Negro Looks at the South*, published posthumously in 2007.

The final collaboration planned between Brown and Botkin reveals their efforts to reprise a shared belief in folklore. But time and circumstance had seemingly passed them by. This moment deepens our understanding of Brown by shedding light on a little-explored facet of his life. Here we see Botkin as less an active participant than one who is forced to hear but not comment on a confession. In early July 1965 Brown, a bit agitated if not mildly manic, consulted with Botkin on a collection that would reassert their authority in the wake of *The Book of Negro Folklore*, edited by Langston Hughes and Arna Bontemps (1958). Brown obsessed on the idea that their selections came from raids on *The Negro Caravan* (1941), which he co-edited with Arthur P. Davis and Ulysses Lee, and Botkin's *Lay My Burden Down* (1945). Brown found enough duplication to give him pause. In the midst of a near-diatribe against these alleged interlopers, he uncharacteristically offered a confessional moment—a rarely articulated intimate view of his innermost feelings and emotions, unmediated by thoughtful reflection. With the spontaneity of suppressed feeling suddenly given voice, Brown recalled his educational experiences at Williams College (1918–22) and Harvard (1922–23 and 1931–32) and a problem he rarely discussed: his sense of alienation from the other students at these two prestigious schools.

Alienation, of course, manifests itself differently, depending on the material circumstances of the subject. At times, Brown experienced a callous indifference: a denial of his presence and personhood, confirming the old axiom that being ignored is one of the cruelest experiences. At other times, he felt alienated by blatant personal discrimination. This was illustrated by his "friendship" with another Phi Beta Kappa student, a white graduate of Dartmouth, with whom he developed an acquaintance at Harvard in 1922–23. Their relationship was warm and cordial until the Dartmouth grad found out that the really fair-skinned Brown was African American. From that moment on, he refused to acknowledge Brown. For Brown, this indignity was a grim reminder of his undergraduate life at Williams College that continued to haunt him in his later years. In other instances, Brown experienced an alienation that was institutionally driven, such as the official policies that Harvard (like Princeton, Williams, Vassar, and other schools) established in the early 1920s. Historian Marcia Graham Synnott wrote that Harvard administrators Charles W. Eliot and A. Lawrence Lowell "both thought racial tension would be decreased if Negroes and whites lived as separate entities under equal protection of the laws" (Synnott 1979: 52). As Synnott further argues, southern whites were considered more valuable to both Lowell and Harvard than blacks were. This belief formed the subtext of Lowell's premise that off-campus (not dormitory) housing was a form of protection for black students.

Brown seldom revealed the depth of these feelings publicly. He projected an outward image of strength and virility. Like all strong men, however, he had his inner fragilities. To dwell on feelings such as alienation would, for him, risk subverting this outward persona. It might reveal a personal weakness, undermine his achievements, or exacerbate an anger that festered just below the surface. In unguarded moments, he sometimes retreated into himself and remembered aloud the feelings he had suppressed. After having a bit too much to drink or in an emotional outburst, he bared his soul to the few who were in his company. But as quickly as he succumbed to the powerful need for self-revelation, he again took refuge in the realm of safe disclosure, usually by praising the high quality of the education he received. The names of luminaries rolled easily from his tongue: George Dutton and Bliss Perry at Williams; George Lyman Kittredge, F.O. Mathiessen, and many others at Harvard. It was as if, on balance, teaching him how to see literature freshly, analytically, and intelligently was compensation for the personal indignity he suffered and endured. Publicly, he refused to play victim to the overt and covert racism that he experienced. Privately, the hurt was embedded in his psyche and in his soul.

In an anecdote he shared with Botkin on that day in July 1965, Brown barely concealed the extent to which he was chagrined by such differential treatment. Resorting to storytelling, he revisited "Rinehart" (or "Reinhardt"), one of Harvard's oldest legends. As described in a *Christian Science Monitor* article (October 19, 1935):

> Back in the dim distant limbo of Harvard glory when students hurried from the Castle Square Theater in Boston to catch the 12 o'clock horsecar at Park Street for Harvard Square there lived one Reinhardt, on the top floor of Thayer Hall, one of the most ancient dormitories in the Yard. Reinhardt had no friends. Each night he heard men standing below the windows of Thayer Hall calling to friends above. Gradually the dormitory would empty of men, until finally he alone remained in his solitary room. Reinhardt was naturally timid. He feared that the other men in the dormitory would realize that he had no friends and as a consequence that he would become a marked man. Finally, his fear crystallized into action.
>
> He formed the habit of hiding himself in the bushes near Thayer in the late evenings and shouting his own name up to his window. Occa-

sionally he would disguise his voice, making it appear that he had several friends who called him each night. But one night the students found out his ruse. Thereafter many voices shouted his name nightly, in teasing fun. (2)

Brown never identified with the Rinehart whose loneliness prompted the charade of having numerous friends among his fellow students; nor did he express an affinity with the Rinehart who became "a marked man," an object of ridicule and scorn. Despite his denials, Brown certainly shared with Rinehart a sense of loneliness, exacerbated in his own case by the alienation precipitated by his racial identification.

Brown carefully orchestrated the manner in which he was to be perceived— or at least he thought so. During the day spent with Botkin, Brown used another strategy to protect his inner self from being exposed: he inverted the personal and made it public. The recollection of the Rinehart story frames an intensely personal revelation, but Brown quickly masks the personal by reframing the story into a public rumination. As in a brainstorming session, Brown vacillates among a number of ideas. For one thing, he said he "never felt compelled to go back" to Harvard.[14] The encouragement of Botkin and Nobel laureate Ralph Bunche convinced him to do otherwise. During the graduation ceremonies, Brown saw Bunche in line with the other members of the Board of Overseers, decked out in "tails and top hats." "I wish I could have been Tom Sawyer," he said in jest, "and knocked it off."[15] In this mischievous comment, Brown betrays a bit of his own feeling about the school. As he meandered around Harvard Yard, "self-pity" and "racism" weighing upon him, he walked around a wrought iron fence: "I was pitying myself until I met an Irishman (a 6th grade dropout) who managed to get me through, since I didn't have a ticket to graduation. This for me was the democracy of the work gang, and it restored my faith in Harvard."[16]

The "democracy of the work gang" captures Brown's allegiance and reaffirms his commitment to an aesthetic and intellectual preoccupation with Americans he felt were historically disenfranchised: African Americans, Irish, and Jews. In using the phrase, he offers a reminder of how his interests in minorities began earlier, when he discovered literary parallels among these groups and sought to explore them systematically in course theses as a doctoral student at Harvard in 1931–32.[17] Arguably, his "rescue" by the Irish worker alerted him to his good experiences at Harvard. But the humor is double-edged. Brown is proud to see how Bunche's earned doctorate in government at Harvard and many other accomplishments merited him a seat on the Board of Overseers. But his pride in Bunche is also tempered by a tinge of envy. Bunche's success reminds Brown how Anglo-Saxon, Old French, Old English—"everything old," he frequently quipped—turned him off and played a role in his decision not to seek a doctorate from Harvard.

On that day in July 1965, Brown deftly inverted the discourse from private to public expression by announcing his intentions to write a series of essays titled "Rinehart Revisited." He envisioned essays on the question: "What Negroes have gone to Harvard and what have they done?" A partial list would include Bunche, historian Rayford Logan, and Howard University president Mordecai Johnson. In this venue, there would be no discussion of alienation. If anything the book would be guided by another permutation of the Rinehart story, the one found in Botkin's *A Treasury of New England Folklore:* " 'Heads out!' was the cry in Walker's day; 'Oh, Rinehart!' began later, after a student of that name had repeatedly been shouted to by noisy friends. In course of time it has become a sort of Harvard battle-cry, and the word is now used to describe any Yard uproar, in which the calling of Mr. Rinehart's undying name is an inevitable feature" (Botkin 1965m: 522). This version best describes the chaos that Brown foregrounds as a rallying cry, not for riotous behavior but for social activism. What has each figure that Brown writes about in his essay collection done to advance the cause of African American citizenship and full participation in the American Dream?

Brown's life and art were a rallying call to resist the dehumanization of people of color and to promote racial pride. Instead of succumbing to social or political defeatism and victimization, he found precept and example in the people Langston Hughes affectionately called "the low down folks."[18] For both writers, black folk were sources of racial and cultural authenticity, people who were unconcerned with being anyone except themselves. Brown sought to identify with this social group.

Bruce Jackson's comment in summarizing the significance of Botkin's life and career can equally be applied to Brown. "Ben," wrote Jackson, "was a scholar, not an academic, so he never suffered that limitation of apparent respectability and he was willing to admit equally the voice of someone he met on the road and the copy on the back of a cereal box" (Jackson 1976: 1). The democratic vision of Botkin manifests itself in a love and admiration of the folk. He was not constrained by the academic impulse to define folklore with "scientific" certitude. For to do so would be to fit the experience into narrow boxes and therefore truncate its malleability, flexibility, and resonance.

Brown, however, had to play the role of scholar because his positioning in the academy forced him into challenging the scholarship that sought to define black life and character narrowly. Nevertheless, as many have observed, he wrote with the soul of a poet. For he spent his entire life trying to free himself from the regimen of teaching and research so that he could concentrate on being a creative writer. Neither Brown nor Botkin would live to see the completion of the magnum opus that each had planned as a summary of his professional life. *American Myths and Symbols* was intended to be the culmination of Botkin's lifelong pursuits. It seems likely that *A Negro Looks at the South* was to be the one book that would mark Brown as a prose writer. Its multigenre or multivocal character was the prose equivalent of his excellent poetry.

Brown and Botkin shared aesthetic beliefs in the possibilities of the folk. To say this is to understand how both rooted themselves in the distilled metaphysic of a people often disparaged or, worse, ignored. *Folk-Say*, appropriately, provides an alembic through which to read their appreciative expression. For it encourages us, as Jackson says of Botkin, to "listen, listen, listen" (Jackson 1976: 6).

Notes

1. Sterling A. Brown, "The Approach of the Creative Artist" ("Conference" 1946: 506). It should be noted that the actual conference occurred in 1942. Shortly after the conference ended, many of the participants were called to take part in the war effort; thus the original proceedings remained in typescript for four years before this condensed version was published.

2. Letter, Charles S. Johnson to Benjamin A. Botkin, May 17, 1929, B. A. Botkin Papers, Special Collections and Preservation, University of Nebraska–Lincoln.

3. Botkin recounted the origins of "folk-say" in a number of essays, including Botkin 1931c and 1935b.

4. James Weldon Johnson, preface to *Book of American Negro Poetry* (1922) (New York: Harcourt Brace and World, Inc., 1931), 41.

5. Letter, Sterling A. Brown to Benjamin A. Botkin, 19 January 1930, B. A. Botkin Papers, Special Collections and Preservation, University of Nebraska–Lincoln.

6. See Steven Shively's excellent discussion of the versions of Brown's "Ma Rainey" in this volume.

7. It is worth noting that Botkin also expresses this idea in *Fighting Words* (1940), selected materials from the Third American Writers' Congress, held in New York, June 2–5, 1939. Editor Donald Ogden Stewart records Botkin's comments this way: "Folklore is not something far away and long ago, but real and living among us and something from which the writer has more than materials, idiom, and forms to gain. He gains a point of view" (Botkin 1940c: 11).

8. "W.P.A. Guidebook Arouses Fuss," in *Appendix to the Congressional Record*, vol. 84, part 12 (April 1939), 1359–60.

9. National Archives (hereafter NA), RG 69 WPA, Box 200, Folder "Incoming Letters by States," Memo Miles to Alsberg, March 4, 1937.

10. NA, RG 69 WPA, Box 201, Folder "Beaufort, S.C.," typescript "Original Beaufort Article," 6.

11. NA, RG 69 FWP, Box 201, Folder "Studies of Negro Survival Types in Coastal Georgia," i.

12. Ibid., 27.

13. NA, RG 69 FWP, Box 201, Folder "Georgia File," Letter from Brown to Granger, February 24, 1938. Brown consults two sociologists for their criticism. See in the same folder the letter from E. Franklin Frazier to Brown, February 1, 1938; and letter from W. O. Brown to Sterling A. Brown, January 28, 1938.

14. Cassette #99 in Benjamin A. Botkin Papers, Special Collections and Preservation, University of Nebraska–Lincoln (July 3, 1965).

15. Ibid.

16. Ibid.

17. John Edgar Tidwell and John S. Wright, "Steady and Unaccusing: An Interview with Sterling A. Brown," *Callaloo* 21.4 (1998): 816.

18. Langston Hughes, "The Negro Artist and the Racial Mountain," *Nation* (June 23, 1926), 693.

PART THREE

Botkin in His Own Words

Essays

Intimate Notebook
City Summer

His mind was a large cool room, full of light, with queer symbols on the walls. His words were delicate brushwork, and his movements were fine penstrokes.

Standing beside him at the foot of the Palisades, on our first Sunday together, looking across at the skyline of the city, from which I had been absent as long as I had been separated from him, I was happy in a rich sense of kinship and communion. We were reunited. Again I was to know the ripe, stimulating satisfaction of two minds striking fire from each other, and to behold dazzling revelations of unsuspected powers and resources within me. Again I was to see things through his clearer, steadier eyes.

He was still teaching mathematics, still creating his symbolic, automatic poems and his tenuous, detached pictures; and those cryptic eyes of the visionary still had an hypnotic effect on me. Being with him and hearing him talk was like a séance, with his look and his tone saying: Relax. Breathe deeply. Let your mind drift. Your eyes are going to close. . . .

This essay appeared in *Space* 1 (July 1934): 35–36, the monthly that Botkin founded and edited between May 1934 and April 1935. The magazine fit the format of the many experimental "little magazines" that proliferated in the 1920s. The title *Space* was consciously chosen to reflect a more modernist orientation than the conventional topics addressed in *Time* magazine. Botkin's account of the friendship between two unnamed male companions reads like a diary entry. It is personal, cryptic, and intimate, even as it evokes the vibrancy of its Coney Island setting. By incorporating personal details that rarely found their way into his prose in a setting as vivid as Coney Island was in the 1930s popular imagination, Botkin produced one of his more curious pieces of writing. Coney Island is a "littered strip of shore" whose liveliness drowns out the "boom of the surf." It emerges as an urban spectacle, a place to observe and be observed that welcomes everyone equally and as such serves as a powerful symbol of the new kind of mass popular culture that Botkin found so worthy of study.

II told him how amazing and beautiful it was that we never really lose the things that are worthwhile, the things that really belong to us. This was life's unconscious fulfillment. I had drifted away from him, not heard from him for two years, and now without any effort on my part, drawn by an irresistible force, I had come back to him.

———

Talking, we picked our way among the campers and picnickers who encumbered our feet like driftwood washed ashore from opposite Manhattan. As animalism anticked in bathing suits, I remarked on the pure joy of physical contact. "Yes, like horses rubbing their necks together," he said—an observation commemorated in his pen and ink sketch of Sunday at the Palisades, entitled "Necking: Horses Do It."

On this littered strip of shore, in full view of the city's skyscrapers, with the beetle-browed cliffs above and behind us—amidst the thick intimacy of city folk on an outing, gregariousness triumphing over solitude—we spoke much of love and friendship. Drawing strength and sweetness from his hardness, like honey out of the rock, I felt that I had outgrown all my other friends and that I was closer to him than ever. What had become, I asked myself, of all the friends I had clung to so importunately, so passionately? I had lost them by the very storm and stress with which I had sought to retain them. There was something destroying and doomed to destruction about these unequal, violent relationships, these voluminous letters of mine, these too ready outpourings of the soul, my too insistent pleading, fussing, and fretting. . . . Quiet and immovable as a rock he stood there beside me, as if he had always been there and always would be there.

———

Young and old cavorted and frolicked about us. In their intense good-timing, they were quite oblivious of us as we paused to study one group after another. Alone and as it were invisible in our detachment, we noted and annotated each striking pose, each comic gesture, in this pretty girl or that prankish young man—the unconscious grace of the children—the heavier, sodden content of their elders. With not so much as a sandwich or a girl between us, we looked on curiously and dispassionately at the gorging and the gamboling. To the strumming of ukeleles and guitars and the diffused mumble of phonographs, we moved among the summer cottages, tents, campfires, and camp tables, like lone spectators at a carnival remaining to eavesdrop on the performers.

———

He told me how pleased he was to find that I had attained to something of his equanimity. His philosophic detachment from life was not ascetic, he explained. He did not reject life. On the contrary, he took all life to him, and yet, by *accepting* everything, good and bad, he was in a position to *reject* everything too.

He ran on in his mesmeric voice, soothing, insinuating, commanding. His voice was doing things to me, as it had done the evening I watched him hypnotize a student in his room in Norman. "Don't pay attention to anything that happens. . . . Do just what I tell you. . . . Sleep, sleep. . . ." His words were fingers, softly, firmly stroking, massaging away the ache in my brow and temples.

About us, we decided, lay the material and the scene of the great American comedy. (He was writing a play.) You can't make these things up, he said. You can only take them from life.

I agreed. It is scenes like this, I said, in which people recognize themselves in all their unconscious absurdities and follies, with little touches of pathos and beauty, that make true, natural comedy.

If everything, he resumed, like the things about us, appears acceptable and equitable to him, then nothing really matters. He can thus get along without any of the things that otherwise might seem so important to him. Take his attitude toward his friends. Call it selfish if you will, but he never goes out of his way for them. He doesn't like letter-writing, and he never writes letters. But, more than that, he cannot become too intimate with a person without somehow losing the stimulus of contact. That was his objection to marriage. The people and things you are with every day, you soon take for granted, like the furniture in your room.

I admitted the attenuating effect of intimacy, by a kind of attrition, but people have more than one point of contact with each other—the people that one would want to have contact with—and as one is worn away another is formed. Or it is like katabolism and anabolism. For every tearing down there is a building up; there is constant loss and renewal. . . . He did not know that I was living for the letter I received every day and in the two letters I wrote daily.

———

All during summer school we appeased our minds and senses by wandering among pleasure-seekers on week-end excursions—always on the outside looking on. Our boat trip to Coney Island was symbolic of our companionship. As the piers slid past us with the clouds, we sat on the deck reading some of my poems, to the accompaniment of the strings of the boat musicians and the slapdash of the waves on the side of the boat, oblivious of everyone and everything except the one rhythm within us and outside us. Life was free; and my thoughts of love and beauty were more free and full than life itself—they *were* life.

What I mean is that the crowds satisfied our thirst for physical contact, for the actual, for concrete variety and excitement, while our inner selves remained apart, communing in a dream, satisfying our need of abstraction, our hunger for the ideal. In the parks, along the river, at the Stadium concerts, at the seashore—on buses, subway trains, ferry-boats, and excursion steamers—we continued to observe and discuss and reflect. In perfect calm and security, buoyed up by the poise and detachment of our contemplation, we were borne upon the surface of an unfathomable seething welter of contacts and impressions; and time and space were a sea that held no terrors for us.

————

The bowl of the Stadium matched the sky, with faces like the countless stars and music like that of the spheres—Strauss's Death and Transfiguration.

The East Side in a bathing suit. Coney Island sent up a roar that drowned out the boom of the surf. As clouds rolled up, black and ominous, and the water grew livid, the wind raised a spray of sand and sea and agitated blowing papers and fleeing bathers.

Why are people on the beach so funny? I asked. If you take the thing seriously and come here to have a strenuous good time, you will probably be disappointed. But if you only look on, it's the greatest cure for the blues. . . . All reformers should be obliged to come here, he said. At the side show, he remarked that the people who came to look were as funny as the freaks; and we were more absorbed in them than we were in Kiki the Billiken, Libbera the double-bodied man, and Eva the serpent-girl.

At night, from our chairs on the upper deck of the return boat, we watched in silence the cool spectacle of sea and sky, where lightning played in orange and violet searchlights, while about us lulling harp and violin throbbed faintly and lovers wrestled hotly in the dark.

————

Then one Sunday I failed to show up, without having let him know in advance. I didn't think he could be affected by such things, but he said afterwards that he had been disappointed. I was, too, when I learned that he had gone to Atlantic Highlands alone. We were like lovers who depended too much on each other and were growing restive under each other's watchfulness, yet were jealous of each other's freedom.

The strain between us increased. Another time I dropped in to tell him that I should have to call off our projected visit to Harlem, since school would be out soon and I should be leaving immediately for Boston. I did not tell him that I had already been to Harlem with another friend on the previous Sunday, when I had been unable to get him on the telephone.

That was the last time I saw him. Immediately after summer school he was leaving for Oklahoma to visit his family, and upon inquiry I felt relieved to know that he would be starting back East before I should return to Norman in the fall, that we might even pass each other on the way.

We had lost our hold on each other. My mind had become too burdened with work and homesickness to "go under" easily any longer. And was I not finding his impassivity too cold, too rare and fine, and beginning to long for more human warmth—trying to assert my independence of him as he constantly asserted his independence of me—trying to test his strength by finding his weakness?

Though in this way and by such arguments I was proving my superiority, not without reluctance I was fighting his will, which gripped mine like bands of steel encased in velvet. Faintly I regretted the loss of that equanimity which for a summer had closed my eyes to the actualities of time and change, the bitterness of conflict and separation, with his "Relax; breathe deeply; everything is everywhere, everywhere is beauty."

Introduction to the Folk-Say Series

The first *Folk-Say* (a paper-bound volume of 151 pages, published in June, 1929, and long out of print) was a local product with aspirations and vibrations beyond the borders of Oklahoma. The work (with few exceptions) of Oklahoma writers, decorated by Oklahoma artists, and printed by the newly established University of Oklahoma Press as its first book, for the Oklahoma Folklore Society *redivivus* as Number I of its *Publications,* the volume attracted a good deal of local interest. The Southwest in general accorded it serious consideration as a statement and demonstration of a new theory of regionalism, but it went virtually unnoticed in the East until the following year, when reviews appeared by Louise Pound, Howard Mumford Jones, and Carey Mc-Williams, the last as late as December 1930, on the eve of the publication of the second volume.

What the critics thought of *Folk-Say* at the time is more or less what I think of it now in looking back over the volume. I am conscious of its limitations, and at the same time of the possibilities that defied and even surmounted these limitations. Not strictly a folklore publication or a work of literature, slightly more than a magazine but not quite a book, it must have piqued, puzzled, and irritated its readers. Yet for the susceptible, there was doubtless some appeal in the sincerity and naïveté of the performance; a challenging and refreshing breath of the West and flavor of the soil in this native medley of

---

This essay originally appeared in the *Southwest Review* 20 (July 1935): 321–29, as part of an article entitled "*Folk-Say* and *Space:* Their Genesis and Exodus." The text is from this edition. It is Botkin's fullest account of how the first book published by the University of Oklahoma Press came to fruition in 1929. He explains the origin of his most famous term, the neologism "folk-say." This coinage, as much as anything Botkin formulated, embodies his belief that folklore mediates among various levels of culture, from the most common to the most erudite. Yet as an indication of Botkin's truest frame of aesthetic and cultural reference, folk-say's vitality remains dependent on its "return to the lower level of the folk." Folk-say reflects Botkin's long-held contention that folklore is ever "in the making," as much a feature of the present as of the past.

Indian legends, tall tales, old-timers' reminiscences, old songs, folk cures, dialect, slang, and local-color sketches and poems, adorned with a buffalo-head colophon and cowboy, Indian, and oil-field motifs.

Perhaps the discerning recognized *Folk-Say* for what it was, the excitement of a tenderfoot discovering the West. In 1921 I had come to the University of Oklahoma to teach English. Encountering a different and more vital variety of word and deed, I soon found my Harvard accent and "indifference" breaking down. The picturesqueness of the local scene, character, speech, custom, and history, and the possibilities of Oklahoma as literary material, struck me with the force of the Oklahoma wind and stuck to me like a sandbur. I inaugurated a series of Thursday evenings on modern poetry and participated in the organization and activities of the campus poetry society. Those first two years of trying to make Oklahoma culture-conscious and Oklahoma-conscious (a twofold pioneering) were varied with summers of communing with Nature in both her Eastern and Western moods. After I had had a chance to compare notes on the two, on a canoe trip in the Adirondacks and a subsequent summer touring the Southwest and hitchhiking on the Coast, the East tempo-rarily won. There followed two *Wanderjahre,* in the course of which I drifted uncertainly and half-heartedly in and out of the Columbia graduate school, an East Side cramming school, a couple of settlement houses, the Village, *Rhythmus,* and the homes and shops of foreigners to whom I taught English from Brooklyn to the Bronx. Then the West recalled me.

In November 1925 I contributed to the *University of Oklahoma Magazine* an article on "The Oklahoma Manner in Poetry." I had taken my cue and title from H. L. Mencken's widely syndicated and publicized statement that "There is almost, indeed, an Oklahoma literature, or, at all events, an Oklahoma manner." Was this, I inquired, earnestly and with as much grace as I could muster, writing from and about a state bordering on the same Mr. Mencken's "Sahara of the Bozart"—was this "the harlequin school of sophisticated lyrists fostered by John McClure, which is after all an exotic transplanted to Okla-homa soil, or the homespun local-color school (a plant of more hardy native stock) in which writers like Stanley Vestal . . . are doing pioneer work with frontier material?"

Upon reading my critique, in which I attempted little more than a rough-and-ready botanical classification, roaming as I might through the whole field of contemporary Oklahoma poetry and stopping to pluck many a wildflower and not a few weeds by the way, Mr. Mencken asked me to collect a number of specimens for the *American Mercury.* The appearance of the "Oklahoma Poets" in May 1926, the first, as it happened, of a series of state anthologies, convinced me that Oklahoma suffered no lack of sweet singers, but that what it and they needed most was a press-agent and promotion.

Having thrown in my lot with the native school, I sought to prove to the readers of the *University of Oklahoma Magazine* for November 1926 that there is a native school, "The Frontier in American Poetry," not only in Oklahoma but in Illinois, Iowa, Nebraska, and New Mexico, and proclaimed it as the hope and promise of an "enlightened regional consciousness."

Out of my loyalty to the native tradition, which was among other things "restoring the oral popular tradition to poetry," grew my interest in folk-song, particularly the play-party song, of which I made an extensive collection among my students during 1926–27. From that time on poetry and folklore went hand in hand. In 1927, as president of Oklahoma Writers, I diverted the programs from the usual shop talk of markets and technique to a consideration of Oklahoma backgrounds and materials. In the same year, as poetry editor of the new State Chamber of Commerce publication, *My Oklahoma,* in a series of critical collections I continued to boom "Oklahoma Poets, Inc." alongside of oil, cotton, alfalfa, broom-corn, and other staples. Finally, in 1928, when I became president of the Oklahoma Folklore Society, I proposed that it issue a publication, after the example of the Texas society.

Then, as at various times, I flirted with the idea of a quarterly, a journal of folklore and folk-motifs, a magazine of native expression, to provide a medium midway between the scholarly journal and the general magazine for the floating material that does not fit into the conventional molds of the market, for the native, regional, and traditional wherever they might be found. Material for the first issue, scheduled for May 1928, was collected in a month; but since the expected endowment was not forthcoming, I had to wait until autumn, when I compromised on an annual. The autumn brought Joseph A. Brandt to the University to assume charge of the University Press. We met one night at a party and immediately confided to each other our dreams—his of a press that would publish books and mine of a book that would find a press. So we pooled our enthusiasm for Oklahoma literature, and the result was the publication of *Folk-Say: A Regional Miscellany.*

I had already coined the title *Folk-Say* the previous spring, by analogy with William Barnes's homely Anglo-Saxon term for preface, "Fore-Say." "The difference between *Folk-Say* and folklore," I wrote, "is the difference between poetry and history." For *Folk-Say* was not a substitute or synonym for folklore, as some have misconstrued it, but an extension of the older term to include literature *about* the folk as well as *of* the folk and to center attention on the oral, story-telling phases of living lore conceived as literary material. In my introduction I considered the relation of lore to literature and tried to make three points: first, that in every age literature moves on two levels, that of the folk and that of "culture," and whenever it is in need of revitalizing it must return to the lower level of the folk; second, that we have in America not one folk group but many folk groups, as many as there are regions and cultural and economic groupings within those regions; and third, that the new region-alists are distinguished from the earlier local-colorists by a more profound interest in culture in the broader sense—folk culture, in particular.

But as the literary material made up only about a third of the volume, and did not even pretend to great literary merit, it failed to bulk very large in the whole, its deficiencies being made more apparent by its isolation in a separate section. Moreover, although I tried to emphasize the contemporary aspects of folklore by including "lore in the making" and by demonstrating the interplay between folk and popular influences, the emphasis seemed to fall on the primitive and frontier past. *Folk-Say* was still in the stage of collection and comment, rather than of interpretation, and still in the "sentimental and anachronistic" stage. To effect a fusion of lore and literature, of folk and regional elements, and to make the book a true medium of native expression rather than merely a source of native material, we should have to increase its size, scope, and variety. Right then, in particular, I saw that I must substantiate my claims with more ample and careful documentation and illustration.

Back East that summer, I conferred with past or prospective contributors and advisers—with Frank Shay, Lynn Riggs, Percy MacKaye, Barrett H. Clark, and Frank Ernest Hill. MacKaye appeared in the role of a guardian spirit, like a character out of one of his own masques, and was to prove the attendant genius of the second volume, prefaced as it was by a quotation from him and including the entire MacKaye family—five strong. He urged the need of pre-serving integrity by freedom from journalism and false sophistication and, above all, by upholding creative standards. For although there would be peo-ple who would try to make me a folklorist or an anthropologist and one thing or another, my one test for material, whether raw or finished, must be: Is it creative? And, ultimately, the personality of the editor must give unity and purpose, shape and tone, to the collection.

Accordingly, my goal became "creative editing"—editing to express editor's and contributors' personalities as one organic whole. I also became interested, through the work of Percy and Benton MacKaye, Howard W. Odum, and Lewis Mumford, in creative conservation of human resources; and as my part in cultural regionalism, I persevered in my intention to make *Folk-Say* the organic focus of the folk and regional movement in America.

All these aims had been expressed or implied in the 1929 "Prospectus and Pronunciamento." Not that I did not mean or want *Folk-Say* to change: it was intended as an experiment, a series of variations on the theme of regionalism, changing in response to changing times, criticism, and my own changing notions of what a regional miscellany should be. I was simply trying to interpret and perhaps occasionally to direct the trend that I perceived; and often enough I was surprised by the turn of events. But beneath the changes in method and emphasis there was a certain organic unity of conception which I felt intuitively and tried to preserve.

The task was now one of integration. The next volume must achieve not only scope and structure but an inter-regional synthesis. After threshing out with myself and others the problem of whether to confine the material to Oklahoma (or Oklahoma and the Southwest), or to take in other regions, I decided on the latter course. That had been inherent in the original conception of a regional miscellany as a miscellany of regions as well as of regional material.

Before we could get anywhere, it seemed necessary to define and clarify our terms. Having encountered considerable variance of opinion as to the meaning of "folk" and its place in art, I asked a number of representative writers, critics, collectors, and scholars, each speaking for his own region and specialty, to contribute to a symposium on the question: Who are the folk in America, and what can they contribute to American language and literature? and on the whole subject of the dangers, limitations, and problems besetting the artist who tries to merge his individual consciousness with that of the group and to convert folk materials into art.

At the time when I read proof on the 1930 volume, which did not appear until November, I was on leave at the University of Nebraska completing my graduate work and doctoral dissertation under Louise Pound. And like my brain, the book was stuffed with facts, dates, references, citations, and arguments. There could be no doubt that *Folk-Say* had sold out to the professors and was in the throes of the scholarly and cultural stage of regionalism. That year the book was published under the imprint of the Press instead of that of the Folklore Society. When the book had been small and priced at a dollar, membership in the Society could very well include a copy. Now that the volume ran to 473 pages and had to be priced at five dollars, the *Publications* of the Society, which had no funds or financial organization, had to be abandoned. To insure the success of the enlarged volume, the Press had spared no expense in publishing and I no pains in editing, and we were rewarded with increased distribution and wide and thorough notices. The comments ranged all the way from "an unholy jumble" to "an orderly and complementary progression." In view of my strenuous efforts at welding a great mass and diversity of material into a semblance of unified sequence—in seven sections, with bibliographical supplement and elaborate notes and index—"orderly jumble" and "unholy progression" would have been more like it.

After reckoning up our losses and gains, we found the latter to be on the side of increased geographical representation and a better understanding of the real business of a regional miscellany, which was "to bring forth significant creative work." This time the creative work received first honors, the answers to my pandemonium of a symposium being generally adjudged, as in my introduction I had already declared them to be, quibbling, conflicting, and evasive. Having got the research bug out of my system, I could now relax and breathe freely in the more congenial atmosphere of literature. I dropped my large and learned advisory board and scrapped the scholarly and critical apparatus. Both the 1931 and 1932 volumes opened and closed with poems, contained a larger proportion of poetry, and were prefaced with poetic inscriptions instead of essays. The last volume even had a poetic sub-title—"The Land Is Ours." By abandoning arbitrary classification into sections, I could now let the material flow as it would, in a rhythmic pattern, with greater flexibility of structure and unity of effect—somewhat like a musical suite or a sequence of moods. I had also learned that the group of sketches and poems rather than the individual sketch or poem is the unit of a miscellany, which should resemble a gallery or an annual exhibit rather than a clearinghouse. Contributors were given not only more liberal representation, in number as well as length of contributions, but greater freedom of treatment. The emphasis was contemporary, on cultural, racial, and class conflicts, rather than on survivals, and the forms were experimental rather than traditional.

To the third volume there still clung a certain amount of quaintness, old-timeyness, and "cute dialect," but a crisper note of lusty, hard-boiled youth was beginning to be heard, with a sharper impact of personality and a stronger and harder personal idiom. The 1932 volume caught up and confirmed these tendencies; it became, in fact, a medium for the discovery of talent and for the free expression of personality and of social ideals in connection with the theme of the relation of individual to environment—of the worker to the soil, of the artist to his horizons.

This volume was temporarily suppressed and the series was ultimately suspended when Oklahomans discovered that folklore and creative writing based

on the folk are not always fit reading for children. Puritanism and its expression in censorship were still forces to be reckoned with by the artist in Oklahoma as elsewhere.

   This outline of the career of *Folk-Say* from 1928 to 1932 may give the reader
the impression that it was a straightforward and clear-cut development. As a
matter of fact, there were many halts, oblique movements, counter-marches,
skirmishes, retreats, losses and recoveries of ground. Thus in 1931 I published a
contribution I had rejected in 1929—and for the same reason: because it was
more *masses* than *folk*. By then I had taken to heart Carey McWilliams's
objection to the first *Folk-Say:* "In times so strenuous as ours, it is rather
annoying to discover intelligent men devoting their talents to such tasks as
listing the animals and plants in Oklahoma folk-cures and noting, with infan-
tile delight, the eroticisms in the folk-speech of taxi-drivers." I had also taken
to heart his other stricture, that in returning to the folk the modern mind
must will to be naïve. By 1932 *Folk-Say* had returned to the modern world—
and it had willed to be conscious, critical, even sophisticated. But was it
still folk? With that question, and partly because of it, *Folk-Say* ended as it
had begun.

Regionalism: Cult or Culture?

I

A "region" is the geographer's term for an "environmental type" in which "the geographic elements are combined in certain definite and constant relations." From the concept of the natural region—physiographic, geological, climatic, biotic, etc.—the human geographer, correlating social with organic and inorganic factors, has developed the concept of the cultural landscape and the human use region. From human geography, in turn, the sociologist and the ethnologist have derived the concepts of the sociological region and the culture area. In the natural, social, and engineering sciences, "regionalism" as a discipline has not only opened up new research leads but supplied the technique of regional planning.

It is when one attempts to transfer regionalism to the psychological or imaginative environment and apply it to literature as a critical or creative approach that it becomes mixed with localism, provincialism, and sectionalism, and is in danger of becoming a cult. There are, in fact, almost as many cults as there are regional cultures, since the regionalists radically disagree as to the sources, methods, and aims of regional literature, and each region tends to interpret regionalism in terms of its own historical shibboleths and local gods.

In this essay, which appeared in the *English Journal* 25 (March 1936): 181–85, Botkin addresses a debate about literary regionalism that was current among American writers. He brings a multidisciplinary perspective to what was generally a literary conversation via his knowledge of scholarship in anthropology, sociology, and literary history. Botkin rejects both the kind of conservative regionalism that privileges one group over another and the Marxist literary critics, who, by occupying a realm of impractical abstraction, ignore just the kind of regional differences in working-class culture that Botkin felt they should be examining. Drawing on cutting-edge cultural anthropology, he urges novelists and poets to focus on "regional 'acceptances and resistances' in relation to the class struggle." For current readers, the essay provides insight into the complexity of debates surrounding the regionalist movement, which is too often remembered as a facile effort to celebrate the virtues of rural life as a means of forestalling the inexorable spread of urban mass culture.

Like humanism, regionalism has given rise to a lively controversy, in which, in this case, not only literary critics but scientists have engaged. Because of its equivocal position between art and science, regional literature has drawn fire from both sides.

II

Thus, on the one hand, the sociological pretensions of literary regionalism have irked the social scientists. To Howard W. Odum, for example, "what is often popularly called the new regionalism in literature. . . . is little more than 'the infatuation of the regionalists for their land and folk.' . . . a sort of sentimental romanticism for the local area or for the historical period." By confusing end with means and exploiting regional differences for their own sake, literary regionalism becomes the very opposite of scientific regionalism, which, starting with the local and the past, uses these as "material for the study of the present and the future," to give "both explanation and power to the whole social fabric as well as to the separate regional units."

On the other hand, the cruder documentary side of self-conscious, antiquarian regionalism gives offense to those refined spiritual natures whose regionalism breathes only the rarefied atmosphere of pure art. To them regionalism is "private tradition" as distinguished from "public tradition" ("sectionalism," or "politics"), "the perpetual participation in the community by the individual" rather than "a philosophy of the community of interest." From "preoccupation with one's own social background which, whether we love it or hate it, we do not take for granted," regionalism is sublimated into Allen Tate's "immediate, organic sense of life in which the fine artist works"—or, more frankly, Glenway Wescott's "patrimony, an unearned inheritance, of knowledge of life, of skeletons in the closet."

Unfortunately, the rattling of the skeletons in the closet prevents even unconscious regionalism from being completely unconscious. "Tradition is not a defense of tradition," but every tradition is unconsciously on the defensive and even consciously apologetic, so that the distinction breaks down, as all distinctions must which rest upon a "dualism of contemplation and action" and a dichotomy between perception and judgment.

A similar fate befalls Donald Davidson's division of southern novelists into "social historians" and "social critics" simply on the basis of loyalty or disloyalty to the southern tradition. Under the combined attack of these "critics" and an invading metropolitan industrialism, the very defenses of the southern tradition crumble; and, despairing of an unconscious regionalism, Mr. Davidson likewise breaks down, to confess that the movement has "already passed far beyond the stage of romantic nostalgia and into the broader field of economics, politics, religion, and social culture." What the southern tradition has to offer in the way of a practical program of reform is shrouded in the mysteries of agrarian economics; but a glimpse of the "reanimation of American life" to result from the new southern "rebellion against uniformity in American life" is afforded by this enumeration of "southern qualities":

> . . . . that southern writing is much nearer to the English tradition than American writing in general, and content to be within that tradition; that it is more restrained and conservative, less wasteful in experiment, perhaps better informed; that it has easiness and warmth, repose, mellowness, humor, maybe the broad sense of the world which comes, paradoxically, from a comparative retirement from the world.

III

The dilemma of the southern agrarians is the dilemma of all regionalists who conceive of regionalism as taking things for granted and accepting as final a certain social order—whether it be the South before the Civil War, the West before the passing of the frontier, or the Indian and Spanish Southwest before the Anglo-American invasion. Yet, in spite of the obvious anachronisms of neo-primitive, Arcadian, and Utopian regional revivals, especially of a genteel-tradition-in-decay-and-at-bay, preaching a theological war between an agrarian god and an industrial devil, regionalism is capable of solid contemporary and forward-looking social significance.

In view of the genuine regional basis and bearing of such proletarian works as *To Make My Bread* and *Tobacco Road,* Marxist critics like V.F. Calverton and Granville Hicks have overreached themselves in their wholesale indictment of regionalism as "escape," in the same category as the agrarian "flight from reality." As Constance Rourke has pointed out, Frederick Jackson Turner's "significance of sections" concerns the economist as much as it does the historian; and if the Marxist is not actually cutting himself off from a valuable ally in regionalism, he cannot afford to overlook regional "acceptances and resistances" in relation to the class struggle. Without this identification of the folk with the proletariat—the folk being basic to regional society—any "intellectual synthesis," whether Marxist or agrarian, is in danger of becoming a myth and an abstraction.

But apart from economic issues, certain cultural and aesthetic values emerge from the smoke of the regionalist conflict. The first and chief of these is the sense of a native tradition growing by folk accretions out of local cultures. In spite of the tendency of the provinces to substitute their local myths for the national myth of Americanism (the *ignis fatuus* of the "national period" of our literature), regionalism has done much to destroy that "all-destroying abstraction, America," and to initiate a new period in American literary history.

Aside from its importance to literary criticism and scholarship, the conception of a regionally differentiated and interregionally related culture has something to offer to literature, namely, a subject matter (the physical and cultural landscape, local customs, character, speech, etc.), a technique (folk and native modes of expression, style, rhythm, imagery, symbolism), a point of view (the social ideal of a planned society and the cultural values derived from tradition as "the liberator, not the confiner").

Seen in this light, regionalism, properly controlled, becomes a valuable social adjunct to literature, along with ethnology, folklore, and Marxist economics. In common with these disciplines, regionalism marks a trend away from the belletristic—pure literature and absolute poetry—toward a social and cultural art—from literary anarchy toward literary collectivism. In this development the regional movement has served to fix attention on the fact that, as individual character and action are inseparable from the social structure, so geographical relationships tend to modify both. Regional coherences exist, to be cultivated by the artist, not for a peculiar glamour of picturesqueness or quaintness or for the false security of "limited solidarities," but as a means to the end of social portraiture and the expression of personality with roots.

In this regional literature a natural division of labor exists between the provincial writer, on the side of the rural and agrarian, and the metropolitan writer, on the side of the urban and industrial. But both are essential to a complete picture of the American scene and the American folk and to the new ideology and mythology emerging alike from our buried cultures and our submerged classes.

WPA and Folklore Research: "Bread and Song"

A New York City field worker was interviewing a Croatian tailor on Jugoslav folk songs. "Business is bad," he said. "I have a big family. I just can't put my head to anything. The chain stores—they just—" and he made a cutting gesture across his throat. "We ought to live, too. Something happen if this keep up. . . . If I could only put my head to it for a few hours, I could make a few songs." "Oh, don't be worried," replied the interviewer. "I understand. You see, I don't come from Park Avenue either. Millions of people have a hard time now. People will be ordering things for Christmas. Cheer up! Think of the folk melodies you sang as a youth. Forget bread for a few hours!" Then to herself she thought: "My, how you lied! You certainly didn't sing when you had no bread! You couldn't remember your own name, never mind about where you lived four years ago. And your voice was so weak the relief investigator told you to take a couple of sips of water to moisten your throat! . . . Great thing this bread and song business! Messy world, messy world! We're all in the same

This essay was first delivered as a paper at the annual meeting of the Modern Language Association and then published in *Southern Folklore Quarterly* 3 (March 1939): 7–14. It contains some of Botkin's most eloquent, vigorous, inspiring, and frequently quoted lines about the role of the folklorist in a democratic society and what knowledge of the nation's diverse lore can offer American culture. On one level it chronicles and vigorously defends WPA folklore programs. On another level it is an invitation to academic folklorists to support and participate in these programs. The essay reflects the WPA Joint Committee on Folklore's efforts to reach out to scholars and to try to make permanent programs that were initially set up to be temporary. That is part of the reason he also spoke to the American Historical Association about "Folklore as a Neglected Source of Social History" and built bridges between the committee and the American Council of Learned Societies. From the opening lines of the essay, Botkin, the engaged scholar, makes points that speak to the social realities of the day as well as to methodological questions. In new forms, those realities and those questions are still with us. He never lets the reader forget that a society and a culture need both bread and song.

boat—Yugoslav, American, Mayflower descendant, all mixed up in this bread and song thing. . . ."

Bread and song have always had an intimate relation to each other in the creation and preservation of folklore, and they have an even more peculiar significance in WPA folklore research. Throughout we stress the relation between art and life, between work and culture. And our security-wage field workers, earning a precarious living of some twenty dollars a week, or much less, need not be taught this lesson. They learned it on the sidewalks of New York skipping rope and bouncing ball:

> Left! Left! I had a good job and I left!
> First the hired me, then they fired me,
> Then by golly I left!
> Left! Left a wife and fourteen kids.
> Right! Right! Right on the kitchen floor.

> I should worry, I should care,
>   I should marry a millionaire.
>   He should die, I should cry,
>   I should marry another guy.

At school they wrote in each other's autograph albums:

> Take a local,
> Take an express.
> Don't get off
> Till you reach success.

And in the shadow of war and hunger they jingled this ironic bit of nonsense:

> Hailie Selassie was a kind old man,
> He lit the match to the frying pan.
> When all the people tasted the beef
> They all trucked off to the home relief.

An inventory of the 355,000 words of New York City folklore copy collected by a staff of 27 workers in 88 working days from September through December 1938 reveals in its titles and text the predominance of industrial and occupational interests in the folklore of the metropolis. The childhood level of playing at work and at being grown-up becomes the adolescent and adult level of work and amusement—the epic of construction, excavation and wrecking (subways, skyscrapers, bridges), transportation (taxi, bus, subway), shipping (railroads, trucking, long-shore and maritime industry), the needle trades (garments, fur, hats), the white collar professions and retail trades (department stores, peddling, markets), and the symphony of New York night life—taxi dance halls, night clubs, honky tonks. . . .

"When we got a little older," says one informant, "we stopped chasing the white horse [a game like Follow the Leader] and started chasing the girls, yeh, and instead of shooting the cannon we began to shoot the dice. And plenty of other things. Yeh, and then I went to college, but it didn't exactly reform me."

For example, the Negro street cries of Harlem are work songs, just as surely as are the Southern Negro's songs of the cotton, cane and tobacco fields, road-construction, sawmill and turpentine camps, and chain gangs. And they have social significance. Thus Mobile Mac, the Hoppin' John King, seasons his invitation to buy with a slap at the boss:

> An' Hoppin' John
> Wit' plenty red-hot sauce
> Will make a po' man
> Tu'n aroun' en slap de boss.

New York Jewish needle workers sing at their work—and like the Negroes of the South they protest against too much or too little work, too little or too much love. "Yes, making a living," said one to an interviewer, "this is like climbing the Alps."

Greenwich Village and the Seamen's Union have both produced their minstrels, whose repertoire is also part of our New York City collection. The more folkish of the two, "Forty Fathoms," describes himself and his songs simply: "I'm just a seaman who writes his stuff for seamen; just a message to seamen." In "Johnny Kane," to the tune of "The Butcher Boy," he has written a classic stanza:

> So dig my grave both wide and deep,
> Place a Union banner at my head and feet.
> And on my heart let my strike card rest
> To show my mates that I did my best.

Bobby Edwards, "King of Greenwich Village," 1913–18, editor of *The Quill,* deliberately sought to keep his songs from becoming folk songs in diffusion, though many of them originated by improvisation and the collaboration of his audience. "I always tried to make my songs as difficult as possible. . . . I used up all the rhymes, so that they couldn't be added to, or improved upon . . . so you see, I deliberately frustrated what might have become a field for a genuine growth of folk songs. Sometimes, though, Harry Kemp or somebody would add a verse or two and burst out with it when I got through, and, well, it if was good enough, I'd keep it and use it—but most of the time what the others wanted to add was *too* good, and would have to be deleted out when we sang for the public." Bread and song—Bobby Edwards sang derisively of Bohemian ladies and bootleggers, of the real-estate speculator's invasion of the Village, and of police raids (to divert attention from the police's short-comings), songs in which the accents of Tin Pan Alley mingled with those of Whiz Bang.

> She was only a bootlegger's daughter,
> And her face it was somber and sad
> As she sat in her golden Packard,
> The only one that she had.

Bread and song. In New England a regional collection is investigating the lives and lore of Connecticut clockmakers and munitions workers, Rhode Island fishermen and French-Canadian textile workers, Maine clam diggers, Vermont Welsh slate workers and Italian granite workers, and a half-dozen additional nationality and occupational types of Massachusetts. In New York, Roland Palmer Gray is collecting canal and lumberjack songs. Pennsylvania is collecting, among other industrial lore, the hero-tales of Joe Magarac, the Hungarian strong man of the steel mills. Tales of railroading, brickmaking, and steel mills from Chicago; tales of the Oklahoma oilfields; tales of the Montana and Arizona copper mines; tales of Southern textile mill-workers and service occupations.

Meanwhile we are not neglecting the lore of the more strictly rural folk, past and present—folk songs of the Cumberlands from Virginia: life histories and lore of the Southern tenant-farmer, of the Conchs and Latin colony of Florida; Negro spirituals and play-party songs from Alabama and South Carolina; Louisiana Voodoo and Creole lore; stories and songs of the Creole pioneers of Indiana; Spanish-American folk songs from New Mexico; oldtimers' and tall tales from Iowa, Idaho, and Washington.

II

"If I could only put my head to it for a few hours, I could make a few songs."

Fortunately, people are never too busy to make and swap and gather folk songs and tales. In the depths of the depression the WPA is not too busy building roads and bridges to collect and study American folklore. And those of us who have come to it from the academic groves feel that we are participating in the greatest educational as well as social experiment of our time.

It is idle to talk of the dangers of vulgarization and amateurishness. If giving back to the people what we have taken from them and what rightfully belongs to them, in a form in which they can understand and use, is vulgarization, then we need more of it. For the task, as we see it, is one not simply of collection but also of assimilation. In its belief in the public support of art and art for the public, in research not for research's sake but for use and enjoyment by the many, the WPA is attempting to assimilate folklore to the local and national life by understanding, in the first place, the relation between the lore and the life out of which it springs; and by translating the lore back into terms of daily living and leisure-time activity. In other words, the WPA looks upon folklore research not as a private but as a public function, and folklore as public, not private property. This function is a collective and cooperative one, a synthesis of anthropology, sociology, psychology, and literature, the results of which are being pooled and cleared for an ever widening public.

Specifically, the folklore program of the WPA falls into two parts; first, the folklore work of the individual projects; and second, the work of the Joint Committee on Folk Arts, WPA, which, with the help and approval of the American Council of Learned Societies, has recently been set up in Washington to integrate and coordinate all the folklore, folk music, folk drama, and folk art and craft activities of the WPA, both within itself and with outside agencies. The original aim of the Joint Committee is to avoid needless duplication and overlapping and to insure complete coverage of the field, but more than that it will provide new directives and objectives in the training of personnel and the utilization of materials.

The Committee is composed of technical (not administrative) representatives of the various branches of the WPA which in any way touch the field of folk culture. These branches include the five arts projects of Federal Project No. 1, which in the latter part of 1935 was organized in the division of Women's and Professional Projects (the non-construction division of the WPA), and four other divisions of the WPA; the Education and Recreation Divisions, the National Youth Administration, and the Technical Services Laboratory.

The particular folklore activities covered by these branches of the WPA, together with their supervisors, are as follows; the Folklore Studies of the Federal Writers' Project, under B. A. Botkin; the Index of American Design of the Federal Art Project, under C. Adolph Glassgold; the folk music recording and social music of the Federal Music Project, under Charles Seeger; the

Folksong and Folklore Department of the National Service Bureau of the Federal Theater Project, under Herbert Halpert; the inventories of the Historical Records Survey, under S. B. Child; the adult and workers' education program of the Education Division, under Ernestine L. Friedman; the leisure-time program of the Recreation Division, under Nicholas Ray; the art project of the NYA, under Grace Falke; and the special skills of the Technical Services Laboratory, under Grete M. Franke.

Consultants are being drawn from government and private agencies. Among these are Donald H. Daugherty, of the Executive Office of the American Council of Learned Societies, who in June 1938 called the first meeting of technical workers in the Arts Projects and so gave the impetus to the formation of the Joint Committee; and Harold Spivacke, chief of the Music Division of the Library of Congress, who is cooperating "in every way consistent with the Library's policy and within the limits of the Library's facilities," specifically through the Archive of American Folksong, which is "ready to receive, shelve, and make available recorded material" and to "aid in the actual recording by supplying discs and lending recording machinery." The list further includes Ralph S. Boggs, George Herzog, Alan Lomax, Louise Pound, and Reed Smith.

To consult and cooperate with the Joint Committee on request, the Executive Committee of the American Council of Learned Societies, on the recommendation of the newly established Committee on American Culture, has approved the appointment of a subcommittee of the Joint Committee on Materials for Research of the American Council of Learned Societies and the Social Science Research Council.

The services offered by the Joint Committee to date are as follows:

(a) the effecting of cooperation among the various workers and their projects;
(b) the preparation of directives for the technical handling of folk arts contacts and materials;
(c) the preparation and issuing of lists and descriptions of informants, materials, intermediaries, technical services and equipment available;
(d) the sponsorship of publications.

As its first field trip the Joint Committee is planning a three-months' recording expedition through the Southeastern region. Using the sound truck of the Federal Theatre Project, Herbert Halpert will collect both musical and speech material and suitable information regarding it from the informants and their communities. The list of informants and intermediaries is being pooled from all available sources. The material collected will be used in the furtherance of various programs, such as the productions of the Federal Music and Federal Theater Projects, the folklore publications of the Federal Writers' Project, and the work of the Education and Recreation Divisions. A complete set of discs, photographs, texts, and accompanying information will be filed with the Library of Congress, which is to provide the necessary materials and duplicates.

III

Basic to the programs of the Joint Committee is the plan and procedure of the Folklore Studies of the Federal Writers' Project, as set forth in the Manual for Folklore Studies, September 1938. Throughout the work the Federal Writers' Project will serve as a clearing-house and central depository, a link between the various projects and between the national and regional committees.

The folklore program of both the Federal Writers' Project and the Joint Committee owes a debt to the sympathetic encouragement and stimulation of Henry G. Alsberg, director of the Federal Writers' Project, who in 1936 initiated our folklore studies under the direction of John A. Lomax. Mr. Lomax served until July 1937 and amassed a great deal of Negro lore and ex-slave interviews and stories and recorded a large number of folksongs. In the folklore publications of the Writers' Project Mr. Alsberg is intent upon maintaining the high standards of accuracy and interest set by the twenty large-city, state, and interstate-route guides already published, most of which contain folklore data or chapters. Since the inception of our present folklore program in August, local, state, regional, and national studies are well under way or nearing completion in 27 states. Scheduled publications include local, state, regional, and national collections: *Idaho Lore, Hard Rock* (Life and Lore of Arizona Mining Towns), *Living Lore in New England, Chase the White Horse* (New York City Songs and Stories from the Life), and *American Folk Stuff* (A National Collection of Folk and Local Tales). In addition, writers are being encouraged to do individual and collective creative work with the folk materials collected.

The benefits of this varied activity are many. In addition to its folkloristic value, its popular interest, and its creative uses, the material collected will have important bearings on the study of American culture in both its historical and functional aspects, including minority groups (ethnic, geographical, and occupational), immigration and internal migration, local history, regional backgrounds and movements, linguistic and dialect phenomena. The knowledge and leads supplied will be of particular interest to students of popular literature, American literature, contemporary literature, present-day English, and the relations of literature and society. Perhaps the most conspicuous benefit to scholarship will be the establishment of the national folklore archive in Washington and possibly of state and regional archives.

But to the success and the very life of the undertaking the support and cooperation of all scholars and their groups are necessary. Their advice and assistance are needed in the vast task of accumulation and evaluation. Beyond this, the most important task confronting the folklorist in America is that of justifying folklore and explaining what it is for, breaking down on the one hand popular resistance to folklore as dead or phony stuff and on the other hand academic resistance to its broader interpretation and utilization. Upon us devolves the tremendous responsibility of studying folklore as a living culture and of understanding its meaning and function not only in its immediate setting but in progressive and democratic society as a whole.

Paul Bunyan Was OK in His Time

*Human history is work history. The heroes of the people
are work heroes.*

Meridel Le Sueur

The Ways of Modern American Folklore

Every hero, whether real or imaginary, is a social expression, embodying in
ideal form the traits and spirit of some heroic age. In America this heroic age is
generally identified with the Frontier, fulfilling as it does the epic require-
ments "of a society cut loose from its roots, of a time of migrations, of the
shifting of populations." Since the frontier is only another name for the shifting fringe of settlement, each successive wave of migration had produced its

---

This essay appeared in *New Masses* (64 [April 23, 1946]: 12–14), the dominant
intellectual journal of the period for the Communist Party. Botkin's wife, Gertrude,
recalled that the journal's editor, Joseph North, asked Botkin to write about labor
folklore. She cautioned her husband about the risks of alienating the government by
publishing in such a venue, but he was undeterred. The connection between Paul
Bunyan and Popular Front cultural politics is more pertinent than it might first
appear. Folklorists would later focus on questions of whether there was an oral
tradition from which Bunyan emerged and on establishing whether Bunyan was a
creation of lumber company promotional campaigns. But Botkin was less interested in issues of origins and the means of transmission of lore than in its actual
function, how it was used in culture. He raised larger questions about the relationship of folk heroes to the social and political realities of American history, a topic
that reflected his long-held interest in the relationship between heroes like Bunyan
and social periods. *A Treasury of American Folklore* commences, for example, with
Davy Crockett material. He sees evidence in Paul Bunyan that industrial workers
were creating new forms of lore that reflected as much about class identity as they
did about mythic notions of American individualism and outdoor work. By implication, Paul Bunyan thus had as much to say about worker and labor issues as Joe
Hill and the International Workers of the World, Ella Mae Wiggins and southern
textile workers, Aunt Molly Jackson and Appalachian miners, and Woody Guthrie
and the Dust Bowl migrants—which together serve as examples of what Botkin
characterized as folklore in the making.

own hero or heroes. And since each wave of migration is correlated with some heroic labor, most of our heroes are work heroes. The work hero is a form of culture hero, who either belongs to history or makes history. The great culture heroes, of course, do not simply change the country but make it a better place to live—they change the world.

In their historical and cultural role, heroes look backward to a vanished era or forward to a new one. In this way they are either anachronistic or prophetic, nostalgic or revolutionary, depending upon whether the Golden Age lies behind or ahead. At the same time every great hero expresses some permanent truth or faith which each new generation or group may reinterpret in its own way, as it reads new meaning into the past or sees new values in the present.

Heroes do not spring up overnight, but are built up over a period of years through the accumulations and variations of oral tradition and popular literature. Hero tales pass from mouth to mouth and are constantly reworked by professional writers as well as by natural story-tellers until they form a cycle or saga. And as new struggles arise and new problems demand new solutions, or old solutions become inadequate, old heroes are made over and new ones are constantly in the making.

This relation of heroes to struggle and the solution of problems is a fundamental one. If the heroes of one age or country seem inadequate by comparison with those of another, the reason may be that their solutions are too easy. It takes great struggles to make great heroes—struggles for survival and freedom, revolts against injustice, and oppression, conflicts between old and new social systems or world orders. Thus the Negro's struggle for freedom has produced some of the noblest creations of American folklore, including the spirituals or freedom songs, the blues and songs of protest, the Br'er Rabbit and John tales, and the steel-driving hero, John Henry, beside whom Paul Bunyan seems a little childish.

The struggle, the heroic age, from which Paul Bunyan springs is the source of all our frontier heroes—the struggle against nature, the conquest of the continent, the epic of wilderness-clearing and land-taking. This experience gave rise to a body of tall tales-brags, lies, and gibes about rich land and poor land, booms and busts, feasts and famines, floods, droughts, blizzards, marvelous hunts, big crops and giant vegetables, and other freaks of nature, human nature, and "unnatural" natural history—which gradually became attached to individual heroes or supermen—at first actual, perhaps, and then legendary.

———

In its conception of a free, resourceful, outdoor, migratory life, self-sufficient and democratic, the Paul Bunyan legend perpetuates the pioneer tradition, which has given us the quasi-legendary, homely figures of the Yankee Peddler, the Backwoodsman, and the Homesteader, as well as solitary, eccentric "heroes of endurance" like Johnny Appleseed. The "last frontier" of the North woods and the Southwest oil fields, to which Paul Bunyan moved on, is only a few steps removed from the hunting and trapping society of Davy Crockett and Mike Fink. The logging fraternity of the generous camp boss and his loyal crew grew out of and reflects the fluid, mobile social relations of the frontier before the tightening of class lines and the sharpening of conflict between worker and boss. Similarly, as Margaret Larkin has remarked about cowboy songs, "the boss rode with the hands" and "every cow puncher was a prospective cowman; all that was needed to start a herd was a stout rope and a running iron."

At the same time the humorous, idyllic fantasy of the Paul Bunyan stories bears an inverted relation to the actual conditions of the logging camp of the past, as if it were history written upside down. For instance, we know that the bunkhouses in Paul Bunyan's time were dirty and vermin-infested. But legend has it that the loggers either made friends with the bedbugs or they didn't last very long. "The story is that the loggers all had their pet bugs that followed them around camp and out in the woods like dogs, some even being trained, it is said, to steal blankets off adjoining bunks for their masters on especially cold nights." After the I.W.W. had cleaned up the camps, a new kind of bedbug (sometimes crumb) story began to go the rounds. This version makes out the bugs and the bosses to be "blood brothers," who take turns bleeding the slaves by day and night. And the bugs keep the slaves "so busy scratching they can't do any thinking" or organizing.

"Paul Bunyan was all right in his time," begins the story of the "Crumbs," "but he didn't have the big shots of today to deal with. . . ." With the great changes that took place in industry and labor as a result of mechanization, centralization, and unionization, the conception of the hero underwent a change. The work hero became a worker hero, who identifies himself with the cause of organized labor in the class struggle that marks a new heroic age.

In this conflict singing has played an important part and at times even seemed to overshadow story-telling, as ballads have celebrated labor's heroes and labor's exploits, union songs championed labor's cause, and strike songs cheered workers on the picket line.

And worker bards, who were also organizers and in many cases martyrs, and so "had what it takes to make songs," became new heroes of labor, from the "Molly Maguire" balladists and Joe Hill to Ella Mae Wiggins and Aunt Molly Jackson. The spirit of Joe Hill's songs is the spirit of his last words as he faced the firing squad in Salt Lake City on November 17, 1915: "The cause I stand for means more than any human life—much more than mine. Let'er go!" At the Third American Writers' Congress, in June 1939, Aunt Molly Jackson, a coal miner's wife from Harlan County, Kentucky, told the Folklore Craft Session how she wrote her songs:

"Anything that touched my heart I liked to compose a song or poem about.

"I composed one a morning in Harlan County, when fifteen of the miners' children went to a soup kitchen in the field. I recognized the voice of Flossie, my sister's child. Blood was coming down through their toes in the rain. Why are these children so naked in the cold rain? I sang the exact situation and surroundings and how I felt at that time. I called it the 'Kentucky Miners' Hungry Blues.' It began, 'I am sad and weary and got the hungry ragged blues.'"

American workers had sung of their grievances in ballads and folk songs long before. For example, in the forecastle song, "Boston," the sailor sang:

> Up comes the skipper from down below,
> And he looks aloft and he looks alow,
> And he looks alow and he looks aloft,
> And it's "Coil up your ropes there, fore and aft."

> Then down to his cabin he quickly crawls,
> And unto his steward he loudly bawls,
> "Go mix me a glass that will make me cough,
> For it's better weather here than it is up aloft."

> We poor sailors standing on the deck,
> With the blasted rain all a-pouring down our necks;
> Not a drop of grog would he to us afford,
> But he damns our eyes with every other word.

> And one thing which we have to crave
> Is that he may have a watery grave,
> So we'll heave him down into some dark hole,
> Where the shark'll have his body and the devil have his soul.

Like new wine in old bottles, new words are written to old tunes and new lines added to old songs. In Joe Hill's parody, Casey Jones is a scab on the S.P. Line, who dies and goes on scabbing until the Angels' Union, Number 23, throws him into hell:

Casey Jones, went to Hell a-flying.
Casey Jones, the Devil said, Oh, fine.
Casey Jones, get busy shoveling sulphur.
That's what you get for scabbing on the S. P. Line.

If this song traduces the name and fame of Casey Jones (whose memory is honored by a monument in Cayce, Kentucky, as well as by the folk song), other heroes have fared better in their new incarnations. Joe Magarac, the steel man, made rails by squeezing the hot steel through his fingers—four rails from each hand—and jumped into a furnace to make better steel, recalling memories of foundation sacrifice rites and stories of men who have fallen into vats of molten steel and been buried with the metal (as in Mike Gold's poem "A Strange Funeral in Braddock" and Joseph Auslander's "Steel"). In a Pittsburgh version, supplied by J. Ernest Wright, Joe Magarac is the class-conscious worker who believes the mills belong to the men rather than the men to the mills:

"And the steel makers say that if a man works for a long time in the mills and does right by his fellow workers he will sometimes be able to see Joe sitting in the furnace, and that if you speak to him he will say 'Hello.' . . .

"And the steel men say that once when some one asked him who owned the mill he worked at he said, 'We own the mills because, we built them, and because we make the steel that comes out of them.' "

In the new folklore of labor even a "bad man" could be a "good guy" if he fought on the right side. Woody Guthrie sings:

The outlaw Jesse James would never rob the poor,
Or frighten a mother with a child. . . .
But he took it from the rich and he gave it to the poor,
And they shot poor Jesse on the sly.

And in "Pretty Boy Floyd":

As through this world I've traveled, there's lots of funny men,
Some rob you with a six-gun, and some with a fountain pen.
I've known lots of outlaws, but I have never known
An Oklahoma outlaw to drive a family from their home.

Though workers' songs have had a wilder circulation because of their more obvious utility and appeal ("the people are on the march and must have songs to sing"), there have also been workers' sayings and stories, some of them of a more esoteric nature, told within the group—in the union hall and wherever

workers congregate. On the Federal Writers' Project of New York City, beginning in 1938, an attempt was made to round up this new urban and industrial
lore, from taxi drivers, sandhogs, plasterers, needle trade workers, shoe workers, hospital workers, stage hands, longshoremen, seamen, marine telegraph
operators, Pullman porters, and the like. Although the study uncovered no
new heroes of the stature of Paul Bunyan and John Henry, it revealed a rich
soil of anecdote, allusion, and character from which future heroes might
spring, in labor's new epic of excavation, construction, manufacturing, transportation, trade, and service.

From Chicago came new tall tales and true stories of industry—railroading,
freight car repair yards, auto plants, bricklaying, sign painting—realistic and
critical in their humorous portrayal of customs like initiation ceremonials and
differences and rivalries between old and new hands, piece workers and day
workers, hand workers and machine workers, backward (in the union sense)
and advanced workers. The favorite butt of satire in auto plants is the worker
from the sticks "who sells his labor at a minimum and sets a pace in getting
out the work." Nelson Algren tells how the time-study man, "that mother
robbin' creeper that watches you from behind dolly trucks and stock boxes . . .
always trying to figger a way to get more work out of you at the same pay" was
almost knocked off the Christmas tree when True-Blue Highpockets from the
forks of the crick "told him he reckoned he could do a sight more than he
was. He was tending a milling machine that worked pretty fast, but it only
took one hand.

"Next thing we know, by Jesus, the time-study man was having the mill-
wright put in another milling machine for Highpockets' left hand, and be
damned if he didn't turn out twicet as much work as before. The timestudy
man has got real fond of him by this time, and hangs around watching and
admiring him. Trouble is, he started in on the rest of us wanting we should do
something about them idle left hands of ours. . . .

"Next, there's a block and tackle business fastened to Highpockets' right
leg, and he's pulling stock pans off one conveyor onto another, slick as you
please. . . .

"It goes from bad to worse, with next a band fastened to Highpockets' *left*
leg, and be damned if he ain't jerking empty fender hooks off another conveyor and piling tem in a dolly box, neat as apple pie. . . .

"We thought Highpockets was speeded to full steam finally, because he's got
a little bar in his teeth and with this he's jerking his head back and forth and
this runs a brush back and forth over new stock coming in and knocks the
dust off it. He's finished, we said he *can't* do no more. He's doing all he can,

and that's all a little red bull can do, boys. He's going like a blind dog in a meathouse, and it's reach (right hand) reach (left hand) kick (right leg) kick (left leg) pull (teeth), reach reach kick kick pull. He goes so fast you can't see him for steam. . . .

"He was true blue, that cornfield canary was, and a credit to the human race. The kind of a man that gets somewhere in this plant. He grins game as a fighting cock and chirps right out loud:

" 'Sure, if you want to stick a broom up behind, I think I could be sweeping the floor!' "

True Blue Highpockets from the forks of the crick, the human machine, is a monstrous and tragic caricature of Paul Bunyan and all the champions and supermen of legend who as the biggest, fastest, and bestest men on the job started pace-setting and the high-ball or speed-up system that takes the bread out of a man's mouth. "Paul Bunyan was all right in his time, but he didn't have the big shots of today to deal with. . . ." Or, as the coal miner said about the mining machine that had replaced his pick: "Only trouble is that a machine can pick coal faster than a man and when it ain't working it don't have to eat."

Applied Folklore: Creating Understanding through Folklore

I

One can hardly pick up a copy of a folklore journal these days without coming across an article on some phase of utilization, from "Folklore in the Schools" to "The Plight of the Folk Tale in the Comics." Utilization adds one more string to the folklorist's bow. And since the word "folklore" already means both the material studied and the study itself, it is time we had a term like "applied folklore" to designate the use of folklore to some end beyond itself. To some end beyond itself, because anyone who does anything with folklore, from the original folk singer or story-teller to the scholar, is *using* it. But as long as the folklorist stays *inside* folklore and regards it "from the point of view of folklore itself," he remains a "pure" folklorist. It is only when he gets *outside* of folklore into social or literary history, education, recreation, or the arts that he becomes an "applied" folklorist.

As an applied folklorist I have always believed that while the study of folklore belongs to the folklorist, the lore itself belongs rather to the people who make it or enjoy it. As to the place of the study of folklore in the hierarchy of knowledge, we know it belongs both to the humanities and to the social

This essay appeared in *Southern Folklore Quarterly* 17 (September 1953): 199–206, during an especially complicated time for Botkin (and most of his friends). With the Cold War raging abroad, a red scare putting everyone on full alert at home, and even the hint of an affiliation with the Popular Front being a sure invitation to a permanent Federal Bureau of Investigation file, it was an era, as historian Richard Pells has observed, that put liberal intellectuals in a conservative mood. Nonetheless, despite having earned his own file, Botkin was intent on promoting just the kind of intercultural understanding at home and sympathy among nations that made him vulnerable to conservative paranoia. He remains committed to promoting applied folklore as a crucial means for creating a sense of community for a pluralistic society. Consistent in his adherence to interdisciplinary intellectual models that serve public audiences, Botkin aims at nothing short of articulating a fresh theory about the role of the folklorist and folklore in American culture.

sciences. But whereas a pure folklorist might tend to think of folklore as an independent discipline, the applied folklorist prefers to think of it as ancillary to the study of culture, of history or literature—of people.

Something like this distinction between pure and applied folklore was in Ralph S. Boggs' mind when in 1942 he distinguished as follows between the scientific and artistic phases of folklore:

> The scientific phase is concerned primarily with a body of materials. It is based upon and gets its unity and derives its identity from the body of materials that it chooses to work with primarily. These materials are gathered, collected [collated?], classified, and typed [that is, related to a type], and then they are analyzed and studied so that discussions can be made to deduce some scientific conclusions or laws which govern the life of these materials.[1]

Other people then try to master the results that science has given them, and, as masters of those results, try to become skilled in their application toward various ends. This is the artistic phase of that body of matter, and it seems to me that most people who have worked in folklore belong to the artists rather than the scientists of the group.

Those ultimate ends to which the immediate results of the investigation of the science of folklore can be applied are various and important. Some of them have been touched upon, but others have not been much exploited. One of the important (because of its timeliness) ultimate results that folk material can be used for is the development of international consciousness and the promotion of international understanding.

By "artistic" Boggs means creative, in the broad sense, since scholarship too may be creative. His emphasis on understanding is good, because folklore is a set of group relations, and the study of folklore is one way of studying group relations, for understanding and the promotion of understanding. That is why applied folklore should take first place in any folk festival discussion program since the folk festival is an important form of utilization and application, for understanding as well as enjoyment, through participation and the celebration of our "commonness"—the "each" in all of us and the "all" in each of us. For what we participate in here is not only a performance and a revival but cultural—intercultural—democracy.

Participation is the most direct and perhaps the best form of applied folklore. It involves an activity—understanding by doing—and the sharing and enriching of experience. What is closer to human experience than the making and breaking of bread? In Walter de la Mare's lines:

It's a very odd thing—
As odd as can be—
That whatever Miss T. eats
Turns into Miss T.

Eating and cooking internationally have always been a feature of international folk festivals like the Festival of Nations at St. Paul. And food has
become part of the curriculum or extra-curricular activities of the folk culture
seminar, which combines the folk festival and the folklore course in the application of folklore to our whole culture. At the Sixth Annual Seminars
on American Culture held by the New York State Historical Association at
Cooperstown, in July 1953, students in a laboratory course on "The American
Frugal Housewife" were able to "participate in baking bread in the brick oven,
the preparation of food on the hearth, churning and cheese making, also soap
making and candle dipping, and in a study of the textiles in the farmhouse." At
the Second Annual Seminars on the Folk Culture of the Pennsylvania Dutch
Country in conjunction with the Fourth Annual Pennsylvania Dutch Folk
Festival at Kutztown, also in July, participants not only lived Pennsylvania
Dutch folk culture but ate it, "sampling a wide variety of . . . specialized dishes,
from *fasnachts* to *drechder-kucha.*"

II

As an activity or experience, applied folklore involves an interchange between cultural groups or levels, between the folk and the student of folklore.
This technique owes most, perhaps, to the anthropologist and his functional
approach—a contribution to which the unfortunate and unnecessary split
between the literary and anthropological folklorists has tended to blind us. It
blinds us further to the fact that the anthropologist is also concerned with "literature" and the literary folklorist with "culture." This means, according to a
functional folklorist, Herbert Halpert, that "folklore does function in a particular setting, which should be analyzed as the anthropologist would analyze
primitive culture and that from this not only do the folk tales elucidate the
culture but in turn knowledge of the culture aids in the study of the aesthetics of
its folklore."[2] Another functional folklorist, Alan Lomax, sees the "geniuses of
the community, the creators and transmitters," as literary artists in their own
right, and believes that the "best interpretations of folklore may be obtained in
the end from the folk themselves."[3] Lomax's *Mister Jelly Roll* (1950) is thus a folk
history of New Orleans jazz and jazzmen and of New Orleans in the jazz era,
based on the recorded and interwoven monologues of Jelly Roll Morton.

In my own conception of applied folklore, the folk-sayer—the folk genius as creator or transmitter—plays an all-important role. The development of my conception of applied folklore follows the development of my conception of "folk-say" from folk literature to folk history.[4] In the beginning I defined "folk-say" as the "oral, linguistic, and story-telling . . . aspects of folklore [in] its living as well as its anachronistic phases," including "literature about the folk as well as literature of the folk." But gradually (especially in conjunction with my work as folklore editor of the Federal Writers' Project [1938–41],[5] where I had to deal with folkways as well as folk-say, first with life histories of folklore informants and then with life histories generally), "folk-say" came to mean what the folk have to say not only *for* but *about* themselves, in their own way and in their own words.

From life history or "own stories" it was only a step (in my thinking) to folk history—history in which the folk are both the history and the historians.[6] My conception of folk-say as folk literature and folk history may perhaps best be illustrated by *Lay My Burden Down: A Folk History of Slavery* (1945), a selection of slave narratives from interviews with former slaves by members of the Federal Writers' Project in seventeen southern, middle western, and southwestern states from 1936 to 1938. The book is applied folklore in still another sense: it gives us a folk's-eye view of slavery as reflected not only in the folk society, folkways, and folklore of the slave but also in the attitudes and traditions, the symbols and myths of the ex-slave looking back on the experience of his youth. In this way folklore becomes the "buried culture" not only of mankind but of the individual, as one layer of experience becomes buried under another. And in this sense folk history, like life history, is "hidden history"—not so much history in the strict sense of the word as the stuff of history—indirect or secondary historical evidence, subject to all the distortions of time, faulty memory, and hearsay.

III

Folklore as experience passes naturally into folklore as understanding. Fittingly enough, it is a Quaker, Rachel Davis DuBois, who has transformed one into the other by bringing the folk festival into the home in the form of a Quaker experience meeting—the Neighborhood Folk Festival. As described in her latest book, *Neighbors in Action* (1950), her techniques are two—the group conversation and the *parranda*. The philosophy behind them is that of creating understanding among groups of different yet common experiences. And if she seems to emphasize differences more than likenesses it is because she believes that unity achieved at the expense of glossing over or underestimating differences is a false and superficial unity. "It's the not me in thee which makes thee valuable to me," goes her Quaker proverb.

The group conversation is applied folklore in two senses. First, it promotes understanding through participation, with the participants, under the guidance of a skilled leader, matching their personal memories of changes of season, food, work, storms, and other themes of universal interest—co-operative enterprises in the home, crises in the life of the individual in relation to nature and the group. In this way she uncovers and works *up* as well as *in* a great deal of folklore in the form of customs and beliefs and so performs a service to the folklorist by locating and stimulating informants, in much the same way as the folk festival. By interpolating songs, dances, and games suggested by the conversation and generally ending with a symbolic song, dance, or ceremony, the group conversation becomes applied folklore in the second sense of festival as ritual.

The group conversation resembles group therapy in that by getting back to their childhood memories the participants try to get back to a time when they accepted their culture and their neighbors, before misunderstanding and mistrust had been built up by education and social imitation. Now this technique may work successfully for the older generation with happy memories of childhood in the old country or in a small community, but, as is pointed out, for the children of this generation, brought up in the tension areas of large cities, it may take more than memory—it may take reeducation and even psychiatric social work—to create understanding.

Recognizing this need of reeducation, Dr. DuBois has developed another technique for bringing children into active participation in the home culture of the neighborhood. This is the *parranda*—a Puerto Rican term for "progressive party," in which several families hold open house and the guests travel from house to house. In the applied *parranda* the children leave the classroom and visit the homes of families of various cultural backgrounds, participating in food, songs, games, and dances and learning about customs, through conversation and interview, which are in turn reported back in the pupils' compositions and integrated into the school experience through intercultural assemblies.

IV

The folk festival, the folk culture seminar, the group conversation, and the *parranda* are only a few examples of the varied uses of applied folklore for creating understanding. The ultimate aim of applied folklore is the restoration to American life of the sense of community—a sense of thinking, feeling, and acting along similar, though not the same, lines—that is in danger of being lost today. Thus applied folklore goes beyond cultural history to cultural strategy, to the end of creating a favorable environment for the liberation of our creative energies and the flourishing of the folk arts among other social, cooperative activities. In a time of increasing standardization it becomes an increasingly important function of the applied folklorist to discover and keep alive folk expressions that might otherwise be lost. And in a country of great regional diversity such as ours, the balanced utilization of regional as well as ethnic resources is vital to the enrichment and fulfillment of American life and expression. In this way the folklorist may outgrow the older "survival" theory of the "partial uselessness" of folklore and renew the continuity and survival values of folklore as the "germ-plasm of society." Survivals survive, according to R.R. Marett, "because they are the constantly renewed symptoms of that life of the folk which alone has the inherent power of surviving in the long run."[7]

By its very nature applied folklore requires the cooperation of the folklorist with other disciplines concerned with the study of society and culture. In restoring the sense of community and continuity to modern life, the folklorist may have to follow the lead of the sociologist and the anthropologist. In securing and making available socially and artistically satisfying examples and versions of folk expression, the folklorist should take the initiative.

In either capacity the folklorist must cease to be an "I" person and become a "we" person, like Frankie in Carson McCullers' *The Member of the Wedding*.

> The trouble with me is that for a long time I have been just an "I" person. All other people can say "we." When Berenice says "we" she means her lodge and church and colored people. Soldiers can say "we" and mean the army. All people belong to a "we." . . .

V

At this moment in history, when the creation of understanding in the world community is essential to survival, students and users of folklore and the folk arts must become "members of the whole world." An unexcelled opportunity for putting applied folklore to work toward what Ralph Boggs in 1942 saw as one of the important and timely "ultimate results" of utilization presented itself at the Third National Conference of the United States National Commission for Unesco held in New York City in January 1952. This took the form of a proposal for a panel on folklore and folk (including primitive and popular) arts in the United States National Commission.[8] Moved by the almost total neglect of the language and visual folk arts at the Third National Conference, Charles Seeger and I drafted the following proposal:

Folklore and the folk arts are a cross-classification of communicative and creative media and techniques. As such they cut across other fields represented in the U.S. National Commission for Unesco, such as the visual arts, music, language and language arts, communications, and education. Folklore and the folk arts are a bridge between the humanities and the social sciences, a key to the understanding of and between cultures, regions, and social and economic groups.

The promotion of understanding in the world community cannot be achieved without (a) knowledge and understanding of group acceptances and resistances and traditional resources, attitudes, and techniques as embodied in folklore and the folk arts (including folksong, folk dance, folk speech, arts and crafts, legend, myth, folkways, and folk beliefs and customs) and (b) the utilization (with proper selection and control) of these resources, attitudes, and techniques for breaking down resistance and building upon acceptance.

We, the undersigned representatives of folklore organizations present at the Third National Conference of the U.S. National Commission for Unesco and other interested groups and individuals, propose, therefore, the setting up of a panel on folklore and the folk arts in the U.S. National Commission for Unesco as a central meeting place and clearing found for the various folklore approaches and interests now scattered and separated in the Commission.

The draft was signed by the following delegates, who constituted themselves an organizing committee for the purpose of bringing the proposal back to their respective organizations for endorsement and implementation: B. A. Botkin, American Folklore Society; Charles Seeger, International Music Council; Elizabeth Burchenal, U.S. National Commission on the Folk Arts; May Gadd, Country Dance Society of America; Mrs. Raymond F. McLain, International Folk Music Council. Also present and in approved were Marshall W. Stearns, Institute for Jazz Studies; Laura Boulton, New York City; and Rachel Davis DuBois, Workshop for Cultural Democracy.

At the annual meeting in December 1952, the American Folklore Society approved the proposal. It seems clear that as "members of the whole world" folklorists have a stake in culture and in the world community, and it is up to them to make themselves heard in the councils of cultural, strategy, or else—. But there must not be an "or else."

Notes

Based on a paper at the Folklore Conference of the National Folk Festival Association held under the auspices of University College, Washington University, St. Louis, April 7–8, 1953, in celebration of the Centennial of Washington University and the Sesquicentennial of the Louisiana Purchase.

1. "Conference on the Character and State of Studies in Folklore," *Journal of American Folklore* 59 (October–December 1946): 502–503.

2. Ibid., pp. 511–512. As a case in point, Halpert cites Ruth Benedict's *Introduction to Zuni Mythology.*

3. Ibid., pp. 507, 509.

4. For a note on the origin and development of the term, see my article on " 'Folk-Say' and Folklore," *American Speech* 6 (August 1931): 404–406. The word was coined in 1928 as an extension of, not, as some have thought mistakenly, a substitute for, the word "folklore." In looking for a title for the first publication of the Oklahoma Folklore Society, I remembered "Fore-Say," the Dorset poet William Barnes' homely counterpart for "preface" in J. S. Udall's *Dorsetshire Folklore*; and out of "folklore" by "fore-say" sprang "folk-say." In 1947, for the first time in any dictionary, Clarence L. Barnhart included "folk-say" in the *American College Dictionary* in the narrow sense of "informal verbal expressions such as proverbs and exclamations, among a relatively unsophisticated group of people:—"narrow" because it accounts for only the linguistic but not the story-telling phases of "folk-say."

5. For accounts of the Folklore Studies of the Federal Writers' Project see my articles "WPA and Folklore Research: 'Bread and Song,' " *Southern Folklore Quarterly* 3 (March 1939): 7–14, and "Living Lore on the New York City Writers' Project," *New York Folklore Quarterly* 2 (November 1946): 252–63.

6. The application of folklore to the study of history as well as of literature belongs to another article. I have touched upon phases of literary applied folklore in "The Folk in Literature: An Introduction to the New Regionalism," in *Folk-Say* (1929), 9–20. In "Folklore as a Neglected Source of Social History," in *The Cultural Approach to History* (1940), edited for the American Historical Association by Caroline F. Ware, 308–15, I have dealt with historical applied folklore. Sociological applied folklore is illustrated by my article on "Folk and Folklore," in *Culture of the South* (1934), edited by W. T. Couch, 570–93. In "The Folk and the Individual: Their Creative Reciprocity," in *English Journal* (College Edition) 27 (February 1938): 121–35, I have considered some of the problems and possibilities of recovering folk values in literature.

7. *Psychology and Folk-lore* (1920) [New York: Macmillan], 26.

8. See "Delegate's Report on the Third National Conference of the United States National Commission for Unesco" by the present author in the *Journal of American Folklore* (July–September 1953): 253–54.

Poems

Vernal Equinox

I heard my bookseller greet the man from
  Across the way:
"The flowers must be blooming in your front
  yard today."

I
Fourth Avenue

Somehow it makes booksellers seem less hard
To Talk, not shop, but flowers in the yard.

And bookstalls bloom like gardens at the door,
Where dingy, browsing folk have wings and soar

And hover—plundering bees and butterflies—
With eager fluttering of their hands and eyes. . . .

Poor city grubs and drones and bookworms stand,
And take their spring, like books, at second hand.

II
Fifth Avenue

Elite and hoi polloi who seek or have a new
Hat or beau or what not haunt the Avenue

Here's pussywillow—in a woman's hand;
And there are violets—on a flower-stand.

Now more than ever people block the way
To stare at dolls or legs and dream of play.

And with the park-waifs sit in equal rows
The laughing lovers—doves among the crows.

From *University of Oklahoma Magazine* 14 (Spring 1926): 22.

III
East Side

The rancor of an old decay is sweet
Where dust of spring blows down the pushing street;

Where fire-escapes and pushcarts press and grope
In brazen gesturing of raucous hope;

And caught in webs of tenements and bridges,
The swarming myriads cling like frantic midges. . . .

O polyglot of phonographs and faces!
The wail and sigh of spring in strange far places.

IV
Riverside

We learn the varied use of bus and bench,
With pretty nursemaids to improve our French

The wistfulness of gulls is in our throats,
And in our limbs the pull of freight and boats.

The mothers ply their needles, books, and tongues,
While children exercise their legs and lungs.

And organ-grinders, with their new-old tunes,
Make monkey-shines of Pierrots and moons.

Sanctuary

Though I remember songs and faces.
Blown to me in windy spaces,
Pricking out old patterns of pain,
Like stinging needle-points of rain;
Though in my throat my passions choke,
Heavy as fog and bitter as smoke;
Though a sudden light or breath torments me,
And yet it is only change contents me,
Because my need of love is greater
Than love itself, a burnt-out crater,
And no one person can satisfy
This hunger for endless life that is I:—
One pure inviolate region I know.
Where, like a leprous slough of snow,
My burdens slip from me entire,
Purged in elemental fire;
Where the scales have fallen from my sight,
And I see clearly in the night;
Where I am I, eternal, unchanged,
Restored to myself that was estranged;
Where love and hate no more can clutch me.
And no, not even you can touch me.
With head thrown high and shining face,
In a magic ring, a moonlit place,
On wings of time and space I stride,
With all eternity at my side,
In the sublime and beautiful, whole
And perfect loneliness of the soul.

From "Oklahoma Poets," ed. H. L. Mencken, *American Mercury* 7 (May 1926): 14.

Spectacle

Down by the river, where the storm clouds lift,
   I watch the curtain rising on a play.
The hills grow lights, and slowly through the rift
   Of sky unfolds the drama of the day.

Behold the spectacle! As huge as fate
   And silent, for here language plays no part.
For shame, you poets! Who can only prate
   Of beauty, while dumb nature shames your art.

From *Opportunity: A Journal of Negro Life* 5 (January 1927): 22.

Going to the Store

Out of the walk he snatches small delights,
Constructing plots and patterns in the streets
And seeing strangeness in accustomed sights,
At whose new sense his heart more quickly beats.
Adventure lurks in purchases; in shops
Whose rounds he makes; in every passing lure
Of windows, signs, and corners where he stops—
Whose hazards make his safe routine more sure.
The paper with its distant war and crime
Grows stale in his hand, but not the small-town thrills
By whose recurrent tide he measures time.
And though an engine switching freight-cars fills
His veins with yearning, he prefers to wonder
How one at home will share the latest plunder.

From *Harp* 4 (March–April 1928): 9 (reprinted in Botkin 1928d: 35).

Track Lover

I

A track was company; it lived and moved
And walked along beside him when he roved.
The blood of distance ran in its steel veins.
Its level was no higher than the plains,
And yet its height was in its length, its ties
Like ladder-rungs could climb into the skies.

II

When he sat down to rest he drew the speed
Of trains from rails and felt no other need
Of travel; when he walked he felt at rest,
Watching slow-moving landscapes he knew best.
This was a journey—to stroll out of town.

III

He watched in passing (to reduce the scale)
Field mouse's, horned toad's, or lizard's tail
Streak out of sight; he often startled quail
With drumming wings, or saw a patient rail
Adjust its pace to caterpillar crawl
Or crablike spider legs—and seem less tall.

IV

For speech the rails clicked; there were singing wires
And—perched like notes on staffs—frail sparrow choirs.
And water-tower sparrows hopped about
With tea-time chatter on its tea-pot spout.
He walked between trains—there were eight a day,
Four north, four south; he had the right-of-way
With space for thought, escaped from narrow street
Of houses, cars, and faces he must greet.

From *Southwest Review* 14 (Spring 1929): 343.

Classroom

A teacher teaches.
A teacher sits at a desk and faces fifty students.
Fifty students sit in one-arm lunch chairs and face a teacher.
Fifty chairs, fifty faces face a desk.
Fifty one-arm lunch chairs think of lunch.
What'll it be to-day? Something in a roll with mustard and picallili?
English—French—mathematics with mustard and picallili?

A teacher talks.
Words come out of his mouth and hang in the air like a balloon of words in a
    comic strip.
A windbag, a stomach with a desk on the end of it.
Wind from a stomach.
Fifty stomachs face a stomach.
It would be better if fifty pairs of buttocks faced another pair of buttocks.

The balloons break away and float over the room,
Fifty balloons—toy balloons—all colors—
An Italian selling toy-balloons.
Fifty faces stick fifty pins into fifty balloons and make fifty pops like fifty
    laughs.
The windbag puffs harder and harder and gets redder and redder in the face,
Blowing up new balloons.
Fifty balloons break away each time and fifty faces pop fifty laughs.

How many brought their books to-day?
Page page page page page what is the page?
Fumble mumble jumble rumble of wind in a stomach.
This is beautiful? How many think it is beautiful?
Is there any question? Is there any answer?

From "A Page of College Verse," *New Masses* 4 (April 1929): 8.

Sender requests an answer. Tick-tick-tick-tick.

Next time and next time and next time.

Page to page to page to page, face to face to buttock to buttock.

Windbag grows tired of blowing, bellowing and belly-aching, pumping the bellows.

Can't hear himself talk for the steady popping.

Fifty laughs of buttock-faces taking the wind out of a desk-stomach.

Balloon-face collapses and sags into open book.

Balloon-stomach swells and swells and nearly bursts when—Brrrnnng! the bell. . . .

A closed book floats out of the room.

Fifty faces, fifty pairs of buttocks leave fifty one-arm lunch chairs staring at an empty desk.

Home Town

The streets were home to him, one long carouse
In sun and common things. To leave the house
That shut him in and roam familiar streets,
Whose houses shut him out, shut out defeats
Of narrow walls and lonely rooms and brought
New glories of small battles daily fought
With his environment; it gave ingress
Into these people's lives; possessionless
And homeless though he felt, the poor defense
Of houses fell before his conquering sense
Of proud possession; with the sky and air
Their lives and property were his to share.

Each day the streets were spun from him afresh,
A web for spidery wonder to enmesh
With shining subtlety new evidence
Of people's likeness and their difference.
What his own life was like he knew; it flattered
His vanity to know the same things mattered
To others, and it teased him that these walls
Held doors and windows opening on halls
Of self which he might glimpse but never know,
Barriers that he could never overthrow.

He steeped his senses in the look, the smell,
The sound of houses; in bright roofs that fell
In shadows on the lawn; in walls and glass
That caught the sun; in color, line, and mass
Of shingles, gravel, brick, paint, grass, and smoke;

From *Prairie Schooner* 4 (February 1930): 34–35.

Snatches of phonographs, pianos; folk
In casual encounters at their doors;
Genie-like tradesmen, women doing chores,
Old men on sticks who hugged the sunny side,
Children on swings and carts and skates who cried
A tuneless song; dogs running out to sniff
Or bark at him; the titillating whiff
Of cooking meals and burning trash; a line
Of blowing clothes in which he could divine
An augury as in the flight of birds;
Milk-jars on steps—stray fragments, hints, mute words,
A jig-saw puzzle, scattered, disconnected—
He pieced together bits that he collected.

Watching the town grow as one builds his house,
He was the rentless tenant, like a mouse
That slips in from the winter fields to gnaw
Through walls and nibble crumbs while men plied saw
And hammer (sounds that thrilled him) to push back
The prairie. He would cross the railroad track
And leave behind the park and power plant,
The smell of gins, the engines' throb and pant,
Exchange the pavement for dirt roads and tang
Of fields and cows, where winds and high wires sang,
To watch the changing and receding line,
Dividing town from prairie. The blue wine
Of wind and distance bubbled in his brain.
He liked to feel himself a moment strain
At his safe leash before the thoroughfares
Absorbed him to repattern plotted squares.

Meteor

More beautiful than ships or planes
Are lightning-flash and thunderbolt
Of runaway night-frightened trains

Swift, brutal in a wild assault
Of frantic wings and flying heels,
They leap from out of the catapult

Of distance, thunder in their wheels
And lightning in their Cyclops' eye
And serpent tail, with warning squeals

As if the shaken stars and sky
Were falling through the holes they rip
In night and silence. Demon cry

And dragon flight, receding, slip
Into the reticence of space—
More terrible than 'plane or ship
In fiery speed and iron grace.

From *Poetry: A Magazine of Verse* 37 (November 1930): 84

Highway West

Great cities rose to meet us from the plain,
　And swam along beside us for a while.
Like them we tried to climb into a sky
　That fell away from us with every mile.

Always the empty road, and in our eyes
　The ache of distance, in our minds a blank;
The rushing in our ears of wind-like waves
　As miles flowed over us until we sank.

From "Some Southwestern Poets," *New Republic* 92 (October 13, 1937): 264.

Bibliography

Adams, Ramon F. 2000. *Cowboy Lingo* (1936). New York: Houghton Mifflin Co.

Allen, Ray, and Ellie M. Hisama, eds. *Ruth Crawford Seeger's Worlds*. Rochester: University of Rochester Press, 2007.

Ames, L. D. 1911. "The Missouri Play-Party." *Journal of American Folklore* 24: 295–318.

Arlt, Gustave O. 1953. "Review of *A Treasury of Western Folklore*." *Journal of American Folklore* 66: 177–78.

Baker, Houston A., Jr. 1987. *Modernism and the Harlem Renaissance*. Chicago: University of Chicago Press.

Banks, Ann. 1980. *First Person America*. New York: Knopf.

Baughman, Ernest W. 1966. *Type and Motif Index of the Folktales of England and North America*. Indiana University Folklore Series No. 20. Bloomington: Indiana University Press.

Bauman, Richard, Roger Abrahams, and Susan Kalcik. 1976. "American Folklore and American Studies." *American Quarterly* 28: 360–77.

Bayard, Samuel P., ed. 1982. *Dance to the Fiddle, March to the Fife*. University Park: Pennsylvania State University Press.

Belden, Henry M., and Arthur Palmer Hudson, eds. 1952. *Folk Songs from North Carolina*. Frank C. Brown Collection of North Carolina Folklore, vol. 3. Durham: Duke University Press.

Bergson, Henri. 1949. *An Introduction to Metaphysics*. Translated by T. E. Hulme. Indianapolis: Bobbs-Merrill.

Bode, Carl, ed. 1977. "Letter to Fielding H. Garrison." In *The New Mencken Letters*, 102. New York: Dial Press.

Botkin, B. A. 1921a. "The Coffin in the Express House" (poem). In *The Poets of the Future, A College Anthology for 1920–1921*, ed. Henry T. Schnittkind, 203–204. Boston: Stratford Co.

——. 1921b. "The Early Life of Thomas Edward Brown: An Introduction to the Study of the Letters and Poems." Master's thesis, Graduate Faculty of Philosophy, Columbia University.

——. 1921c. "Field Wireless" (poem). *New York Evening Post*, Aug. 3.

——. 1921d. "The Robbery" (poem). *New York Evening Post*, July 27.

——. 1921e. "The Swimmer" (poem). In "The Bowling Green," ed. Christopher Morley. *New York Evening Post*, July 23.

——. 1922a. "Prescription" (poem). In "The Bowling Green," ed. Christopher Morley. *New York Evening Post*, July 21.

———. 1922b. "Witter Bynner." *University of Oklahoma Magazine* 10 (Mar.): 17.

———. 1923a. "Folk Motif" (poem). From the Yiddish of J. L. Peretz. *Jewish Forum* (May): 44.

———. 1923b. "The Gift of Singing" (edited by Lynn Riggs). *University of Oklahoma Magazine* 2 (Mar.): 14.

———. 1923c. Seven poems. In "The Lyric Art of B.A. Botkin," ed. Lynn Riggs. *University of Oklahoma Magazine* 11 (Jan.): 14.

———. 1924a. "Field Wireless" (poem). Reprinted in *The Bowling Green, An Anthology of Verse,* selected by Christopher Morley, 31–32. Garden City, N.Y.: Doubleday, Page and Co.

———. 1924b. (Review) *One Little Boy.* By Hugh de Sélincourt. *Told by an Idiot.* By Rose Macaulay. *Stratford Monthly* n.s. 2 (July): 93–94.

———. 1924c. (Review) *So Big.* By Edna Ferber. *Country People.* By Ruth Suckow. *The New Candide.* By John Cournos. *Stratford Monthly* n.s. 3 (Nov.): 188–90.

———. 1924d. Seven poems. Reprinted in *University Anthology,* ed. Joseph Francis Paxton, 16–19. *University of Oklahoma Bulletin* n.s. 290. Norman: University of Oklahoma.

———. 1925a. "The 'Oklahoma Manner' in Poetry." *University of Oklahoma Magazine* 14 (Nov.): 27–31.

———. 1925b. "On the Way Home" (four poems, with "An Appreciation" by Adeline Rubin). *University of Oklahoma Magazine* 14 (Nov.): 22.

———. 1925c. (Review) *The Autobiography of an Attitude.* By George Jean Nathan. *Daily Oklahoman,* Dec. 27.

———. 1926a. "Faculty Recital" (poem). *Harlow's Weekly* 29 (Nov. 6): 9.

———. 1926b. "Field Wireless" (poem, illustrated). Reprinted in *University of Oklahoma Magazine* 14 (Spring): 4.

———. 1926c. "The Frontier in American Poetry." *University of Oklahoma Magazine* 15 (Nov.): 9–10.

———. 1926d. "The Haunted Wood" (fifteen poems). *University of Oklahoma Magazine* 15 (Feb.): 12–13.

———. 1926e. "Kreymborg to Visit in State before Long." *Daily Oklahoman,* Oct. 17.

———. 1926f. "Lovers Tonight" (poem). *Stratford Magazine* 1 (Sept.): 20.

———. 1926g. "Moon Poems." *University of Oklahoma Magazine* 15 (Nov.): 16.

———. 1926h. (Review) *The Aristocratic West.* By Katherine Fullerton Gerould. *Daily Oklahoman,* Mar. 14.

———. 1926i. (Review) *Collected Poems.* By Vachel Lindsay. *Daily Oklahoman,* May 16.

———. 1926j. (Review) *Color.* By Countée Cullen. *Daily Oklahoman,* Apr. 11.

———. 1926k. (Review) *Cyclops' Eye.* By Joseph Auslander. *Daily Oklahoman,* Sept. 12.

———. 1926l. (Review) *Selected Poems.* By Arthur Davison Ficke. *Daily Oklahoman,* Nov. 28.

———. 1926m. "Sanctuary." In "Oklahoma Poets," ed. H. L. Mencken with the assistance of B. A. Botkin. *American Mercury* 7 (May): 14.

———. 1926n. "A Tale of Peter Panhandler." *Library* 2 (Dec. 15): 4. Roswell: New Mexico Military Institute.

———. 1926o. "Two Poems from the Armenian." By Lootfi Minas, English versions by Lootfi Minas and B. A Botkin. *Stratford Magazine* 1 (May): 22–23.

———. 1926p. "Vernal Equinox" (seven poems). *University of Oklahoma Magazine* 14 (Spring): 22.

———. 1927a. "Children of the Sun" (poem in commemoration of the fifteenth anniversary of Phi Beta Delta). *Tripod of Phi Beta Delta* 1 (May): 2.

———. 1927b. "Complaint" (poem). *Library* 3 (Jan. 15): 3.

———. 1927c. "Complaint" (poem). Reprinted in *University of Oklahoma Magazine* 16 (Nov.): 26.

———. 1927d. "Elizabeth Ball-Dream Singer." In "Oklahoma Poets No. 2." *My Oklahoma* (Dec.): 34.

———. 1927e. "Folk-Lore Songs Are Found at the Play-Parties in Oklahoma." *Oklahoma Daily*, Mar. 20, 5.

———. 1927f. "The Frontier in American Poetry." Reprinted in *Tripod of Phi Beta Delta* 1 (Dec.): 11–12.

———. 1927g. "Give and Take" (poem, illustrated). *University of Oklahoma Magazine* 15 (June): 4.

———. 1927h. "Lynn Riggs, Poet-Playwright." In "Oklahoma Poets No. 1." *My Oklahoma* 1 (Nov.): 29–31, 53.

———. 1927i. "Moon-Miracle" (poem). *Southwest Review* 12 (Jan.): 131.

———. 1927j. "Oklahoma Poets, Inc." *My Oklahoma* 1 (July): 28–31, 63.

———. 1927k. "Party Games Hold Place in Lore of State." *Daily Oklahoman*, Apr. 3.

———. 1927l. "Perverse" (poem). *University of Oklahoma Magazine* 15 (Mar.): 30.

———. 1927m. "Piano (Chopin's Berceuse)" (poem). *Oklahoma Woman* 1 (Apr.): 9.

———. 1927n. (Review) *The American Caravan.* Ed. Van Wyck Brooks, Alfred Kreymborg, Lewis Mumford, and Paul Rosenfeld. *Daily Oklahoman*, Dec. 4.

———. 1927o. (Review) *Big Lake.* By Lynn Riggs. *Daily Oklahoman*, Oct. 23.

———. 1927p. (Review) *Collected Poems of James Stephens: Hail and Farewell.* By George Moore. *Daily Oklahoman*, Jan. 16.

———. 1927q. (Review) *Fandango.* By Stanley Vestal. *Daily Oklahoman*, Apr. 24.

———. 1927r. (Review) *Lamb of God.* By Paul Horgan. *Daily Oklahoman*, May 1.

———. 1927s. (Review) *A New Testament.* By Sherwood Anderson. *Daily Oklahoman*, Dec. 25.

———. 1927t. (Review) *Poems.* By T. S. Eliot. *Ports of Call.* By Lena Whitaker Blakeney. *Daily Oklahoman*, Mar. 6.

———. 1927u. (Review) *Singing Youth.* Ed. Mabel Mountsier. *Daily Oklahoman*, Sept. 25.

———. 1927v. (Review) *Tristram.* By Edwin Arlington Robinson. *Daily Oklahoman*, May 29.

———. 1927w. "Self-Portraiture and Social Criticism in Negro Folk-Song" (rev. article, *Negro Workaday Songs* by Howard W. Odum and Guy B. Johnson). *Opportunity: A Journal of Negro Life* 5 (Feb.): 38–42.

———. 1927x. "Spectacle" (poem). *Opportunity: A Journal of Negro Life* 5 (Jan.): 22.

———. 1927y. "Train in the Mist" (poem). *Oklahoma Daily*, Oct. 2.

———. 1927z. "Travel Song" (poem). *University of Oklahoma Magazine* 15 (Jan.): 4.

——. 1927aa. "Weathercock" (eleven poems). *University of Oklahoma Magazine* 15 (Mar.): 10.

——. 1928a. "The Case for the Ballad" (Stanley Vestal). In "Oklahoma Poets No. 3." *My Oklahoma* 2 (Jan.): 27, 49.

——. 1928b. "The Fish" (poem). *Vanguard* 1 (Feb.): 28.

——. 1928c. "Going to the Store" (poem). *Harp* 4 (Mar.–Apr.): 9.

——. 1928d. "Going to the Store" (poem). Reprinted in *Anthology of Magazine Verse for 1928 and Yearbook of American Poetry,* ed. William Stanley Braithwaite, 35. New York: Harold Vinal, Ltd.

——. 1928e. "Kenneth C. Kaufman." In "Oklahoma Poets No. 4." *My Oklahoma* 2 (Apr.): 42.

——. 1928f. "People Riding" (poem). *Vanguard* 1 (Apr.): 11.

——. 1928g. "The Play-Party in Oklahoma." In *Foller de Drinkin' Gou'd: Publications of the Texas Folk-Lore Society No. VII,* ed. J. Frank Dobie, 7–24. Austin: Texas Folklore Society.

——. 1928h. (Review) *The Answering Voice.* Ed. Sara Teasdale. *Daily Oklahoman,* Sept. 16.

——. 1928i. (Review) *Armed with Madness.* By Mary Butts. *Daily Oklahoman,* Oct. 14.

——. 1928j. (Review) *The Best Poems of 1927.* Ed. L.A.G. Strong. *Daily Oklahoman,* April 8.

——. 1928k. (Review) *The Boy in the Sun.* By Paul Rosenfeld. *Daily Oklahoman,* Nov. 25.

——. 1928l. (Review) *The Bright Doom.* By John Hall Wheelock. *Steep Ascent.* By Jean Starr Untermeyer. *Ballads for Sale.* By Amy Lowell. *Happy Ending.* By Louise Imogene Guiney. *Dick Turpin's Ride and Other Poems.* By Alfred Noyes. *Requiem.* By Humbert Wolfe. *The Cyder Feast and Other Poems.* By Sacheverell Sitwell. *Trinc.* By H. Phelps Putnam. *Daily Oklahoman,* Feb. 26.

——. 1928m. (Review) *The Bronze Treasury.* Ed. Harry Kemp. *Daily Oklahoman,* Sept. 30

——. 1928n. (Review) *Brook Evans.* By Susan Glaspell. *Daily Oklahoman,* Aug. 26.

——. 1928o. (Review) *The Buck in the Snow and Other Poems.* By Edna St. Vincent Millay. *Daily Oklahoman,* Dec. 9.

——. 1928p. (Review) *Caroling Dusk.* Ed. Countée Cullen. *Daily Oklahoman,* May 13.

——. 1928q. (Review) *Cities and Men.* By Ludwig Lewisohn. *Daily Oklahoman,* May 20.

——. 1928r. (Review) *England Reclaimed.* By Osbert Sitwell. *Spring Plowing.* By Charles Malam. *The Seventh Hill.* By Robert Hillyer. *Exile and Other Poems.* By Theodore Maynard. *To Youth.* By John V. A. Weaver. *The Joy Ride and Other Poems.* By Warren Gilbert. *The King of Spain and Other Poems.* By Maxwell Bodenheim. *Poems.* By Clinch Calkins. *Wind Out of Betelgeuse.* By Margaret Todd Ritter. *Burning Bush.* By Louis Untermeyer. *Daily Oklahoman,* May 27.

——. 1928s. (Review) *François Villon.* By D.B. Wyndham Lewis. *Daily Oklahoman,* Oct. 28.

———. 1928t. (Review) *Georgie May*. By Maxwell Bodenheim. *Daily Oklahoman*, July 29.

———. 1928u. (Review) *The Gobbler of God*. By Percy MacKaye. *Daily Oklahoman*, June 24.

———. 1928v. (Review) *A History of English Literature*. Vol. 2. By Louis Cazamian. *Daily Oklahoman*, Apr. 15.

———. 1928w. (Review) *Jealous of Dead Leaves*. By Shaemas O'Sheel. *Daily Oklahoman*, Aug. 5.

———. 1928x. (Review) *Literary Blasphemies*. By Ernest Boyd. *Daily Oklahoman*, May 6.

———. 1928y. (Review) *The Lyric South*. Ed. Addison Hibbard. *Daily Oklahoman*, Oct. 7.

———. 1928z. (Review) *Man Possessed*. By William Rose Benét. *Daily Oklahoman*, July 22.

———. 1928aa. (Review) *Men Atwhiles Are Sober*. By Stephen Raushenbush. *Daily Oklahoman*, Sept. 9.

———. 1928bb. (Review) *Ol' Man Adam an' His Chillun*. By Roark Bradford. *Daily Oklahoman*, Nov. 11.

———. 1928cc. (Review) *Rainbow Round My Shoulder*. By Howard W. Odum. *Daily Oklahoman*, Apr. 22.

———. 1928dd. (Review) *The Saga of Cap'n John Smith*. By Christopher Ward. *Daily Oklahoman*, Aug. 19.

———. 1928ee. (Review) *The Sea and April*. By John Richard Moreland. *Southwest Review* 14 (Autumn): xviii, xix, xxi.

———. 1928ff. (Review) *The Second American Caravan*. Ed. Alfred Kreymborg, Lewis Mumford, and Paul Rosenfeld. *Daily Oklahoman*, Dec. 30.

———. 1928gg. (Review) *The Silk Purse*. By Elizabeth Sanxay Holding. *Daily Oklahoman*, Oct. 21.

———. 1928hh. (Review) *Stone Dust*. By Frank Ernest Hill. *Daily Oklahoman*, Sept. 23.

———. 1928ii. (Review) *The Temptation of Anthony*. By Isidor Schneider. *Daily Oklahoman*, Dec. 23.

———. 1928jj. (Review) *The Tower*. By W.B. Yeats. *Daily Oklahoman*, Nov. 18.

———. 1928kk. (Review) *The Turquoise Trail*. Ed. Alice Corbin Henderson. *Daily Oklahoman*, Sept. 9.

———. 1928ll. (Review) *The Woman Who Rode Away and Other Stories*. By D. H. Lawrence. *Daily Oklahoman*, Sept. 2.

———. 1928mm. "Spiders" (poem). *Stratford Magazine* 3 (June): 15–16.

———. 1929a. "Classroom" (poem). In "A Page of College Verse." *New Masses* 4 (Apr.): 8.

———. 1929b. "The Folk in Literature: An Introduction to the New Regionalism." In *Folk-Say: A Regional Miscellany*, 9–20.

———, ed. 1929c. *Folk-Say: A Regional Miscellany*. Norman: Oklahoma Folklore Society. Printed by the University of Oklahoma Press.

———. 1929d. "The Indian Log-Rolling." As told by Cliff Frank. In *Folk-Say: A Regional Miscellany*, 79–85.

——. 1929e. Nine poems. Reprinted in *The Oklahoma Anthology for 1929,* ed. Joseph Francis Paxton, 16–20. Studies Series No. 33. Norman: University of Oklahoma Bulletin.

——. 1929f. "Paul Bunyan on the Water Pipeline." As told by Wayne Martin, with a "Paul Bunyan Bibliography." In *Folk-Say: A Regional Miscellany,* 50–63.

——. 1929g. (Review) *American Criticism.* By Norman Foerster. *Daily Oklahoman,* Feb. 10.

——. 1929h. (Review) *Anthology of Magazine Verse for 1928.* Ed. William Stanley Braithwaite. *Daily Oklahoman,* Apr. 7.

——. 1929i. (Review) *The Best Poems of 1928.* Ed. Thomas Moult. *Daily Oklahoman,* Jan. 13.

——. 1929j. (Review) *Blue Juniata.* By Malcolm Cowley. *Daily Oklahoman,* Nov. 17.

——. 1929k. (Review) *Buckaroo Ballads.* By S. Omar Barker. *Compass Rose.* By Elizabeth Coatsworth. *Silver in the Sun.* By Grace Noll Crowell. *Star Dust and Stone.* By Glenn Ward Dresbach. *Mountain against Mountain.* By Arthur Davison Ficke. *The Turquoise Trail.* Ed. Alice Corbin Henderson. *A Bronco Pegasus.* By Charles F. Lummis. *Red Heels.* By Lexie Dean Robertson. *Along Old Trails.* By William Haskell Simpson. *Southwest Review* 15 (July): xii.

——. 1929l. (Review) *Destinations.* By Gorham B. Munson. *Daily Oklahoman,* Mar. 10.

——. 1929m. (Review) *Homer in the Sagebrush.* By James Stevens. *Daily Oklahoman,* Feb. 3.

——. 1929n. (Review) *The Life and Private History of Emily Jane Bronte.* By Romer Wilson. *Daily Oklahoman,* Feb. 24.

——. 1929o. (Review) *Moods Cadenced and Declaimed.* By Theodore Dreiser. *Daily Oklahoman,* Nov. 24.

——. 1929p. (Review) *Prophet and Fool.* By Louis Golding. *Daily Oklahoman,* Apr. 7.

——. 1929q. (Review) *Sonnets, 1889–1927.* By Edwin Arlington Robinson. *Daily Oklahoman,* Mar. 17.

——. 1929r. (Review) *A Son of Earth.* By William Ellery Leonard. *Daily Oklahoman,* Oct. 6.

——. 1929s. (Review) *A Voyage to Pagany.* By William Carlos Williams. *Daily Oklahoman,* May 19.

——. 1929t. (Review) *West-Running Brook.* By Robert Frost. *Daily Oklahoman,* Mar. 3.

——. 1929u. "Serenity and Light." Symposium on "Regional Culture in the Southwest." *Southwest Review* 15 (July): 492–93.

——. 1929v. "Track Lover" (poem). *Southwest Review* 14 (Spring): 343.

——. 1929w. "Track Lover" (poem). Reprinted in *Anthology of Magazine Verse for 1929,* ed. William Stanley Braithwaite, 24–25. New York: George Sully and Co.

——. 1929x. "The Verse Racket." *Southwest Review* 14 (Jan.): 158–67.

——. 1929y. "The Wolf Boy, a Kiowa Tale." As told by Tsa-to-ke. In *Folk-Say: A Regional Miscellany,* 32–36.

——. 1930a. "Back Home in Indiana." As told by Cliff Frank. In *Folk-Say: A Regional Miscellany: 1930,* 67–83.

——. 1930b. "Burying-Ground by Railroad" (poem). *Harp* 6 (July–Aug.): 6.

——, ed., with an introduction. 1930c. *Folk-Say: A Regional Miscellany: 1930*. Norman: University of Oklahoma Press.

——. 1930d. "The Gulls: Provincetown Harbor" (poem). *Prairie Schooner* 4 (Fall): 229.

——. 1930e. "Home Town" (poem). *Prairie Schooner* 4 (Feb.): 34–35.

——. 1930f. "I'd Like to Have Written—*Punch: The Immortal Liar; Documents in His History.*" By Conrad Aiken. *Tulsa World* (Book Page), Jan. 5.

——. 1930g. "The Lore of the Lizzie Label." *American Speech* 6 (Dec.): 81–93.

——. 1930h. "Meteor" (poem). *Poetry: A Magazine of Verse* 37 (Nov.): 85.

——. 1930i. "The Oklahoma Literary Society." As told by W. L. Wilkerson. In *Folk-Say: A Regional Miscellany: 1930*, 266–71.

——. 1930j. (Review) *The Black Christ and Other Poems.* By Countée Cullen. *Daily Oklahoman*, Feb. 9.

——. 1930k. (Review) *The Golden Stallion.* Ed. D. Maitland Bushby. *Southwest Review* 15 (Jan.): viii–ix.

——. 1930l. (Review) *The Hobo's Hornbook.* By George Milburn. *Daily Oklahoman*, July 27.

——. 1930m. (Review) *Indian Earth.* By Witter Bynner. *Southwest Review* 15 (Spring): vii–viii.

——. 1930n. (Review) *Indian Stories from the Pueblos.* By Frank G. Applegate. *Daily Oklahoman*, Jan. 19.

——. 1930o. (Review) *The New American Caravan.* Ed. Alfred Kreymborg, Lewis Mumford, and Paul Rosenfeld. *Daily Oklahoman*, Jan 19.

——. 1930p. (Review) *O City, Cities.* By R. Ellsworth Larson. *Daily Oklahoman*, Apr. 6.

——. 1930q. (Review) *Phases of English Poetry.* By Herbert Read. *Daily Oklahoman*, Mar. 23.

——. 1930r. (Review) *Walter De La Mare.* By Forrest Reid. *Daily Oklahoman*, Mar. 30.

——. 1930s. Two poems. *Morada* 3 (Spring): 83.

——. 1931a. "An Anthology of Lizzie Labels." *American Speech* (Oct.): 32–39.

——. 1931b. "Courting." As told by Cliff Frank. In *Folk-Say: A Regional Miscellany: 1931*, 278–83.

——. 1931c. " 'Folk-Say' and Folklore." *American Speech* 6 (Aug.): 404–6.

——, ed. 1931d. *Folk-Say: A Regional Miscellany: 1931.* Norman: University of Oklahoma Press.

——. 1931e. "Folk Speech in the Kentucky Mountain Cycle of Percy MacKaye." *American Speech* 7 (Apr.): 224–76.

——. 1931f. "The Gulls: Provincetown Harbor" (poem). Reprinted in *Cap and Gown: Some College Verse,* selected by R. L. Paget, 26. 4th series. Boston: L.C. Page and Co.

——. 1931g. "Literary Headlines." *American Speech* 7 (Dec.): 156–58.

——. 1931h. "Old man, what are you planting?" (poem). In *Folk-Say: A Regional Miscellany: 1931*, 5.

——, ed. 1931i. *The Southwest Scene: An Anthology of Regional Verse*. Oklahoma City: Economy Co.

——, ed. 1932a. *Folk-Say IV: The Land Is Ours*. Norman: University of Oklahoma Press.

——. 1932b. "Symbols and Horizons" (poem). In *Folk-Say IV: The Land Is Ours*, 5.

——. 1933a. "From a Western Anthology." *Panorama* (Nov.): 3.

——. 1933b. "The New Mexico Round Table on Regionalism." *New Mexico Quarterly* 3 (Aug.): 152–59.

——. 1933c. "Serenity and Light." Reprinted in *America in the Southwest*, ed. T. M. Pearce and Telfair Hendon, 139–41. Albuquerque: University of New Mexico Press.

——. 1933d. "Tall Talk and Tall Tales of the Southwest." *Candle* 9 (June 283): 3.

——. 1933e. Three poems. *Panorama* 1 (Oct.): 3.

——. 1933f. "We Talk about Regionalism—North, East, South and West." *Frontier* 13 (May): 286–96.

——. 1933g. "Writers' Round Table Not Only Rounds Up Writers of Region but Also Molds Materials and Methods into Philosophy of Regionalism." *Candle* (July 12): 3.

——. 1934a. "As One Reader to Another." *Space* (Nov.): 80.

——. 1934b. "Biography" (poem). *Panorama* 1 (Aug.): 2.

——. 1934c. "Commencement: 'I Want to Say a Few Words.'" As heard by B. A. Botkin. *Panorama* 8 (June): 4.

——. 1934d. "Folk and Folklore." In *Culture in the South*, ed. W. T. Couch, 570–93. Chapel Hill: University of North Carolina Press.

——. 1934e. "I Fall in Love with My Mother." *Panorama* 7 (Apr.): 7.

——. 1934f. "Intimate Notebook: City Summer." *Space* 1 (July): 35–36.

——. 1934g. "Mary Austin" (memorial note). *Space* 1 (Sept.): 64.

——. 1934h. "Regionalism: The Next Step." *Space* 2 (Dec.): 86–88.

——. 1934i. (Review) *Human Geography of the South*. By Rupert B. Vance. *Southwest Review* 19 (July): 12–13.

——. 1934j. "Simple Confession." *Panorama* 6 (Mar.): 6.

——, ed. 1934k. *Space* (monthly, May through December). Norman, Okla.

——. 1935a. "Critical Notebook—The Paradox of the Little Magazine: A Postscript." *Space* (Apr.): 113–15.

——. 1935b. "*Folk-Say* and *Space:* Their Genesis and Exodus." *Southwest Review* 20 (July): 321–35.

——. 1935c. "In Oklahoma" (three poems). Reprinted in *Arkansas and Oklahoma Poets: An Anthology of 29 Contemporaries*, with forewords by Rosa Zagnoni Marinoni and Hala Jean Hammond, ed. by the House of Henry Harrison, 49–51. New York: Henry Harrison.

——. 1935d. "The Last Word." *Space* (Apr.): 113.

——. 1935e. "Morning Walk" (poem). *Space* 1 (Mar.): 112.

——. 1935f. (Review) *American Ballads and Folk Songs*. Ed. John A. Lomax and Alan Lomax. *Frontier and Midland* 15 (Summer): 323–24.

——. 1935g. (Review) *Pittsburgh Memoranda*. By Haniel Long, *Daily Oklahoman*, Oct. 27.

———. 1935h. (Review) *Those Who Perish*. By Edward Dahlberg. *Windsor Quarterly* 3 (Fall): 87–88.

———, ed. 1935i. *Space* (monthly, Jan. through Apr.). Norman, Okla.

———. 1935j. "Unliterary Literature." *Trend* 2 (Jan.–Feb.): 234–35.

———. 1936. "Regionalism: Cult or Culture?" *English Journal* 25 (Mar.): 181–85.

———. 1937a. "The Air Waves, or It Can't Happen Here." *American Prefaces* 2 (Summer): 172–73.

———. 1937b. *The American Play-Party Song with a Collection of Oklahoma Texts and Tunes*. Ph.D. dissertation. Lincoln, Nebraska. Published as University Studies of the University of Nebraska, 38, Nos. 1–4. Lincoln: University of Nebraska.

———. 1937c. "The Folkness of the Folk." *English Journal* 26 (June): 461–69.

———. 1937d. "Highway West" (poem). In "Some Southwestern Poets." *New Republic* 92 (Oct. 13): 264.

———. 1937e. "The New Regionalism" (excerpt from "The Folk in Literature: An Introduction to the New Regionalism"). Reprinted in *The American Mind*, ed. Harry N. Warfel, Ralph H. Gabriel, and Stanley T. Williams, 1331–32. New York: American Book Co.

———. 1937f. "Regionalism and Culture." In *The Writer in a Changing World*, ed. Henry Hart. 140–57. New York: Equinox Cooperative Press.

———. 1938a. "Carnival" (poem). *Frontier and Midland* 18 (Summer): 227.

———. 1938b. "The Folk and the Individual: Their Creative Reciprocity." *English Journal* 27 (Feb.): 121–35.

———. 1938c. "The Function of a Folk Festival." *Washington Post*, Supplement, Apr. 25, 1938, [Fifth Annual] *Folk Festival Edition*, 3.

——— (contributor). 1938d. "Regionalism in Contemporary American Literature." In *The Problems of a Changing Population*, 247–49. Report of the Committee on Population Problems to the National Resources Committee (May). Washington, D.C.: United States Government Printing Office.

———. 1938e. (Review) *Madness in the Heart*. By Edward Donahoe. *Southern Review* 3 (Winter): 621–24.

———. 1938f. *Supplementary Instructions to the American Guide Manual: Manual for Folklore Studies* (mimeographed). Washington, D.C.: WPA, Federal Writers' Project. (Unsigned.)

———. 1939a. "Folklore" in the chapter "Folklore and Folkways." In *Nebraska: A Guide to the Cornhusker State*, 105–11. American Guide Series. New York: Viking Press.

———. 1939b. (Review) *Folk Dances of Tennessee*. By Lucien L. and Flora Lassiter McDowell. *Southern Folklore Quarterly* 3 (Sept.): 194–95.

———. 1939c. (Review) *The Negro in American Fiction, Negro Poetry and Drama*. By Sterling A. Brown. *Opportunity* 17 (June): 184.

———. 1939d. "Selected Folklore Bibliography" (mimeographed, Mar. 20). Professional and Service Letter No. 1. Washington, D.C.: WPA, Federal Writers' Project.

———. 1939e. "WPA and Folklore Research: 'Bread and Song.'" *Southern Folklore Quarterly* 3 (Mar.): 7–14.

——. 1940a. "The Folk Basis of Writing." In "Convention Summaries." *English Journal* 29 (Feb.), part 2: 15–16.

——. 1940b. "Folklore as a Neglected Source of Social History." In *The Cultural Approach to History,* ed. Caroline F. Ware for the American Historical Association, 308–15. New York: Columbia University Press.

——. 1940c. "Introduction to Folklore Craft Session, Third American Writers' Congress." In *Fighting Words,* ed. Donald Ogden Stewart, 11–14. New York: Harcourt, Brace.

——. 1941. (Review) *Straight Texas.* Ed. J. Frank Dobie and Mody C. Boatright. *Journal of American Folklore* 64 (Jan.–June): 99–100.

——. 1942. "Nebraska Folklore." Reprinted from "Folklore" in *Nebraska: A Guide to the Cornhusker State,* in *Of the People,* ed. Harry T. Warfel and Elizabeth W. Manwaring, 499–507. New York: Oxford University Press.

——. 1943a. "Folk Song Record Albums." *Music Educators Journal* 29 (Apr.): 21.

——. 1943b. "Oklahoma Folklore Society." In "North American Folklore Societies," compiled by Wayland Hand. *Journal of American Folklore* 61 (July–Sept.): 179–80.

——. 1943c. "The People's Music, U.S.A." *American Music Lover* 10 (Nov.): 67–68.

——. 1943d. (Review) *Americans and Their Songs.* By Frank Luther. *New York Times Book Review,* Apr. 11, 8.

——. 1943e. (Review) *Short Grass Country.* By Stanley Vestal. *California Folklore Quarterly* 2 (Oct.): 335–37.

——. 1944a. "American Songs for American Children, M.E.N.C. Committee on Folk Music of the United States." *Music Educators Journal* 30 (Jan.): 24–25.

——. 1944b. "American Songs for American Children, United States Folk-Song Series." *Music Educators Journal* 30, no. 2 (Feb.–Mar.): 39; no. 3 (Apr.): 27; no. 4 (Sept.–Oct.): 39.

——. 1944c. "America's Heirloom Stories." Reprinted from *A Treasury of American Folklore, Blue Book* 79 (Oct., Nov., Dec.): 1–22.

——. 1944d. "Archive of American Folk-Song." *Music Educators Journal* 30 (Sept.–Oct.): 64–65.

——. 1944e. "Dust on the Folklorists." *Journal of American Folklore* 57 (Apr.–June): 139.

——. 1944f. "Folklore for Children: American Heritage of History and Humor." *New York Post, Annual Christmas Book Section, Books at the Post,* Nov. 30, l3B.

——. 1944g. (Review) *Guide to Life and Literature of the Southwest.* By J. Frank Dobie. *California Folklore Quarterly* 3 (Jan.): 66–68.

——. 1944h. *The Sky's the Limit: A Selection from "A Treasury of American Folklore."* Ed. Louis Untermeyer. New York: Editions for the Armed Services, Inc.

——. 1944i. "The Slave as His Own Interpreter." *Library of Congress Quarterly Journal of Current Acquisitions* 2 (Nov.): 37–62.

——, ed., with an introduction. 1944j. *A Treasury of American Folklore: Stories, Ballads and Traditions of the People.* With a foreword by Carl Sandburg. New York: Crown Publishers.

——, ed. 1945a. Album 7, *Anglo-American Ballads,* Records No. AAFS 31–35; Album 8, *Negro Work Songs and Calls,* Records No. AAFS 36–40; Album 9, *Play and Dance Songs and Tunes,* Records No. AAFS 41–45; Album 10, *Negro Religious Songs and Services,* Records No. AAFS 45–50, *Folk Music of the United States from Records in the Archive of American Folk Song.* Washington, D.C.: Library of Congress.

——. 1945b. "American Songs for American Children: No. 5." *Music Educators Journal* 31 (Jan.): 36.

——. 1945c. "America's Heirloom Stories." Reprinted from *A Treasury of American Folklore, Blue Book* 80 (Jan., Feb., Mar., Apr., May, June, July, Aug., Sept.).

——. 1945d. "The Archive of American Folk Song" (with bibliography). *Library of Congress Quarterly Journal of Current Acquisitions* 2 (June): 61–69.

——. 1945e. "Foreword." In *Humorous Folk Tales of the South Carolina Negro,* by J. Mason Brewer, xvii–xviii. Orangeburg: South Carolina Negro Folklore Guild, Claflin College.

——. 1945f. "Introduction." In *Mid Country: Writings from the Heart of America,* ed. Lowry C. Wimberly, 11–14. Lincoln: University of Nebraska Press.

——, ed., with a preface and introduction. 1945g. *Lay My Burden Down: A Folk History of Slavery* (illustrated). Chicago: University of Chicago Press.

——. 1945h. (Review) *Norwegian-American Studies and Records,* vol. 4. Managing ed. Theodore C. Blegen. *United States Quarterly Book List* 1 (Mar.): 28–29.

——. 1945i. "Special Qualities of Midland Writing." *Chicago Sun Book Week, Midwest Christmas Annual* 4 (Dec. 2): 5.

——. 1946a. "American Folk Forms in Literature." In *Encyclopedia of the Arts,* ed. Dagobert D. Runes and Harry G. Schrickel, 33–34. New York: Philosophical Library.

——. 1946b. "American Folk Forms in Music." In *Encyclopedia of the Arts,* ed. Dagobert D. Runes and Harry G. Schrickel, 34–36. New York: Philosophical Library.

——. 1946c. *The American People in Their Stories, Legends, Tall Tales, Traditions, Ballads and Songs* (abridged edition of *A Treasury of American Folklore*). London: Pilot Press, Ltd.

——. 1946d. "Living Lore on the New York City Writers' Project." *New York Folklore Quarterly* 2 (Nov.): 252–63.

——. 1946e. "Paul Bunyan Was OK in His Time." *New Masses* 64 (Apr. 23): 12–14.

——. 1946f. "Publication." In "Conference on the Character and State of Studies in Folklore." *Journal of American Folklore* 59 (Oct.–Dec.): 520–22, and remarks passim.

——. 1946g. "Rediscovering America." *Book Find News* (July): 10–11.

——. 1946h. (Review) *Play Songs of the Deep South.* By Altona Trent-Johns. *California Folklore Quarterly* 5 (Oct.): 411–12.

——. 1946i. "Tradition Challenges the Negro." *Negro Digest* 4 (June): 81–82.

——. 1947a. "Art of Retelling Folk Tales." *Philadelphia Inquirer, Christmas Book Section,* Dec. 7, 29.

——. 1947b. "Coffee Grows on White Oak Trees." Reprinted from *The American Play-Party Song,* in *Folk Song: U.S.A.,* ed. Alan Lomax, Charles Seeger, and Ruth Crawford Seeger, 100–102. New York: Duell, Sloan, and Pearce.

——. 1947c. "Folklore, American." In *Ten Eventful Years,* 364–67. Chicago: University of Chicago, Encyclopaedia Britannica, Inc.

——. 1947d. "The Folksay of Freedom Songs." *New Masses* 65 (Oct. 21): 14–16.

——. 1947e. (Review) *The American Imagination at Work.* By Ben C. Clough. *Philadelphia Inquirer Books,* Aug. 24, 4.

——. 1947f. (Review) *Jonathan Draws the Long Bow.* By Richard M. Dorson. *New York Folklore Quarterly* 3 (Spring): 78–81.

——. 1947g. (Review) *Song of Robin Hood.* Ed. Ann Malcolmson. *New York Times Book Review,* Dec. 21, 13.

——, ed., with an introduction. 1947h. *A Treasury of New England Folklore: Stories, Ballads, and Traditions of the Yankee People.* New York: Crown Publishers.

——. 1948a. "Buffalo Girls," "Jim Along Josie," and "Walk Along John." Reprinted from *The American Play-Party Song,* in *American Folk Songs for Children,* ed. Ruth Crawford Seeger, 31–32, 72–75, 134–35. Garden City, N.Y.: Doubleday and Co., Inc.

——. 1948b. "Foreword." In *New England Bean-Pot,* by M. Jagendorf, xvii–xviii. New York: Vanguard Press, Inc.

——. 1948c. "Jewish Salt on Jewish Wounds" (rev. article: *A Treasury of Jewish Folklore,* by Nathan Ausubel). *Jewish Life* 3 (Nov.), part 2, Cultural Supplement: 27–28.

——. 1948d. "Wit and Myth and American Literature." *Vogue* 111 (Feb. 1): 196, 270–71, 273.

——. 1949a. "American Folklore." In *Funk & Wagnalls Standard Dictionary of Folklore, Mythology and Legend,* vol. 1, 43–48. New York: Funk & Wagnalls Co.

——. 1949b. "The Country of the Word." *Southern Packet* 5 (Oct.): 1–4.

——. 1949c. "Folk Music." In *Collier's Encyclopedia,* vol. 8, 206–207. New York: P.F. Collier and Son Corp.

——. 1949d. (Review) *Pennsylvania Songs and Legends.* By George Korson. *Notes,* 2nd series, 7 (Dec.): 113–15.

——. 1949e. Thirteen short articles ("Almanacs," "Anecdotes," "Arkansas Traveler," "Bad Man," "Brer Rabbit," "Comics," "Cracks and Slams," "Crockett," "Fearsome Critters," "Febold Feboldson," "Folklore," "Folk-Say," and "Industrial Lore"). In *Funk & Wagnalls Standard Dictionary of Folklore, Mythology and Legend.* New York: Funk & Wagnalls Co.

——, ed., with an introduction. 1949f. *A Treasury of Southern Folklore: Stories, Ballads, Traditions and Folkways of the People of the South.* With a foreword by Douglas Southall Freeman. New York: Crown Publishers.

——. 1950a. "Colorado Trail." *New York Folklore Quarterly* 6 (Winter): 268–72.

——. 1950b. "Cooperstown Experiment," "Folklore and History," and "—And All Around the Map" (notes on folklore and folk, local, and regional culture). *New York Folklore Quarterly* 6 (Autumn): 195–99.

——. 1950c. "From Trailer to Barn" (Sam Eskin). *New York Folklore Quarterly* 6 (Summer): 115–18.

——. 1950d. "Intercultural Relations" (through folklore). *New York Folklore Quarterly* 6 (Spring): 48–50.

——. 1950e. "Over the Hill" (Ruth Ann Musick). *New York Folklore Quarterly* 6 (Winter): 272.

——, ed. 1950f. *A Pocket Treasury of American Folklore.* Reduced and revised ed., with a new introduction. New York: Pocket Books, Inc.

——. 1950g. (Review) *American Folklore Fancies.* By Franz B. May. *New York Folklore Quarterly* 6 (Summer): 118.

——. 1950h. (Review) *A Harvest of World Folk Tales.* By Milton Rugoff. *New York Folklore Quarterly* 6 (Summer): 113–14.

——. 1950i. (Review) *Selected Writings of Louise Pound. New York Folklore Quarterly* 6 (Summer): 114–15.

——. 1950j. Thirty-four short articles ("Jiggs Strip," "Joe Magarac," "John or Old John," "Johnny Appleseed," "Jonathan," "Liars and Lying Tales," "Little Moron," "Lizzie Labels," "Lovers' Leap," "Mickey Mouse," "Mike Fink," "Paul Bunyan," "Pioneer and Pioneering Lore," "Play-Party," "Railroad Bill," "Ring-tailed Roarer," "Rip Van Winkle," "Salt River," "Sells," "Sheepmen Stories," "Shmoo," "Slappy Hooper," "Slow Train Humor," "Stackalee," "Stormalong," "Street Cries," "Subway Lore," "Superman," "Tall Talk," "Tony Beaver," "Uncle Remus," "Uncle Sam," "Washington Myth," "Yankee Doodle"). In *Funk & Wagnalls Standard Dictionary of Folklore, Mythology and Legend,* vol. 2. New York: Funk and Wagnalls Co.

——. 1951a. "ACLS Folklore." *New York Folklore Quarterly* 7 (Summer): 158–59.

——. 1951b. "After the Ballad Is Over" (Maude Karpeles revisits the Southern Appalachians). *New York Folklore Quarterly* 7 (Spring): 79–81.

——. 1951c. " 'A Little Christian Civility' " (improving public relations among folklorists). *New York Folklore Quarterly* 7 (Spring): 78–79.

——. 1951d. (Review) *A Guide to American Folklore.* By Levette J. Davidson. *New York Folklore Quarterly* 7 (Summer): 159.

——. 1951e. (Review) *Selected Writings of Louise Pound. Midwest Folklore* 1 (Apr.): 63–65.

——. 1951f. *A Treasury of American Folklore.* Garden City Books Reprint. Garden City, N.Y.: Garden City Books.

——, ed., with an introduction and with special introductions for the Rocky Mountain States and California regional editions. 1951g. *A Treasury of Western Folklore.* Foreword by Bernard DeVoto. New York: Crown Publishers.

——. 1952a. "All Upstairs" and "Sitting Down Together" (a visit with Harry Siemsen). *New York Folklore Quarterly* 8 (Winter): 313–15.

——. 1952b. "Battle of the Books" (war of the folklorists). *New York Folklore Quarterly* 8 (Autumn): 235.

——. 1952c. "Delegate's Report on the 34th Annual Meeting of the American Council of Learned Societies." *Journal of American Folklore* 65 (Apr.–June): 182–83.

——. 1952d. "Folklore and Culture"; "The Future of Culture"; "What Is Your Rye-Q?"; "Popular Arts and Public Taste"; and "Folklore and World Understanding" (cultural notes). *New York Folklore Quarterly* 8 (Summer): 153–57.

——. 1952e. "Good Neighbors" and "Person-to-Person" (local folklore societies and publications). *New York Folklore Quarterly* 8 (Spring): 73–75.

——. 1952f. "Out of the East" (The Westerners, New York Posse). *New York Folklore Quarterly* 8 (Autumn): 233–34.

——. 1952g. (Review) *Another Sheaf of White Spirituals*. By George Pullen Jackson. *United States Quarterly Book Review* 8 (Dec.): 362. (Unsigned.)

——. 1952h. (Review) *Bloodstoppers and Bearwalkers*. By Richard M. Dorson. *United States Quarterly Book Review* 8 (Dec.): 412–13. (Unsigned.)

——. 1952i. (Review) *Early Wisconsin through the Comic Looking-Glass*. By Jonathan W. Curvin. *New York Folklore Quarterly* 8 (Spring): 74.

——. 1952j. (Review) *The Frank C. Brown Collection of North Carolina Folklore*, vols. 1–3. Gen. ed. Newman Ivey White. *United States Quarterly Book Review* 8 (Dec.): 413–14. (Unsigned.)

——. 1952k. (Review) *Selected Writings of Louise Pound*. *Western Folklore* 11 (Oct.): 302–304.

——. 1952l. "A Saga of a Singer" (Oscar Brand). *New York Folklore Quarterly* 8 (Winter): 316–17.

——. 1952m. "A Sudden Man" (George S. Brooks family anecdote). *New York Folklore Quarterly* 8 (Spring): 73–75.

——. 1953a. "Applied Folklore: Creating Understanding through Folklore." *Southern Folklore Quarterly* 17 (Sept.): 199–206.

——. 1953b. Cultural and Folklore Approach to Jazz in Symposium on "New Directions in Jazz Research: The New York Seminar" (remarks). *Record Changer*, special issue, "The Institute of Jazz Studies" (July–Aug.): 9–13, 50–51.

——. 1953c. "Delegate's Report on the Third National Conference of the United States National Commission for Unesco." *Journal of American Folklore* 66 (July–Sept.): 253–54.

——. 1953d. "Delegate's Report on the 35th Annual Meeting of the American Council of Learned Societies." *New York Folklore Quarterly* [issue no. not available]: 252–53.

——. 1953e. "Eye to Eye" (Paul Vanderbilt and iconography). *New York Folklore Quarterly* 9 (Winter) 316–17.

——. 1953f. "Middle Atlantic Regionalism and Folklore." *New York Folklore Quarterly* 9 (Spring): 71–72.

——. 1953g. "More Neighbors" (two New Hampshire place-name stories). *New York Folklore Quarterly* 9 (Winter): 316.

——. 1953h. (Review) *American Folksongs of Protest*. By John Greenway. *United States Quarterly Book Review* 9 (Dec.): 415–16. (Unsigned.)

——. 1953i. (Review) *American Nonsinging Games*. By Paul G. Brewster. *United States Quarterly Book Review* 9 (June): 153. (Unsigned.)

——. 1953j. (Review) *Down in the Holler*. By Vance Randolph and George Pickett Wilson. *United States Quarterly Book Review* 9 (Sept.): 296–97. (Unsigned.)

———. 1953k. (Review) *Hell on Horses and Women.* By Alice Marriott. *United States Quarterly Book Review* 9 (Dec.): 428. (Unsigned.)

———. 1953l. (Review) *Music in the Southwest, 1825–1950.* By Howard Swan. *United States Quarterly Book Review* 9 (June): 152–53. (Unsigned.)

———. 1953m. (Review) *Paul Bunyan, Last of the Frontier Demigods.* By Daniel G. Hoffman. *New York Folklore Quarterly* 9 (Spring): 73–74.

———. 1953n. (Review) *Shanghai Pierce.* By Chris Emmett. *United States Quarterly Book Review* 9 (Dec.): 392. (Unsigned.)

———. 1953o. (Review) *The Typical Texan.* By Joseph Leach. *New York Folklore Quarterly* 9 (Spring): 72–73.

———. 1953p. (Review) *Who Blowed Up the Church House? and Other Ozark Folk Tales.* By Vance Randolph. *United States Quarterly Book Review* 9 (Mar.): 30. (Unsigned.)

———. 1953q. (Review) *The World's Great Folk Tales.* By James R. Foster. *New York Times Book Review,* Aug. 9, 16.

———. 1953r. "The Spiels of New York." *New York Folklore Quarterly* 9 (Autumn): 165–75.

———, ed., with an introduction. 1953s. *A Treasury of Railroad Folklore: The Stories, Tall Tales, Traditions, Ballads and Songs of the American Railroad Man* (illustrated). With Alvin F. Harlow. New York: Crown Publishers.

———. 1953t. "Upstate, Downstate." *New York Folklore Quarterly* 9 (Summer): 153–54.

———. 1954a. "City Children's Lore." *New York Folklore Quarterly* 10 (Summer): 155.

———. 1954b. "Cultural Symbolism and the Automobile." *New York Folklore Quarterly* 10 (Autumn): 235–36.

———. 1954c. "First Lady of Intercultural Education" (Rachel Davis DuBois). *New York Folklore Quarterly* 10 (Spring): 71–72.

———. 1954d. "Folklore and People: Highlights of a Conference" (City Folklore and Its Uses). *New York Folklore Quarterly* 10 (Summer): 153–55.

———. 1954e. "Joke Town: U.S.A." In *Sidewalks of America: Folklore, Legends, Sagas, Traditions, Customs, Songs, Stories and Sayings of City Folk,* 481–83. Indianapolis and New York: Bobbs-Merrill Co., Inc.

———. 1954f. "Point of View" (a personal statement of the author's folklore approach). *New York Folklore Quarterly* 10 (Autumn): 233–35.

———. 1954g. "Ralph Boggs on Folklore." *New York Folklore Quarterly* 10 (Winter): 316–17.

———. 1954h. (Review) *American Ways of Life.* By George Stewart. *New York Times Book Review,* July 18, 3.

———. 1954i. (Review) *Ballads Migrant in New England.* Ed. Helen Hartness Flanders and Marguerite Olney. *United States Quarterly Book Review* 10 (Mar.): 44–45. (Unsigned.)

———. 1954j. (Review) *Greener Fields.* By Alice Marriott. *United States Quarterly Book Review* 10 (Mar.): 8. (Unsigned.)

———. 1954k. (Review) *Negro Slave Songs in the United States.* By Miles Mark Fisher. *New York Times Book Review,* Jan. 24, 28.

———. 1954l. (Review) *The Old Country Store.* By Gerald Carson. *Nation* 178 (Apr. 24): 364.

——. 1954m. "Ruth Crawford Seeger" (memorial note). *New York Folklore Quarterly* 10 (Spring): 73–74.

——, ed., with an introduction. 1954n. *Sidewalks of America: Folklore, Legends, Sagas, Traditions, Customs, Songs, Stories and Sayings of City Folk* (illustrated). Indianapolis and New York: Bobbs-Merrill Co., Inc.

——. 1954o. "Tom Glazer's Blend." *New York Folklore Quarterly* 10 (Winter): 315–16.

——. 1954p. "Will Geer's Folk Say" (Mark Twain readings). *New York Folklore Quarterly* 10 (Winter): 314–15.

——. 1955a. "Folklore and History." *Manuscripts* 7 (Summer 1955): 256–60.

——. 1955b. "Foreword." In *Fightin' Mose*, by Harold W. Felton, vii–x. New York: Alfred A. Knopf.

——. 1955c. "Knishes and Pasteles Calientes" (Conference on Puerto Rican Folkways: Pathways to Understanding). *New York Folklore Quarterly* 11 (Spring): 73–74.

——. 1955d. "Last of the Showboatmen" (Captain Billy Menke). *Westerners New York Posse Brand Book* 2: 81, 94.

——. 1955e. "Love and Learning" (66th Annual Meeting of the American Folklore Society). *New York Folklore Quarterly* 11 (Spring): 74–75.

——. 1955f. "Number Two and Number Three." (Harold W. Thompson retires as editor of *NYFQ*). *New York Folklore Quarterly* 11 (Winter): 310.

——. 1955g. (Review) *American Heroes: Myth and Reality*. By Marshall W. Fishwick. *United States Quarterly Book Review* 11 (Mar.): 52. (Unsigned.)

——. 1955h. (Review) *Amishland*. By Kiehl Newswanger and Christian Newswanger. *New York Times Book Review*, Jan. 16, 29.

——. 1955i. (Review) *The Devil's Pretty Daughter, and Other Ozark Folk Tales*. By Vance Randolph. *United States Quarterly Book Review* 11 (Sept.): 341. (Unsigned.)

——. 1955j. (Review) *Ghosts in American Houses*. By James Reynolds. *New York Times Book Review*, Dec. 4, 30.

——. 1955k. (Review) *Johnny Appleseed: Man and Myth*. By Robert Price. *United States Quarterly Book Review* 11 (Mar.): 13–14.

——. 1955l. (Review) *South from Hell-fer-Sartin*. By Leonard W. Roberts. *United States Quarterly Book Review* 11 (Sept.): 342.

——. 1955m. (Review) *The Susquehanna*. By Carl Carmer. *United States Quarterly Book Review* 11 (June): 249. (Unsigned.)

——. 1955n. (Review) *Texas Folk and Folklore*. Ed. Mody C. Boatright, Wilson M. Hudson, and Allen Maxwell. *New York Times Book Review*, Apr. 24, 36.

—— ed., with an introduction and special introductions for the Upper Mississippi, Ohio River, and Lower Mississippi regional editions. 1955o. *A Treasury of Mississippi River Folklore: Stories, Ballads, Traditions and Folkways of the Mid-American River Country* (illustrated). Foreword by Carl Carmer. New York: Crown Publishers.

——. 1955p. "TV Crockett" and "Add Crockettiana." *New York Folklore Quarterly* 11 (Autumn): 231–34.

——. 1956a. "Cornhusker Bee" (Nebraska visit). *New York Folklore Quarterly* 12 (Autumn): 227–28.

——, ed., with an introduction. 1956b. *New York City Folklore: Legends, Tall Tales, Anecdotes, Stories, Sagas, Heroes and Characters, Customs, Traditions, and Sayings* (illustrated). New York: Random House.

——. 1956c. "The Nine Lives of Crockett." *New York Folklore Quarterly* 12 (Spring): 74–75.

——. 1956d. "On the Loose" (folklore and linguistic change). *New York Folklore Quarterly* 12 (Autumn): 228.

——. 1956e. (Review) *David Crockett: The Man and the Legend*. By James Atkins Shackford. Ed. John B. Shackford. *New York Times Book Review*, Sept. 2, 3.

——. 1956f. (Review) *Half Horse Half Alligator*. Ed. Walter Blair and Franklin J. Meine. *New York Times Book Review*, Oct. 7, 28.

——. 1956g. (Review) *The Roads of Home*. By Henry Charlton Beck. *New York Herald Tribune Book Review*, Dec. 9, 4.

——. 1956h. (Review) *The Story of American Folk Song*. By Russell Ames. *New York Folklore Quarterly* 12 (Autumn): 226.

——. 1956i. (Review) *Tales of Old-Time Texas*. By J. Frank Dobie. *United States Quarterly Book Review* 12 (Mar.): 43. (Unsigned.)

——. 1956j. "Saranac Sage" (William Chapman White, memorial note). *New York Folklore Quarterly* 12 (Autumn): 225–26.

——. 1956k. *The Search* (TV film on "The Two Sisters" produced by Irving Gitlin). *New York Folklore Quarterly* 12 (Spring): 72–73.

——. 1956l. "Such a Getting Upstairs," "Sandy Land," and "Sandy Land." Reprinted from *The American Play-Party Song*, in *Music for Living: Book Two, In Our Town*, ed. James L. Mursell et al., 26; *Book Three, Now and Long Ago*, 49; and *Book Four, Near and Far*, 34. Morristown, N.J.: Silver Burdett Co.

——. 1957a. "Captain Jinks." Reprinted from *The American Play-Party Song*, in *Voices of America*, ed. Max T. Krone, 98. Chicago: Follett Publishing Co.

——. 1957b. "Edith Allaire" (memorial note). *New York Folklore Quarterly* 13 (Summer): 148.

——. 1957c. "Many Faces" (Hans Hacker and New York enthusiasts). *New York Folklore Quarterly* 13 (Spring): 64–65.

——. 1957d. "The Nostalgic Fallacy and the Good Old Days." *New York Folklore Quarterly* 13 (Summer): 145–46.

——. 1957e. "Out of Canada" (Edith Fulton Fowke). *New York Folklore Quarterly* 13 (Winter): 311–12.

——. 1957f. "Passing of the *USQBR*." *New York Folklore Quarterly* 13 (Spring): 65.

——. 1957g. "Retrospective—1957" (Louise Pound). In *Roundup: A Nebraska Reader*, ed. Virginia Faulkner, 232–35. Lincoln: University of Nebraska Press.

——. 1957h. (Review) *Sounds of My City* (record). By Tony Schwartz. *New York Folklore Quarterly* 13 (Spring): 63–64.

——. 1957i. (Review) *Whistlin' Woman and Crowin' Hen*. By Julian Lee Rayford. *New York Folklore Quarterly* 13 (Summer): 146–47.

——. 1957j. (Review) *Why the Chisholm Trail Forks, and Other Tales of the Cattle Country.* By Andy Adams. Ed. Wilson M. Hudson. *New York Folklore Quarterly* 13 (Summer): 147.

——, ed., with an introduction. 1957k. *A Treasury of American Anecdotes: Sly, Salty, Shaggy Stories of Heroes and Hellions, Beguilers and Buffoons, Spellbinders and Scapegoats, Gagsters, and Gossips, from the Grassroots and Sidewalks of America.* New York: Random House.

——. 1958a. "From Many Roots." *What's New* 209 (Christmas): 29–32.

——, ed., with an introduction. 1958b. *The Illustrated Book of American Folklore: Stories, Legends, Tall Tales, Riddles, and Rhymes.* With Carl Withers. Illustrated by Irv Docktor. New York: Grosset and Dunlap.

——. 1958c. "In Memoriam" (Levette J. Davidson). *New York Folklore Quarterly* 14 (Spring): 68–69.

——, ed. 1958d. *Lay My Burden Down.* Reprinted (with index). Phoenix Books (paperback). Chicago: University of Chicago Press.

——. 1958e. "Lincolniana," "Lincoln National Life Foundation," and "Culture in Fort Wayne." *New York Folklore Quarterly* 14 (Spring): 66–68.

——. 1958f. "The Liveliest Art" (Lee Shaw's *Caravan*). *New York Folklore Quarterly* 14 (Summer): 152–54.

——. 1958g. "The Man from Wilkes-Barre" (George Korson). *New York Folklore Quarterly* 14 (Summer): 154–55.

——. 1958h. "Never Go Back: In the Short Grass Country with Walter Campbell (1887–1957)—A Personal Reminiscence of a Trip with the Late Writer, Historian and Teacher." *Westerners New York Posse Brand Book* 5: 39, 46.

——. 1958i. (Review) *American Murder Ballads and Their Stories.* By Olive Woolley Burt. *New York Times Book Review,* Sept. 21, 3.

——. 1958j. "We Called It 'Living Lore.' " *New York Folklore Quarterly* 14.3 (Fall): 189–201.

——. 1958k. "We Called It 'Living Lore.' " In *Whatever Makes Papa Laugh: A Folklore Sheaf Honoring Harold W. Thompson,* ed. Warren S. Walker, 29–41. Cooperstown, N.Y.: New York Folklore Society.

——. 1959a. "Caravan" (Billy Faier takes over). *New York Folklore Quarterly* 15 (Summer): 153–54.

——. 1959b. "The Carnegie Corporation and the Archive of Folksong." *New York Folklore Quarterly* 15 (Summer): 154–55.

——. 1959c. "Louise Pound (1872–1958)" (memorial notice). *Western Folklore* 18 (July): 201–202.

——. 1959d. "More on the Problems and Purposes of the State Folklore Journal." *New York Folklore Quarterly* 15 (Summer): 151–53.

——. 1959e. "New York at the AFS Meeting" and "Accent on Youth" (new trends at the 70th annual meeting). *New York Folklore Quarterly* 15 (Spring): 71–72.

——. 1959f. "Pound Sterling: Letters from a Lady Professor." *Prairie Schooner* 33 (Spring): 20–31.

——. 1959g. (Review) *The American Folklore Reader.* Ed. John T. Flanagan and Arthur Palmer Hudson. *New York Herald Tribune Book Review,* Jan. 4, 7.

——. 1959h. (Review) *The Book of Negro Folklore*. Ed. Langston Hughes and Arna Bontemps. *New York Herald Tribune Book Review*, Feb. 1, 3.

——. 1959i. (Review) *Nebraska Folklore*. By Louise Pound. *New York Folklore Quarterly* 15 (Autumn): 234–35.

——. 1959j. (Review) *A Pioneer Songster*. By Harold W. Thompson and Edith E. Cutting. *New York Folklore Quarterly* 15 (Autumn): 234.

——. 1959k. (Review) *Sticks in the Knapsack*. By Vance Randolph. *Tales from the Cloud-Walking Country*. By Marie Campbell. *New York Times Book Review*, Jan. 18, 5.

——. 1960a. "Apple Cider 'n 'Simmon Beer." Reprinted from *What's New* (Christmas, 1957), in *The Abbott Christmas Book*, ed. Herbert W. Luthin, 17–19. Garden City, N.Y.: Doubleday and Co., Inc.

——, ed., with an introduction. 1960b. *A Civil War Treasury of Tales, Legends and Folklore*. Illustrated by Warren Chappell. New York: Random House, 1960.

——. 1960c. "Newspaperman as Storyteller" (Allan M. Trout). *New York Folklore Quarterly* 16 (Spring): 69–71.

——. 1960d. (Review) *Been Here and Gone*. By Frederic Ramsey, Jr. *New York Times Book Review*, Aug. 28, 7.

——. 1960e. (Review) *The Block*. By Ralph Schoenstein. *New York Folklore Quarterly* 16 (Winter): 302–303.

——. 1960f. (Review) *The Joe Miller of the Near East*. By Albert Rapp, with preface and notes by Nat Schmulowitz. *New York Folklore Quarterly* 16 (Winter): 302–303.

——. 1960g. (Review) *Meyer Berger's New York*. *New York Folklore Quarterly* 16 (Spring): 68–69.

——. 1960h. (Review) *Our Last Family Countess and Related Stories*. By Antonio Barolini. *Croton-Cortlandt News* (Croton-on-Hudson, N.Y.), Feb. 18, 4.

——. 1960i. (Review) *Three Circles of Light*. By Pietro di Donato. *New York Folklore Quarterly* 16 (Spring): 68.

——. 1960j. "Sandy Land." From *The American Play-Party Song*, in *Songs from Music for Living, Silver Burdett Company Records That Teach: Book 4, Music Near and Far*, Album 2, Side 2, 54097, P84, T30.

——. 1960k. "Such a Getting Upstairs." From *The American Play-Party Song*, in *Songs from Music for Living, Silver Burdett Company Records That Teach: Book Two, Music in Our Town*, Album 15, Side I, FR992, P26, T22.

——. 1960l. "Your Turn for Sugar and Tea." From *The American Play-Party Song*, in *Songs from Music for Living, Silver Burdett Company Records That Teach: Book Two, Music in Our Town*, Album 12, Side 2, FR987, P25, T20.

——. 1961a. "Civil War Collector" and "Some Lee Stories" (Rosanna A. Blake). *New York Folklore Quarterly* 17 (Spring): 69–72.

——. 1961b. "A Civil War Sampler" (from *A Civil War Treasury of Tales, Legends, and Folklore*). *New York Folklore Quarterly* 17 (Spring): 10–13.

——. 1961c. "Educated Folklore." *New York Folklore Quarterly* 17 (Winter): 297–98.

——. 1961d. "A Good War Dies Hard." *Croton-Cortlandt News* (Croton-on-Hudson, N.Y.), Jan. 19, 1.

——. 1961e. "Hey Jim Along Josie." Reprinted from *The American Play-Party Song*, in *The Oxford School Music Books: Pupils' Book I, Beginners*, ed. Gordon Reynolds, 4. London: Oxford University Press.

——. 1961f. "[Jewish] Folklore as Recall and Renewal" (guest editor's editorial). *Recall* (Los Angeles, Jewish Heritage Foundation) 2 (Winter): 1–3.

——. 1961g. "Jim Along Josie." Reprinted in *Sing for Joy*, ed. Norman and Margaret Mealy, 124. Greenwich, Conn.: Seabury Press.

——, ed. consultant. 1961h. *The Life Treasury of American Folklore*. By the Editors of *Life*, with paintings by James Lewicki. New York: Time, Inc.

——. 1961i. "Proposal for an Applied Folklore Center." *New York Folklore Quarterly* 17 (Summer): 151–54.

——. 1961j. (Review) *Blues Fell This Morning*. By Paul Oliver. *New York Times Book Review*, Nov. 12, 46.

——. 1961k. (Review) *Joel Chandler Harris, Uncle Remus Stories* (record). As told by Morris Mitchell. *New York Folklore Quarterly* 17 (Winter): 299–300.

——. 1961l. (Review) *Ruth Rubin Sings Yiddish Folk Songs* (record). *New York Folklore Quarterly* 17 (Winter): 300–301.

——. 1961m. (Review) *Two for a Horse: A Pictorial History, Grave and Comic, of Patent Medicines*. By Gerald Carson. *New York Folklore Quarterly* 17 (Winter): 298–99.

——. 1961n. "Some Northern [Civil War] Recollections." (Corporal William H. Gay). *New York Folklore Quarterly* 17 (Spring): 72–73.

——. 1962a. "Charles Francis Potter" (memorial note). *New York Folklore Quarterly* 18 (Winter): 305–306.

——. 1962b. "Down in Alabama." Reprinted from *The American Play-Party Song*, in *Birchard Music Series: Book Three*, ed. Sylvesta M. Wassum et al., 30. Evanston, Ill.: Summy-Birchard Co.

——. 1962c. "The Folkness of the Folk" and "Applied Folklore." Reprinted in *Folklore in Action: Essays for Discussion in Honor of MacEdward Leach*, ed. Horace P. Beck, 44–57. Publications of the American Folklore Society, Bibliographical and Special Series, vol. 14. Philadelphia: American Folklore Society, Inc.

——. 1962d. "Hello, Susie Brown." Reprinted from *The American Play-Party Song*, in *Birchard Music Series: Book Six*, ed. Sylvesta M. Wassum et al, 95. Evanston, Ill.: Summy-Birchard Co.

——. 1962e. "The Making of a Folklorist" (Harold W. Thompson). *New York Folklore Quarterly* 18 (Winter): 306–307.

——. 1962f. "News from Nebraska," "Predecessors and Precedents," "A Challenge and an Opportunity," and "The Role of the State Folklore Society." *New York Folklore Quarterly* 18 (Spring): 76–79.

——. 1962g. (Review) *The Ballad Mongers*. By Oscar Brand. *New York Folklore Quarterly* 18 (Winter): 304–305.

——. 1962h. "Speech Values as a Cultural Resource," " 'Tells' from England," "Overheards," and "Greetings from Old Kentucky" (folk-say). *New York Folklore Quarterly* 18 (Summer): 149–53.

——. 1962i. "Two Anecdotes of Immigrant Life." By J. Gorelick, translated from the Yiddish by B. A. Botkin. *New York Folklore Quarterly* 18 (Spring): 65–67.

——. 1962j. "Walk Along, John." Reprinted from *The American Play-Party Song,* in *Birchard Music Series: Book One,* ed. Sylvesta M. Wassum et al., 153. Evanston, Ill.: Summy-Birchard Co.

——. 1962k. "Your Turn for Sugar and Tea." Reprinted from *The American Play-Party Song,* in *The Story of Music Education and Silver Burdett Co.,* 13. Morristown, N.J.: Silver Burdett Co.

——. 1963a. *The American Play-Party Song.* Reprinted, with a new preface. New York: Frederick Ungar Publishing Co.

——. 1963b. *Die Stimme des Negers: Befreite Sklaven erzählen* (a German-language selection from *Lay My Burden Down*). Translated by Hans Wollschläger. Ed. and with an introduction by Kurt Heinrich Hansen. Hamburg: Nannen-Verlag.

——. 1963c. "DK and the CDS" (Country Dance Society Party for Douglas Kennedy). *New York Folklore Quarterly* 29 (Sept.): 226–28.

——, ed. consultant, with an introduction. 1963d. "The Folklore of the Badman" and "Notes on the Songs." In *The Badmen: Songs, Stories and Pictures of the Western Outlaws from Backhills to Border, 1865–1900,* 11–16, 54–60. The Columbia Records Legacy Collection, produced by Goddard Lieberson. New York: Columbia Records, Inc.

——, moderator's introduction and remarks. 1963e. "The Folksong Revival: A Symposium." *New York Folklore Quarterly* 29 (June 1963): 83–85 and 86–142 passim.

——. 1963f. "Little Magazines of the Folksong Revival." *New York Folklore Quarterly* 29 (Mar.): 62–66.

——. 1963g. "A Sampler of Western Folklore and Songs." In *The Book of the American West,* ed. Jay Monaghan, 503–60. New York: Julian Messner, Inc.

——. 1963h. "Scary Stories for Scared Children." *New York Folklore Quarterly* 29 (Sept.): 229–30.

——, ed., with an introduction. 1963i. *A Treasury of Railroad Folklore.* With Alvin F. Harlow. Reprint. New York: Bonanza Books.

——. 1964a. "Country People and Yankee Storytellers: New Hampshire Local Anecdotes" (from *A Treasury of New England Folklore,* revised ed.). *New York Folklore Quarterly* 20 (Dec.): 263–69.

——. 1964b. Excerpts from *Lay My Burden Down.* Reprinted in *In White America.* Original Cast Recording. Columbia Masterworks, KOL 6030.

——. 1964c. Excerpts from *Lay My Burden Down.* Reprinted in *In White America: A Documentary Play,* by Martin B. Duberman, 15–18, 35–36. Boston: Houghton Mifflin Co. First presented at the Sheridan Square Playhouse, New York City, Oct. 31, 1963.

——. 1964d. "Folklore Values" (questions of the meaning and uses of tradition in the present revival). *New York Folklore Quarterly* 20 (June): 139–40.

——. 1964e. "*Folksay*" (letter). *Columbia University Forum* 7 (Winter): 3.

———. 1964f. "The Folksong Revival: Cult or Culture?" *Folk Music & Dance: Newsletter of the U.S. National Committee, International Folk Music Council* 4 (Apr.): 1–4.

———. 1964g. "Obiter Dicta: Harold Thompson as Seen in His New York Folklore Society Correspondence." *New York Folklore Quarterly* 20 (Sept.): 223–28.

———. 1964h. (Review) *Folklore Keeps the Past Alive.* By Arthur Palmer Hudson. *New York Folklore Quarterly* 20 (June): 141.

———. 1964i. (Review) *From Rags to Riches: Horatio Alger, Jr., and the American Dream.* By John Tebbel. *New York Folklore Quarterly* 20 (June): 142–43.

———. 1964j. (Review) *In White America* (drama). By Martin B. Duberman. *New York Folklore Quarterly* 20 (June): 141–42.

———. 1964k. (Review) *Larry Gorman: The Man Who Made the Songs.* By Edward D. Ives. *New York Folklore Quarterly* 20 (Dec.): 296–97.

———. 1964l. (Review) *Play-Party Games from Kansas.* By S. J. Sackett. *Western Folklore* 23.1 (Jan.): 65–66.

———. 1964m. (Review) *Tree of Arrows.* By Louis A. Brennan. *New York Folklore Quarterly* 20 (Dec.): 297–98.

———. 1964n. "Sandy Land." Reprinted from *The American Play-Party Song*, in *Making Music Your Own*, ed. Beatrice Landeck et al., vols. 2 and 3: 5 and 41. Morristown, N.J.: Silver Burdett Co.

———. 1964o. "Speaking of Books" (the animal tall tale). *New York Times Book Review*, Apr. 26, 2.

———. 1965a. " 'Applied Folklore' Once More." *New York Folklore Quarterly* 21 (Mar.): 65–66.

———. 1965b. "The Folk Roots of Dick Gregory's Humor." *New York Folklore Quarterly* 21 (June): 145–48.

———. 1965c. "The Folk Song Revival: Cult or Culture." Reprinted from *Folk Music and Dance*, in *Sing Out!* 15 (Mar.): 30–32.

———. 1965d. "Love in the City." As told by Fanya Del Bourgo. *New York Folklore Quarterly* 21 (Sept.): 165–78, 231–32.

———. 1965e. "L. Zemljanova on Folklore and Democracy." *Journal of the Folklore Institute* 2 (June): 225–26.

———. 1965f. " 'Make a Job or Take a Job': A Yankee Work Saga." As told by Fred Mills. In *A Treasury of New England Folklore*, 44–51. Revised ed. New York: Crown Publishers.

———. 1965g. "More 'Conflict and Promise in Folklore.' " *New York Folklore Quarterly* 21 (Mar.): 65.

———. 1965h. (Review) *Deep Down in the Jungle . . . Negro Narrative Folklore from the Streets of Philadelphia.* By Roger D. Abrahams. *New York Folklore Quarterly* 21 (Mar.): 66–67.

———. 1965i. (Review) *A Guide for Field Workers in Folklore.* By Kenneth S. Goldstein. *New York Folklore Quarterly* 21 (Mar.): 67–68.

———. 1965j. "Sandy Land." Reprinted from *The American Play-Party Song*, in *Making Music Your Own*, vol. 4: 21. Morristown, N.J.: Silver Burdett Co.

———. 1965k. "A Sentimental Gentleman of Folk Music" (Frank M. Warner). *New York Folklore Quarterly* 21 (June): 148–49.

——. 1965l. "*Space*—After Thirty Years." *Carleton Miscellany* 6 (Winter): 26–31.

——, ed., with a new introduction. 1965m. *A Treasury of New England Folklore*. Revised ed. New York: Crown Publishers.

——. 1966a. "Folk Songs and the Top 40" (symposium). *Sing Out!* 16 (Feb.–Mar.): 14–15.

——. 1966b. (Review) *Born to Win*. By Woody Guthrie. Ed. Robert Sheldon. *New York Folklore Quarterly* 22 (Mar.): 59–61.

——. 1966c. (Review) *Rebel Voices: An I.W.W. Anthology*. Ed. Joyce L. Kornbluh. *Western Folklore* 25 (July): 205–206.

——. 1967a. "Applied Folklore: A Semantic-Dynamic Approach." Manuscript.

——. 1967b. (Review) *Ain't You Got a Right to the Tree of Life?: The People of Johns Island, South Carolina: Their Faces, Their Words, and Their Songs*. Ed. Guy Carawan and Candie Carawan. *New York Folklore Quarterly* 23 (Mar.): 60–61.

——. 1968a. "Automobile Humor: From the Horseless Carriage to the Compact Car." *Journal of Popular Culture* 1.4 (Spring): 395–402.

——. 1968b. (Review) *The Negro and His Folklore in Nineteenth Century Periodicals*. By Bruce Jackson. *New York Folklore Quarterly* 24 (Mar.): 71–72.

Brewster, Paul G. 1939. "Folksongs from Indiana." *Southern Folklore Quarterly* 3.4 (Dec.): 201–22.

Brooks, Van Wyck. 1968. *Van Wyck Brooks, the Early Years: A Selection from His Works*. Ed. Claire Sprague. New York: Harper Torchbooks.

Brown, Sterling A. 1930. "The Blues as Folk Poetry." In *Folk-Say: A Regional Miscellany II*, ed. Benjamin A. Botkin, 324–39. Norman: University of Oklahoma Press.

——. 1930–32. Letters to Benjamin A. Botkin. Sterling Brown Papers, Moorland-Spingarn Research Center, Howard University, Washington, D.C.

——. 1937. "The Negro in Washington." *Washington: City and Capital*. Federal Writers' Project. Washington, D.C.: U.S. Government Printing Office.

——. 1955. "The New Negro in Literature, 1925–1955." In *The New Negro Thirty Years Afterward*, ed. Rayford W. Logan, 57–72. Washington, D.C.: Howard University Press.

——. 1980. *The Collected Poems of Sterling A. Brown*. Ed. Michael S. Harper. Evanston: Northwestern University Press. Rpt. 1996.

——. 1996. "The New Negro in Literature." In *A Son's Return: Selected Essays of Sterling A. Brown*, ed. Mark A. Sanders, 184–203. Boston: Northeastern University Press.

Brown, Sterling A., Arthur P. Davis, and Ulysses Lee, eds. 1969. *The Negro Caravan* (1941). New York: Arno.

Brown, Sterling A., and Alain Locke. 1930. "Folk Values in a New Medium." In *Folk-Say II*, ed. Benjamin A. Botkin, 340–45. Norman: University of Oklahoma Press.

Canter, Elmer A. 1931. Letter to Sterling A. Brown. July 30. Sterling Brown Papers, Moorland-Spingarn Research Center, Howard University, Washington, D.C.

Cantwell, Robert. 1996. *When We Were Good: The Folk Revival*. Cambridge, Mass.: Harvard University Press.

Chappell, William. 1965. *Popular Music of the Olden Time.* 2 vols. London: Chappell and Co., 1859; reprint, New York: Dover Publications.

Colcord, Joanna C. 1938. *Songs of American Sailormen.* New York: Norton.

"Conference on the Character and State of Studies in Folklore." 1946. *Journal of American Folklore* 59 (Oct.–Dec.): 497–527.

Conn, Philip W. 1978. "Traditional Courtship and Marriage Customs of the Appalachian South." In *Glimpses of Southern Appalachian Folk Culture: Papers in Memory of Norbert F. Riedl,* 34–42. Chattanooga: Tennessee Anthropological Association.

Cowell, Henry, ed. 1933. *American Composers on American Music.* Stanford: Stanford University Press.

Crawford Seeger, Ruth. 1948. *American Folk Songs for Children.* New York: Doubleday.

———. 1950. *Animal Folk Songs for Children.* New York: Doubleday.

———. 1953. *American Folk Songs for Christmas.* New York: Doubleday.

———. 2001. *The Music of American Folk Song and Selected Other Writings on American Folk Music.* Ed. Larry Polansky with Judith Tick. Rochester, N.Y.: University of Rochester Press.

Cunningham, Keith. 1972. "Another Look at the Play-Party." *AFFword* 2: 12–23.

———. 1996. "Play-Party." In *American Folklore: An Encyclopedia,* ed. Jan Harold Brunvand, 562–64. New York: Garland Publishing.

Davis, Angela Y. 1998. *Blues Legacies and Black Feminism.* New York: Pantheon.

Davis, Arthur Kyle, Jr. 1929. *Folksongs of Virginia: A Descriptive Index and Classification.* Durham: Duke University Press.

Davis, Charles T., and Henry Louis Gates. 1985. *The Slave's Narrative.* New York: Oxford University Press.

Davis, Francis. 1995. *The History of the Blues.* New York: Hyperion.

Denning, Michael. 1996. *The Cultural Front: The Laboring of American Culture in the Twentieth Century.* London: Verso.

Dorman, Robert L. 1993. *Revolt of the Provinces: The Regionalist Movement in America, 1920–45.* Chapel Hill: University of North Carolina Press.

Dorson, Richard M. 1948. Review of *A Treasury of New England Folklore,* ed. B. A. Botkin. *American Literature* 20: 76–80.

———. 1950a. "Folklore and Fake Lore." *American Mercury* 70: 335–43.

———. 1950b. Review of *A Treasury of Southern Folklore,* by Benjamin A. Botkin, ed. *Journal of American Folklore* 63: 480–82.

———. 1950c. Review of *A Treasury of Southern Folklore,* ed. B. A. Botkin. *Mississippi Valley Historical Review* 37: 354–55.

———. 1959. "A Theory for American Folklore." *Journal of American Folklore* 72: 200–201.

———. 1971a. *American Folklore and the Historian.* Chicago: University of Chicago Press.

———. 1971b. "Applied Folklore." In *Papers on Applied Folklore,* ed. Dick Sweterlitsch, 40–42. *Folklore Forum,* Bibliographic and Special Studies No. 8. Bloomington: Folklore Forum.

——, ed. 1974. *America in Legend: Folklore from the Colonial Period to the Present.* New York: Pantheon.

——. 1976. *Folklore & Fakelore: Essays toward a Discipline of Folklore Studies.* Cambridge, Mass.: Harvard University Press.

Dunaway, David K. 1980. "Charles Seeger Carl Sands: The Composers' Collective Years." *Ethnomusicology* 42 (May): 159–68.

Dwyer-Shick, Susan. 1976. "Review Essay: Folklore and Government Support." *Journal of American Folklore* 89 (Oct.–Dec.): 476–86.

Eliot, T. S. 1962. *Collected Poems, 1909–1962.* New York: Harcourt, Brace and Co.

Evans, David. 2007. "Bessie Smith's 'Back-Water Blues': The Story behind the Song." *Popular Music* 26.1 : 97–116.

Filene, Benjamin. 2000. *Public Memory and American Roots Music.* Chapel Hill: University of North Carolina Press.

Gabbin, Joanne V. 1985. *Sterling A. Brown: Building the Black Aesthetic Tradition.* Westport, Conn.: Greenwood.

Gardner, Emelyn E. 1938. "Review of *The American Play-Party Song* by Benjamin A. Botkin." *Journal of American Folklore* 51: 356–57.

Gates, Henry Louis, Jr. 1987. *Figures in Black: Words, Signs, and the "Racial" Self.* New York, Oxford University Press.

Green, Archie. 1979. Obituary of Charles Seeger. *Journal of American Folklore* 92: 391–99.

Greer, Taylor A. 1998. *A Question of Balance: Charles Seeger's Philosophy of Music.* Berkeley: University of California Press.

Halpert, Herbert. 1995. "The Devil, the Fiddle, and Dancing." In *Fields of Folklore: Essays in Honor of Kenneth S. Goldstein,* ed. Roger D. Abrahams, 44–54. Bloomington, Ind.: Trickster Press.

Hand, Wayland D. 1945. Review of *A Treasury of American Folklore* by Benjamin A. Botkin. *Journal of American Folklore* 58: 56–57.

Harbison, Katherine. 1938. "In the Great Meadow and the Lone Prairie." *Southern Folklore Quarterly* 2.3 (Sept.): 149–56.

Harper, Michael S. 1996. "Preface." In *The Collected Poems of Sterling A. Brown,* ed. Michael S. Harper, xi–xii. Evanston: Northwestern University Press.

Hawes, Bess Lomax. 1974. "Folksongs and Function: Some Thoughts on the American Lullaby." *Journal American Folklore* 87: 140–48.

Herzog, George. 1937. "Play-Party Song." *American Speech* 12.3: 215–17.

Hirsch, Jerrold. 1989. "Foreword." In *Lay My Burden Down: A Folk History of Slavery* (1945), ed. B. A. Botkin, ix–xxx. Athens: University of Georgia Press.

——. 1987. "Folklore in the Making: B.A. Botkin." *Journal of American Folklore.* 100: 3–38.

——. 1996. " 'My Harvard Accent' and 'Indifference': Notes toward the Biography of B.A. Botkin." *Journal of American Folklore* 109: 308–19.

——. 2003a. *Portrait of America: A Cultural History of the Federal Writers' Project.* Chapel Hill: University of North Carolina Press.

——. 2003b. "T. S. Eliot, B. A. Botkin, and the Politics of Cultural Representation: Folklore, Modernity, and Pluralism." In *Race and the Modern Artist,* ed.

Heather Hathaway, Josef Jarab, and Jeffrey Melnick, 16–41. Oxford: Oxford University Press.

———. 2007. " 'Cultural Strategy': The Seegers and B. A. Botkin as Friends and Allies." In *Ruth Crawford Seeger's Worlds: Innovation and Tradition in Twentieth-Century Music,* ed. Ray Allen and Ellie M. Hisama, 196–223. Rochester: University of Rochester Press.

Hisama, Ellie M. 2000. *Gendering Musical Modernism: The Music of Ruth Crawford, Marion Bauer, and Miriam Gideon.* New York: Cambridge University Press.

Hudson, Arthur Palmer. 1936. *Folksongs of Mississippi and Their Background.* Chapel Hill: University of North Carolina Press.

Hughes, Langston. 1930. Letter to Sterling Brown. Apr. 30. Sterling Brown Papers, Moorland-Spingarn Research Center, Howard University, Washington, D.C.

Hughes, Langston, and Arna Bontemps, eds. 1958. *The Book of Negro Folklore.* New York: Dodd, Mead.

Hutchinson, George. 1995. *The Harlem Renaissance in Black and White.* Cambridge, Mass.: Belknap Press of Harvard University Press.

Jackson, Bruce, ed. 1966. *Folklore & Society: Essays in Honor of Benj. A. Botkin.* Hatboro, Pa.: Folklore Associates.

———. 1976. "Benjamin A. Botkin, 1901–1975." *Journal of American Folklore* 89: 1–6.

———. 1996. "Botkin, Benjamin A. (1901–1975)." In *American Folklore: An Encyclopedia,* ed. Jan Harold Brunvand, 101. New York: Garland Publishing.

Jackson, George Pullen. 1944. Review of *A Treasury of American Folklore,* by B. A. Botkin, ed. *Musical Quarterly* 30: 496.

Jenson, Merrill, ed. 1951. *Regionalism in America.* Madison: University of Wisconsin Press.

Johnson, Charles S. 1929. Letter to Benjamin A. Botkin. May 17. Benjamin A. Botkin Collection of Applied American Folklore, Archives and Special Collections, University of Nebraska–Lincoln.

Johnson, James Weldon. 1996. "Introduction to the First Edition [of *Southern Road*]." In *The Collected Poems of Sterling A. Brown,* ed. Michael S. Harper, 6–19. Evanston: Northwestern University Press.

Joyner, Charles. 1940. "Introduction." In *Drums and Shadows,* ed. Georgia Writers' Project, ix–xxvii. Athens: University of Georgia Press. Rpt. 1986.

Kolakowski, Leszek. 1985. *Bergson.* Oxford: Oxford University Press.

List, George. 1991. *Singing about It: Folk Song in Southern Indiana.* Indianapolis: Indiana Historical Society.

Lomax, Alan. 1960. *The Folk Songs of North America.* New York: Doubleday and Co., Inc.

———, ed. 1966. *The Penguin Book of American Folk Songs* (1964). Baltimore: Penguin Books.

———. 1982. "Folk Music in the Roosevelt Era." In *Folk Music in the Roosevelts' White House: An Evening of Song, Recollections, and Dance, January 31, 1982,* 92–106. Program Booklet for the Commemorative Program Presented by the Office of Folklife Programs. Washington, D.C.: Smithsonian Institution.

MacLeish, Archibald. 1939. *America Was Promises*. New York: Duell, Sloan and Pearce.

Mangione, Gerre. 1972. *The Dream and the Deal: The Federal Writers' Project, 1935–1943*. Boston: Little, Brown and Co.

McClure, John. 1918. *Airs and Ballads*. New York: Alfred A. Knopf.

McDonald, William F. 1969. *Federal Relief Administration and the Arts: The Origins and Administrative History of the Arts Project of the Works Progress Administration*. Columbus: Ohio State University Press.

McIntosh, David S. 1974. *Folk Songs and Singing Games of the Illinois Ozarks*. Carbondale: Southern Illinois University Press.

McLendon, Altha Lea. 1944. "A Finding List of Play-Party Games." *Southern Folklore Quarterly* 8.3 (Sept.): 201–35.

Mencken, H. L. 1919. *Prejudices: First Series*. New York: Alfred A Knopf.

——. 1920. "Sahara of the Bozart." In *Prejudices: Second Series*, 135–44. New York: Alfred A Knopf.

——. 1925. "Geographical Adventure That Reveals More 'Saharas of the Bozart.'" *Baltimore Evening Sun*, May 9, 9.

——. 1926. "Oklahoma Poets." *American Mercury* 8.29 (May): 14–17.

Morris, Alton C. 1990. *Folksongs of Florida* (1950). Gainesville: University of Florida Press.

Newell, William Wells. 1888. "On the Field and Work of a Journal of American Folklore." *Journal of American Folklore* 1.

——. 1963. *Games and Songs of American Children* (1883). New York: Harper and Brothers Publishers. Reprint. New York: Dover Publications.

New York Folklore Society (NYFS). 1985. "New Organization Features Urban Folklore." *New York Folklore Newsletter* 6.4: 1–2.

"A Notable New Book." 1932. *New York Times Book Review*, May 15, 13.

Odum, Howard, and Harry Estill Moore. 1938. *American Regionalism*. New York: H. Holt.

Oliver, Paul. 1961. *Blues Fell This Morning: The Meaning of the Blues*. New York: Horizon.

Owens, William A. 1936. *Swing and Turn: Texas Play-Party Games*. Dallas: Tardy Publishing Co.

Pearson, Karl. 1957. *The Grammar of Science*. New York: Meridian Books.

Penkower, Monty Noam. 1977. *The Federal Writers' Project: A Study in Government Patronage of the Arts*. Chicago: University of Illinois Press.

Pescatello, Ann M. 1992. *Charles Seeger: A Life in American Music*. Pittsburgh: University of Pittsburgh Press.

Piper, Edwin F. 1915. "Some Play-Party Games of the Middle West." *Journal of American Folklore* 28: 262–89.

Pitts, Lilla Belle. 1942. "Music Education Advances to a New Front." *Music Educators Journal* 28: 26–28.

Randolph, Vance. 1946. *Ozark Folksongs*. 4 vols. Columbia: State Historical Society of Missouri.

Rao, Nancy Yunhwa. 1997. "Partnership in Modern Music: Charles Seeger and Ruth Crawford, 1929–1931." *American Music* 15, no. 3: 352–80.

Redding, J. Saunders. 1973. "The New Negro Poet in the Twenties." In *Modern Black Poets,* ed. Donald B. Gibson, 13–29. Englewood Cliffs: Prentice-Hall.

Richmond, W. Edson, and William Tillson, eds. 1959. *The Play-Party in Indiana.* Indiana Historical Society Publications 20.2. Indianapolis: Indiana Historical Society.

Ritchie, Jean. 1963. *Singing Family of the Cumberlands* (1955). New York: Oxford University Press. Reprint. New York: Oak Publications.

Rodgers, Lawrence. 2000–2001. "H.L. Mencken and the 'Oklahoma Style' of Literature." *Chronicles of Oklahoma* 78.4: 468–83.

Rosenberg, Bruce A. 1991. *Folklore and Literature: Rival Siblings.* Knoxville: University of Tennessee Press.

Ross, Alex. 1994. "A Female Deer? Looking for Sex in the Sound of Music." *Lingua Franca* (July–Aug.): 53–60.

Rourke, Constance. 1933. "The Significance of Sections." *New Republic* 20 (Sept.): 149.

Russell, Bertrand. 1985. *The Collected Papers of Bertrand Russell.* Vol. 12, *Contemplation and Action, 1902–14.* Edited by Richard Rempel, Andrew Brink, and Margaret Moran. London: George Allen and Unwin.

Ryan, Grace L. 1928. *Dances of Our Pioneers.* New York: A.S. Barnes and Co.

Sackett, S. J. 1961. "Play-Party Games from Kansas." *Heritage of Kansas* 5.3: 2–61.

Sandburg, Carl. 1927. *The American Songbag.* New York: Harcourt, Brace and World, Inc.

Sanders, Mark A. 1999. *Afro-Modernist Aesthetics and the Poetry of Sterling A. Brown.* Athens: University of Georgia Press.

Seeger, Charles. 1930. "On Dissonant Counterpoint." *Modern Music* 7, no. 4 (June/July): 25–31.

———. 1942. "American Music for American Children." *Music Educators Journal* 29.2 (Nov.–Dec.): 41–44.

———. 1972. "Reminiscences of an American Musicologist." Interviewed by Adelaide Tusler and Ann Briegleb, Oral History Program, University of California at Los Angeles.

———. 1978. *Studies in Musicology, 1935–1975.* Berkeley: University of California Press.

———. 1994. *Studies in Musicology II: 1929–1979.* Edited by Ann Pescatello. Berkeley: University of California Press.

Smethurst, James E. 2003. "The Strong Men Gittin' Stronger: Sterling Brown's *Southern Road* and the Representation and Re-Creation of the Southern Folk Voice." In *Race and the Modern Artist,* ed. Heather Hathaway, Josef Jarab, and Jeffrey Melnick, 69–91. Oxford: Oxford University Press.

Spaeth, Sigmund. 1927. *Read 'Em and Weep: The Songs You Forgot to Remember.* New York: Doubleday, Page and Co.

Spurgeon, Alan L. 2005. *Waltz the Hall: The American Play-Party.* Jackson: University Press of Mississippi.

Stekert, Ellen J. 1975. "Obituary: Benjamin A. Botkin, 1901–1975." *Western Folklore* 34: 335–38.

Stevens, Phillips, Jr. 1985. "Reflections on Forty Years: Editor's Introduction, 40th Anniversary Issue." *New York Folklore* 11.1–4: 1–24.

Stocking, George. 1968. *Race, Culture, and Evolution: Essays in the History of Anthropology*. New York: Free Press.

Synnott, Marcia Graham. 1979. *The Half-Opened Door: Discrimination and Admissions at Harvard, Yale, and Princeton, 1900–1970*. Westport, Conn.: Greenwood Press.

Thomas, John L. 1990. "The Uses of Catastrophism: Lewis Mumford, Vernon L. Parrington, Van Wyck Brooks, and the End of American Regionalism." *American Quarterly* 42.2: 223–51.

Thompson, Stith, ed. 1953. *Four Symposia in Folklore*. Bloomington: Indiana University Press.

Tick, Judith. 1997. *Ruth Crawford Seeger: A Composer's Search for American Music*. New York: Oxford University Press.

Tidwell, John Edgar, and Mark A. Sanders. 2007. "Looking at Sterling A. Brown's South." In *A Negro Looks at the South*, by Sterling A. Brown, 3–15. Oxford: Oxford University Press.

Tobias, Richard. 1988. "T.E. Brown." In *Victorian Poets*, 16–20. 2nd ed. Vol. 35 of *Dictionary of Literary Biography*. Detroit: Gale.

Tolman, Albert H. 1916. "Some Songs Traditional in the United States." *Journal of American Folklore* 29: 155–97.

Untermeyer, Louis. 1932. "New Light from an Old Mine." *Opportunity* 10: 250–51.

Waters, Lorrain E. 1941. "The Utilization of Folk Music in Public School Education." *Music Teachers National Association Proceedings* (Pittsburgh MTNA): 52–57.

Widner, Ronna Lee. 1986. "Lore for the Folk: Benjamin A. Botkin and the Development of Folklore Scholarship in America." *New York Folklore* 12.3–4: 1–22.

Wilgus, D. K. 1959. *Anglo American Folksong Scholarship since 1898*. New Brunswick, N.J.: Rutgers University Press.

Williams, John Alexander. 1975. "Radicalism and Professionalism in Folklore Studies: A Comparative Perspective." *Journal of the Folklore Institute* 11: 211–34.

Williams, William Carlos. 1970. "Kenneth Burke." In *Imaginations*, 357–59. New York: New Directions.

Wilson, August. 1985. *Ma Rainey's Black Bottom*. New York: Penguin.

Wixson, Douglas. 1994. *Worker-Writer in America: Jack Conroy and the Tradition of Midwestern Literary Radicalism, 1898–1990*. Urbana: University of Illinois Press.

Wolford, Leah Jackson. 1916. *The Play-Party in Indiana*. Indianapolis: Indiana Historical Commission.

———. 1959. *The Play-Party in Indiana*. Edited and revised by W.Edson Richmond and William Tillson. Indiana Historical Society Publications 20 (2). Indianapolis: Indiana Historical Society.

Yung, Bell, and Helen Rees, eds. 1999. *Understanding Charles Seeger: Pioneer in American Musicology*. Urbana: University of Illinois Press.

Zumwalt, Rosemary. 1988. *American Folklore Scholarship: A Dialogue of Dissent*. Bloomington: Indiana University Press.

Contributors

Lawrence Rodgers was on the faculty of Kansas State University for two decades before becoming dean of the College of Liberal Arts and professor of English at Oregon State University, Corvallis. In addition to numerous articles on twentieth-century American literature, he has published *Canaan Bound: The African-American Great Migration Novel* (Champaign-Urbana: University of Illinois Press, 1997) and introduced novels by Edna Ferber, Booth Tarkington, Edwin Lanham, and Sanora Babb.

Jerrold Hirsch is professor of history at Truman State University. His most recent book is *Portrait of America: A Cultural History of the Federal Writers' Project* (Chapel Hill: University of North Carolina Press, 2003). He has also published numerous articles about B. A. Botkin, the Federal Writers' Project, and oral, southern, African American, and disability history.

Daniel B. Botkin is professor (emeritus) in the Department of Ecology, Evolution, and Marine Biology at the University of California, Santa Barbara. He is also president of the Center for the Study of the Environment, a non-profit and education and scientific organization. He lives in New York City and maintains a website at http://www.danielbbotkin.com/.

Taylor Greer is associate professor at the Penn State University School of Music. Much of his research has focused on the thought of Charles L. Seeger, which culminated in his book *A Question of Balance: Charles Seeger's Philosophy of Music* (Berkeley: University of California Press, 1998). Recently, Greer has explored the American folksong tradition in "Philosophical Counterpoint: A Comparison of Charles Seeger's Composition Treatise and Ruth Crawford Seeger's Folk Song Appendix," in *Ruth Crawford Seeger's Worlds: Innovation and Tradition in Twentieth-Century American Music,* ed. Ray Allen and Ellie M. Hisama (Rochester: University of Rochester Press, 2007).

Bruce Jackson is SUNY Distinguished Professor of English. Since 1972, he has been director of the Center for Studies in American Culture at the State University of New York at Buffalo. Author of more than two dozen books and two hundred articles, he is one of the country's leading and most widely honored folklore scholars.

Nancy Cassell McEntire is associate professor of English at Indiana State University, where she specializes in folklore and ethnomusicology. She edits the journal *Folklore Historian* and directs the Indiana State University Folklore Archives. Her recent publications include *Orkney: Land, Sea, and Community* (Edinburgh: School of Scottish Studies, 2004) and *The Lotus Dickey Songbook,* 2nd ed. (Bloomington: Indiana University Press, 2005).

Dorothy B. Rosenthal (née Botkin) is a retired science educator and former associate professor of science education at California State University, Long Beach. She lives in Florence, Massachusetts, and can be reached at dottie rose@comcast.net.

Ronna Lee (Widner) Sharpe has been a regional folklorist working for the Colorado Council on the Arts (CCA) since 1989. She holds an M.A. in American Studies and Folklore from George Washington University and has worked at the Smithsonian Institution and National Endowment for the Arts. Based at the Museum of Western Colorado in Grand Junction, Colorado, she administers grant programs for CCA, presents public programs, curates exhibits, and leads cultural heritage tours in Colorado.

Steven B. Shively is an assistant professor in the Department of English at Utah State University, where he teaches courses in English education and American literature. He is co-editor of *Teaching Cather* and has published critical and pedagogical articles on various American literary figures.

Ellen Stekert is professor of English emerita and adjunct professor emerita of American Studies at the University of Minnesota. During her distinguished career as a folklore scholar, she also taught at the University of California–Berkeley, University of Oregon, and Wayne State. As a long-time friend and informal student of Botkin's, she is well known both as a folksinger and for her many publications on music, tradition, and change in American life.

Judith Tick is Matthews Distinguished University Professor at Northeastern University. She is a music historian with a specialization in women's history and American music. She has written on Charles Ives, among many others, and is author of the biography *Ruth Crawford Seeger: A Composer's Search for American Music* (New York: Oxford University Press, 1997).

John Edgar Tidwell is associate professor of English at the University of Kansas. Awards from the National Endowment for the Humanities, the American Council of Learned Societies, and others have enabled him to publish widely on African American literature, especially on poets Sterling A. Brown, Langston Hughes, and Frank Marshall Davis and photographer-writer Gordon Parks. His books include his editions of Davis's *Livin' the Blues: Memoirs of a Black Journalist and Poet* (Madison: University of Wisconsin Press, 1992),

Black Moods: Collected Poems (Chicago: University of Illinois Press, 2002), and *Writings of Frank Marshall Davis: A Voice of the Black Press* (Jackson: University Press of Mississippi); Brown's previously unpublished travelogue *A Negro Looks at the South*, with Mark A. Sanders (New York: Oxford University Press, 2007); and the essay collection *Montage of a Dream: The Art and Life of Langston Hughes* (Columbia: University of Missouri Press, 2007).

Index

Academic folklorist, 72, 117n11
African American literature, 154
African American poetry, 16, 157
Alexander, Lewis, 154
Algren, Nelson, 9
Alsberg, Henry (director, FWP), 55n1, 61
America in Legend: Folklore from the Colonial Period to the Present (Dorson), 70
American Council of Learned Societies. *See* Botkin projects
American Folklife Center, 12–13
American folklore, 1–3, 8–10, 13–14, 32, 32n, 36, 41–44, 47–49, 51, 55, 57–59, 62–67, 70, 70n2, 73, 118; anthology, of 62–63, 66; interpretation of, 62, 65; study of, 2, 67, 69; understanding of living, 49, 59
American Folklore Society (AFS), 9, 11, 40, 55n1, 66, 73, 79
American folklore studies, 57–58, 70
American folklorist, 2, 8, 60, 70
American Folk Society (AFS), 40
American folksong, 96, 105, 121
American Folk Song's of Children (R. C. Seeger), 94, 105–6, 108, 114, 117
American Folk Songs for Christmas (R. C. Seeger), 94, 112–14
American Mercury, 26, 195
American Historical Association, 205, 227n6
American myths and symbols, 182
American Play Party, The, 15, 65, 75, 93, 99, 102, 104–105, 109, 121
American Songs for American Children (R. C. Seeger), 101–102, 104, 118n17
Ames, L. D., 137
America's folklore scholarship, 35–36, 41, 47, 51
Animal Folk Songs for Children (R. C. Seeger), 94, 111, 114
Anthropological methodology, 36–37

Applied folklore, 52–54, 73, 76, 80, 103, 166n2
Applied Folklore Center, 52
Applied folklorist, 73
Archives. *See* Botkin Archives
Arlt, Gustave O., 45–46
Arnold, Matthew, 152
Aswell, James, 62
Austen, Mary, 30–32

"Backwater Blues," 158, 161–62
"Backwoods Boaster," 42, 65
Baker, Huston, Jr., 16, 149, 150, 166n3
Ballads, Child, 104–105, 107–78, 118n21, 136, 215–16
"Battle of the Books/War of the Folklorists," 42
Banks, Ann, 173
Bayard, Samuel ("The Girl I Left Behind Me"), 138
Beginning lore, 22, 58
Bergson, Henri, 145-6
Big Lake. See Riggs, Lynn
Billings, William, 100
Blitzstein, Marc, 95, 117n5
Blues, 76, 141, 151, 155–56, 158–59,160, 162, 163, 166n1; "Backwater Blues," 161; "The Blues as Folk Poetry," 154; "Jackhammer Blues," 116; "Mother of Blues," 159; "Riverbank Blues," 153; "Southern Blues," 156; "Worried Man," 105
Boas, Franz, 4, 16, 17n2, 144
Boasian style, 4, 57
Boggs, Ralph, 63, 67
Bontemps, Arna, 155, 178
Book of Negro Folklore, The, 178
Botkin, B. A. (Benjamin Albert), anniversary, 51; archives, 2, 10, 62, 85, 101–102, 113; awards, 13; birth, 2, 51, 141, 151, 169; brother of, 4; career, 3, 4, 10, 24, 34, 40,